CW00482261

THE
ABCs
OF
Armageddon

THE
ABCs
OF
Armageddon

The Language of the Nuclear Age

DONALD J. COLEN

WORLD ALMANAC
AN IMPRINT OF PHAROS BOOKS • A SCRIPPS HOWARD COMPANY
NEW YORK

FOR BEN, ALICIA, AND NICKY

Cover and interior design by Elyse Strongin

Copyright © 1988 by Donald J. Colen

First published in 1988.

Distributed in the United States by Ballantine Books, a division of Random House, Inc., and in Canada by Random House of Canada, Ltd.

Library of Congress Cataloging-in-Publication Data

Colen, Donald J.
The ABCs of Armageddon.

Bibliography: p.
Includes index.
1. Nuclear warfare—Dictionaries.   I. Title.
U263.C64   1988   355'.0217'0321   87-50913
Pharos Books ISBN 0-88687-336-3
Ballantine Books ISBN 0-345-35224-6

Printed in the United States of America

Pharos Books
A Scripps Howard Company
200 Park Avenue
New York, NY 10166

10 9 8 7 6 5 4 3 2 1

CONTENTS

If the future resembles the past, the assumptions our planners make about which contingencies we will face, how specific weapons will perform in wartime, and what exchange calculations can be anticipated may prove to be inaccurate.[1]

Caspar W. Weinberger,
Secretary of Defense.

A complete defense is completely impossible. To rely on such a defense would be even more completely absurd.[2]

Edward Teller
Physicist, Presidential Advisor

The American discussion of strategic matters has been reduced on the public level to a series of deceptive slogans and political hoaxes.[3]

Zbigniew Brzezinski
National Security Adviser

What in the name of God is "strategic superiority?" What is the significance of it politically, militarily, operationally, at these levels of numbers? What do you do with it?[4]

Henry Kissinger
National Security Advisor

I don't know what it all means...all of this is speculation and hypothesis. Who the hell ever tested these things [nuclear weapons]? You couldn't sell a toaster to the American public without exposing it to continued tests, and yet here we talk loosely about what nuclear weapons can do or not do on the basis of no data at all.[5]

James B. Schlesinger
Secretary of Defense

PREFACE

America is a nation of packagers. We put potato chips in cans, panty hose in plastic eggs, and everything from pills to publications into shrink packs. We encapsulate history into decades like the Roaring Twenties or the Soaring Sixties. We wrap our national policies in such easy-to-remember notions as *Detente, Containment,* and *Reaganomics.* And we explain how it all works in oversimplifications like the Laffer Curve or the Domino Theory.

It is not difficult to pierce through the packaging of most products, for we are helped enormously by Pure Food and Drug laws and labeling acts—laws that compel the packager to say specifically what his package contains. But in the political arena, it is difficult to find the preservative in the Spirit of Camp David or the monosodium glutamate in Reaganomics. Still, if we are not as well educated as Thomas Jefferson believed citizens ought to be, we have had sufficient information to reach political decisions with some degree of assurance. Until recently. Now the average citizen doesn't know enough even to guess. For in the summer of 1945, America began what it has packaged ever since as the Atomic Age.

At Alamogordo, New Mexico, in July 1945, scientists proved that the atom could release its energy in cataclysmic amounts from a bomb transportable in an airplane. (Over the years it would be reduced to a package that could be carried in a soldier's knapsack, called *Davy Crockett.*) In August 1945, at Hiroshima and Nagasaki, the military demonstrated that this "primitive" bomb, equivalent to 12,000 tons of TNT, could kill 100,000 people instantly. Hundreds of these bombs, with infinitely more power, could incinerate millions. Thousands could destroy the earth, if not immediately, then more slowly in what would come to be known as *nuclear winter.* Later we would call the instant deaths *prompt* fatalities. Those who took a little longer to die the lingering death of radiation poisoning would be known as *soft* fatalities.

In the ensuing 40 years, several tendencies would develop.

First, Alamogordo-Hiroshima-Nagasaki became a chant of tribal guilt that was intoned whenever anyone asked why we had opened the Pandora's box of nuclear destruction. Today, the box is still open and the chant has been updated to "Midgetman-Trident-Tomahawk-Stealth," with a *Star Wars* on the end. Indeed, on the eve of Star Wars, one prominent academic observer would note that we have "built the most complex technological apparatus ever conceived without thinking through its purpose or how to control it ... the necessary system of command and control has not been constructed. It has not been built because no one has any idea of how to build it. Instead, an ever-widening chasm between strategic ideas and the command structure's ability to carry them out has developed."[1] What is more, in those 40 years, our penchant for packaging has wrapped the whole subject of nuclear strategy in an inexplicable, sometimes obscene language.

That's what this book is all about. It seeks to provide a minimal vocabulary for understanding the language of destruction that "experts" use so glibly. The experts have always been the specialists in the universities, the *think tanks,* the State Department, and the Pentagon. They are mathematicians, physicists, military historians, philosophers, engineers—technologists all. Regardless of their political proclivities, they have in common a willingness to "think the unthinkable," as one of them put it, and a penchant for playing war games on *computers.* Unfortunately, while "garbage in, garbage out" may subvert the Federal Reserve clearing system so that it pays an undeserving bank $29 billion to use overnight as it sees fit, the wrong glitch in the wrong computer program could mean nuclear holocaust. And it should always be kept in mind that there are no true experts. There are specialists and professionals who make a career of analyzing nuclear *strategy* and "what if" alternatives. But there are no experts. No one has ever fought a nuclear war nor tested the prescribed weaponry under battle conditions.

As the Atomic Age enters its fifth decade, its history and, hence, its lessons can be told in many ways. Like street thugs whose pockets bulge with Saturday Night Specials, the superpowers are still pushing and shoving. Neither has fired on the other, although the United States has threatened nuclear action on 19 separate occasions.[2] The "evil empire," as Ronald Reagan called the Soviet Union, has shaken its nuclear stick twice: during the Suez crisis in 1956, when it didn't have any *ICBMs,* and during the 1962 Cuban missile crisis, when it had exactly 4 missiles and the U.S. had 50. So much for the notorious missile gap. Looking at the history of the past 40 years, it may just be as the French foreign minister Talleyrand said of those allied against Napoleon: they were "too frightened to fight one another, too stupid to agree."

On 13 separate occasions, the U.S. and Soviet leaders have come together in so-called summits. A very few have produced concrete results in the form of economic and practical treaties. Several of the summits were without results; a few have even increased tensions. *Arms control* agreements like *SALT* I and *SALT* II, about which there is still considerable acrimonious debate, were signed at two of the meetings. And the *arms race* continues. But because of the way in which the CIA and the Pentagon compare superpower forces, there is some evidence that the U.S. may be racing against itself (see *Bean counts*).

What started with three American atomic bombs in 1945 and one Russian bomb in 1949 had become 50,000 *nukes* by 1985, some with as much as 60 times the explosive force of the Hiroshima bomb. If each side lobbed 200 megaton bombs at the other, over 200,000,000 people would die on both sides. The flights of technology have been awesome: a missile that packs a dozen warheads that can be aimed separately, nuclear-powered submarines that hide from detection and carry missiles with the explosive power of five World War IIs, orbiting satellites that photograph any ground movement that comes within their view. How all this works has become increasingly incomprehensible, as we have progressed from the notion of "soft targets" (people) to "hard targets" (weapons) to the ultimate obscenity of "Peacekeeper," a missile that carries the equivalent of 300,000 tons of TNT—25 times as potent as the bomb that killed 100,000 people at Hiroshima.

"The debate is about definitions and implementation; the debaters massage the symbols, polish them to try to catch public attention and even get people to see them a bit differently,"[3] the political analyst Richard Reeves observed. Sometimes it seems as if the designers of this verbal legerdemain themselves don't quite know what they are talking about. According to former secretary of defense Harold Brown, "We will not have much confidence that more than a small percentage of our silo-based missiles can survive a Soviet preemptive attack."[4] And in the same Department of Defense Annual Report, on the same page, Brown writes: "The Soviets could not be at all confident of destroying the bulk of our missiles."[5] When they do speak with some assurance, it is often with the intended goal of disinformation, PR's latest triumph, which enthrones Humpty Dumpty as the ultimate referee: "When I use a word, it means just what I choose it to mean."

Now, with the arrival of Star Wars, understanding has again taken a back seat to packaging and sales promotion programs vastly larger than anything that preceded them. For example, among the $690 billion worth of Department of Defense goodies that have been bought since 1981 (constant '87 dollars), KEW *(Kinetic Energy Weapon)* is getting a big nod.[6] Secretary of Defense Caspar Weinberger includes among the best of KEW a "smart hyper-velocity gun projectile . . . 'smart seekers' that get to a target in a hurry." Then press takes up the cry of "kinetic kill." But KEW are nothing more than high-tech slingshots: a rock, a bullet, anything that can be thrown or shot is a Kinetic Energy Weapon. Equally zany are the words and pseudo words in the Department of Defense Glossary of Acronyms, where it is not uncommon to find acronyms within acronyms. (See *Acronyms.*)

As the words and their offspring chased each other down through the Atomic Age, some voices of protest were raised. In the early 1970s, Fred Ikle, who would head up the Arms Control and Disarmament Agency and later become undersecretary of defense in the Reagan administration skewered his profession:

> The jargon of American strategic analysis works like a narcotic. It dulls our sense of moral outrage about the tragic confrontation of nuclear arsenals, primed and constantly perfected to unleash widespread genocide. It fosters the current smug complaceny about the soundness and stability of mutual deterrence. It blinds us to the fact that our method of preventing nuclear war rests on a form of warfare universally condemned since the dark ages—the mass killing of hostages.[7]

Across the ocean a decade later, Lawrence Freedman, one-time head of Policy Studies at Britain's International Institute for Strategic Studies and now Professor of War Studies at Kings College, London, reached much the same conclusion and emphasized the sloppy thinking that produced the sloppy jargon:

> [The products of strategic analysis] still consisted of abstract speculative theorising about unlikely contingencies bolstered by technical details and force comparisons . . . the strategic analyses now wielded as potent political weapons were often quite dubious. They depended on questionable assumptions about the reliabilty and performance of unproven new technologies, about the implementation of

subtle and ingenious tactics in the most fraught military environment imaginable, and about the attitudes and behavior of national leaders in the most extreme circumstances.[8]

In short, people and politics are being left out while the fate of the world is being settled within a verbal cloud of obfuscation. Nevertheless, the meanings of the words, as well as the acronyms, are vitally important in understanding exactly how the superpowers are leading each other and the rest of the world toward Armageddon, which is, after all, the ultimate package.

ACKNOWLEDGMENTS

It was difficult to bring this book to a close for two reasons. First, hardly a day passes without another outrageous example of the obscene nuclear embrace with which the superpowers have smothered each other and the world. And second, it seems as if each day brings another book in the long line of books since Alamogordo and Hiroshima, all attempting to explain the nuclear scene from one broadly researched viewpoint or another. It is to these studies that I am greatly indebted. Without them, this book could not have been written, for *The ABCs of Armageddon* tells the story of nuclear weapons and confrontation in the words used most often by these studies.

Every writer needs an editor to bring order out of chaos. Hana Lane's assistance was invaluable, especially in keeping me away from the brink of bias.

Donald J. Colen
August 21,1987

INTRODUCTION

Hiroshima was more than a catastrophic event that produced a strangely mixed reaction of awe and official glee, as President Harry Truman characterized the atomic bombing of Japan "the greatest thing in history."[1] Its effect was hypnotic. The West, especially America, cheered. Japan surrendered. "The American Century" that Henry Luce's *Life* magazine had proclaimed prematurely in 1941 began in earnest, as the United States found itself producing over 40 percent of the world's GNP and in sole possession of an awesome weapon which, it was thought, would guard the world from another Hitler, Hirohito, or Stalin—especially Stalin. In short order, however, questions were raised about whether the bomb should have been used at Hiroshima and Nagasaki, and anger greeted Stalin's refusal to join in an international agreement to outlaw the use of nuclear explosives for all time.

By 1947, when Winston Churchill banged down the Iron Curtain, the *Cold War* had begun, and, with it, the *arms race* and a mad search for security. To achieve that goal, suggestions have ranged from the complete obliteration of the Soviet Union by a quick overwhelming *attack* to total disarmament. If no one talks of obliteration anymore, the ideal of a *"first strike"* and victory in a "prolonged" nuclear war still beats fiercely in Pentagon breasts. Complete nuclear disarmament never had a chance, for a nuclear *deterrent* is indispensable in a world where college students can design a usable bomb from declassified publications and terrorists can carry it in a suitcase. Nor does the security lie at the end of the arms race. Along the way lies only the care and feeding of the *military-industrial complex* and, then, Apocalypse.

What we have done in the name of security is appalling. In Western Europe, where America has stationed over 300,000 troops to protect *NATO* forces against a Soviet attack, we have littered the countryside with "battlefield" *nuclear weapons*. But no one has been able to suggest why the Soviets should mount such an attack, and, for over 30 years, Western intelligence sources have reiterated time and again that this event is altogether unlikely. Nor does the U.S. contribute one whit to security with its unbelievable commitment to subject its own homeland and people to complete destruction in exchange for, say, Hamburg. But with every twitch of the

13

Russian bear, the arms race proceeds apace, pauperizing the Soviet economy and pushing the U.S. deficit ever higher. So it is with security around the world.

In the Middle East, it is alleged that the Iranian revolution and the Soviet invasion of Afghanistan have presented the U.S. with a crisis of major dimensions—that a Soviet invasion of Iran is a certainty, threatening America's oil supply in the Persian Gulf and her national security in the process. And so there is a "need" for enhanced "rapid deployment forces"—helicopters that will operate in the desert, nuclear weapons that can be carried by foot soldiers, and so forth. All this is sold in the name of security in the face of British, American, even Russian studies concluding almost unanimously that such an attack by the Soviets would be the sheerest folly and undoubtedly would fail.[2]

Security will be found neither in the heavens, with President Reagan's vision of an impregnable shield in outer space, nor in more and better nuclear arms. If the Soviets are not put off by the unimaginable destructive power of 25,000 nuclear *warheads,* there will never be security for anyone, any place, any time. Both superpowers are caught up in thinking about the future in terms that are uselessly part of the past—about winning and losing, about being ahead or behind in the nuclear arms race, about inferiority and *superiority.* And to accustom ourselves to the unthinkable, we play games like "Ultimatum: A Game of Nuclear Confrontation," which its distributors, Yaquinto Publications of Dallas, Texas, say has as its object "to destroy relatively more of the enemy's population while minimizing harm to one's own population . . . . The winner is generally the one who has destroyed more of his enemy's population than he himself lost."[3]

Such is security in one sense. In another sense, as one SDI *(Strategic Defense Initiative)* researcher put it: "The days when we were the only bully on the block with a big stick have gone. Some of the advocates of SDI believe that if we can take Russia's stick away and go back to being the only bully on the block, then we'll be all right again."[4]

We have a nagging feeling that this is not the road to national security, nor is every problem along the way the work of the Russians, as many public opinion polls around the world attest. The growing support for a *nuclear freeze* in Europe and the U.S. indicates that the public, at least, believes that the road, leads instead toward international accommodation. It lies in the direction of the last appeal that Albert Einstein signed against the development of nuclear arms: "We appeal to you as human beings to human beings: Remember your humanity, and forget the rest."[5] Nevertheless, the arms race proceeds.

Bigger Bangs for Bigger Bucks

All through the nuclear-*strategy* literature of the past 40 years, the word "feasible" occurs persistently. It is usually used as a synonym for "possible," as in "economically feasible" (is it affordable?) or "technically feasible" (will it work?). In both instances, it tells volumes about each superpower's nuclear, military state.

On both sides, none of the nuclear and conventional equipment is economical; too much of it performs badly or not at all, and no one knows whether a lot of the nuclear equipment will ever work. Obviously, we know more about the American defense experience than about the Russian record. But we know enough of both to say that we share similar experiences, given the Chernobyl and *Challenger* disasters, not to mention the young West German amateur flyer who was able to land his small plane within the Kremlin walls after a flight of some 450 miles through heavily monitored Soviet skies.

How "feasible" are those some 1,000 missiles stored in concrete silos on the Western plains of the United States, which Harvard analyst Professor Thomas Schelling calls "an embarrassment?"[6] And how accurate are they?

The U.S. Air Force has never successfully launched a solid-fuel rocket (Minuteman) from an operational silo. During the 1960s, four attempts were made. Three times the boosters wouldn't ignite; the fourth time the rocket blew up. After that, tests were conducted much more carefully. The rocket was extracted from the silo, placed on a flat-bed carrier, and shipped to the Vandenberg Air Force Base in California.[7] There it was fired west toward the South Pacific. This is the "success" the public reads about. But that success is hardly a valid barometer of future performance. In any nuclear confrontation, unlike the east-west trajectories used in the tests, missiles will be fired on north-south trajectories, where the pull of gravitational forces vary and where it is impossible to say precisely what those variances will be. Thus systematic errors build up in navigational equipment, playing havoc with targeting.[8] Indeed, targeting leaves much room for error on both sides.

Pentagon tests of U.S. strategic missiles show almost as great a reliability problem as the ones that confronted NASA during the launch failures that followed the *Challenger* tragedy. The Navy's Poseidon missile has failed 7 percent of the time and has a major second-stage problem. The Navy's latest, the *Trident* missile, has a first-stage engine problem. Retired Air Force personnel report Air Force failure rates of up to 10 percent. NASA engineers who know all about solid-fuel propellent problems from experience think the talk of first-strike capabilities is "amusing."[9]

Soviet missiles aren't any more accurate. In a test of the SS-N-8, a submarine-launched missile, fired from northeastern Russia toward the test range on the Kamchatka Peninsula, the missile missed its mark by 1,500 miles and landed in China. Reportedly, "something went wrong with the guidance."[10]

But even if U.S. missiles reach their targets, there may be some questions about the efficacy of the warheads. According to recent reports, the U.S. system that produces nuclear material for warheads and submarine propulsion units is "antiquated, ailing and sloppy." The story of the way in which plants run by the Department of Energy are being managed also sounds like a page out of the investigations of NASA after the *Challenger* episode. Environmental problems are being described as nearly insurmountable.[11]

Indeed, both superpowers have booster problems. Tests of the Soviets' new SS-18 missile (believed to be the one they expect to use through the 1990s) ended in explosions in April and August 1986. In the first test, it was propelled from its silo, didn't work, and never got any farther. In August it exploded in mid-flight, and U.S. authorities believe the second failure is a clear setback for the Soviets, as the SS-18 is designed to bash U.S. *ICBM* silos.[12] Similarly, in October 1986, a Soviet warning *satellite* was placed in the wrong orbit[13] and in January 1987 a reconnaissance satellite blew up. At the same time, the Soviets lost a Proton booster, their largest.[14]

Simultaneously, the U.S. was having trouble with its strategic missiles. In August 1986, the Air Force announced it had had to blow up an ICBM being tested over the Pacific because problems were caused by what the Pentagon likes to call an "anomaly." In September, the launch of an Atlas-E rocket was postponed for the fifteenth time; leaking fuel was blamed in that instance.

But if the missiles would work and could be relied upon to reach their targets, who will tell them when to start? Communications, it seems, is not one of the Pentagon's strong points. According to a classified Defense Department assessment of the invasion of Grenada, the operation was a botched job that was nearly crippled by lack of communications among the Army, Navy, Marine, and Air Force units. Army and Navy radios are incompatible, and "the net result was a lack of communications during critical stages of the operation."[15]

Apparently, the breakdown in interservice communications affects the highest level. The military chain of command reaches down from the president through the secretary of defense to the joint chiefs and then to the area commands. But the radio systems in *Air Force One,* the president's plane, and the plane used by Secretary Weinberger, are incompatible. Thus the president and Weinberger discussed plans to force down an Egyptian plane carrying the *Achille-Lauro* highjackers on an open line that could have been picked up by ham radio operators—and was.[16] Allegedly, during a Superpower crisis, when the President has been whisked away to his airborne command post (*NEACP,* called "Kneecap"), he will be able to communicate directly by voice with regional commanders in their airborne posts—if it doesn't rain. This system has been found to be susceptible to interference from heavy rain.[17] "*Looking glass,*" the Strategic Air Force Command Post, does not have a radio range wide enough to reach *TACAMO,* an airborne system that ties into the submarine fleet, "with confidence, in a nuclear and jamming environment."[18] President Jimmy Carter was appalled by the poor state of command-and-control procedures. Suspecting a fiasco, he ordered a test run of the procedures to get the president out of Washington, with Zbigniew Brzezinski, his national security advisor, sitting in for the chief executive. Carter was right. The exercise was a fiasco, probably because no other president had taken the problem seriously.[19]

Back on the battlefield, things are not much better. Everyone wants the Stinger, a shoulder-fired surfaced-to-air missile (SAM). The Contras in Nicaragua want it, as do the Afghans. It's a heat-seeking weapon designed to be used against low-flying aircraft and helicopters by individual infantrymen. Unfortunately, it's the arthritic of weapons; it abhors dampness. Apparently, the Stinger's reputation results from the alleged performance of the SAM-7, a

Soviet shoulder-fired weapon that is supposed to have turned the tide in the Yom Kippur War of 1973. Most of the Israeli losses were caused by old-fashioned guns—of the 5,000 SAMs fired by the Arabs, only 28 hit their targets.[20]

Along with the Stinger, the Bradley Fighting Vehicle and the Sergeant York anti-aircraft gun have become legendary, gold-plated disasters, while questions about the M-1 have persisted since its introduction. The Bradley is supposed to carry soldiers into battle, cross rivers, and be equipped so that its passengers can fight. In tests, it cooked its occupants, nearly drowned them fording rivers, and was virtually unusable.[21] The Army refuses to give it up, although the military could have bought the West German Marder, which carries more men and does the same things that the Bradley is supposed to do at one-third the cost. Nor is there any thought of giving up the M-1 Abrams, which has been called the Cadillac of tanks, despite the fact that it has a serious failure every 34 miles. In a 178-mile test of 39 tanks at Fort Hood, Texas, 47 percent didn't complete the course because they had broken down.[22]

The story of the Sergeant York anti-aircraft gun is equally disturbing. When it was cancelled, it had already cost $1.8 billion and was "so ludicrously incapable of hitting maneuvering aircraft that it had become a painful embarrassment."[23]

Such is a sample of the nagging story of "feasibility" that has persisted since the Eisenhower administration first promoted "a bigger bang for the buck," and bought the cheaper version of national defense, the nuclear weapon. In those days, the U.S. maintained an overwhelming superiority in nuclear arms that allowed it to neglect conventional arms, thereby saving the national budget. Now the superiority has disappeared, the paraphernalia of "indescribable" destruction is questionable, and old standbys like minesweepers have been neglected shamefully, as the Persian Gulf experience of July 1987 attested. An addictive mentality seems to have crept into high places, as the policy of the quick technological fix persists, driven by the search for security, the arms race, and the uncertainties of what parades as "foreign policy."

Policy's Many Faces

"We are mad not only individually but nationally. We check manslaughter and isolated murders; but what of war and the much vaunted crime of slaughtering whole peoples." So said Seneca, the Roman philosopher-statesman, at the dawn of the Christian era. Since the dawn of the Atomic era, unfortunately, the U.S. has been deaf to Seneca and searched instead through a screen of *disinformation* for the means of "slaughtering whole peoples." It was called nuclear strategy and trumpeted as "policy." It still is.

Over the years, there have been various attempts to formulate policies that would fit into a nuclear age. In the view of one analyst, there have been five waves of policy:

1. The original policy of *containment* enunciated by George Kennan and, in a modified form, carried through the Truman administration.

2. The Eisenhower "new look" with its emphasis on *massive retaliation* as a substitute for foreign policy, which continued until 1961.

3. The Kennedy-Johnson *flexible response,* which shaped the way America looked at the world until Johnson left office.

4. The Nixon-Kissinger notion of *detente,* which continued under Ford and Carter until the Russians invaded Afghanistan in 1979.

5. The congeries of "visions," initiatives, doctrines, and *BMD* strategies that have paraded as the Reagan policy.[24]

Aside from the original policy of containment and detente, which Kissinger described as a "national-interest-based foreign policy,"[25] the intervals between those two major thrusts were times of the search for nuclear strength. Kissinger pointed out that the claim during those periods was, "when we have positions of strength, the negotiating position [with the Soviets] will improve." But, he demanded, "What were we going to do with the negotiating position—what were we going to ask of the Russians if they came to the conference table—I defy anybody to find one statement."[26] This attitude—almost strength-for-strength's-sake—is rampant today in the Pentagon's corridors, where Secretary Weinberger once searched for ways to spend the Kremlin into oblivion. He called it "competitive strategies." But the Kremlin may have beaten Weinberger to the punch, if the Toshiba incident of early 1987 is any indication. Apparently, a Japanese company, the Toshiba Corporation, sold advanced U.S.-technology machine tools to the Soviets, enabling them to build quiet submarine propellers, thereby considerably improving the Soviet submarine's ability to escape detection. A special Pentagon study puts the cost of developing a new technology of this kind at between $8 and $60 billion.[27]

Regardless of the way in which policy has been delineated, successive postwar administrations have viewed *arms control* as a way to cap the arms race and even reduce the superpower nuclear arsenals. However, there have been many approaches to arms control, and its theory and practice have changed continuously since the *Baruch Plan* was aborted in the late 1940s. Conceptually, arms control, defense policy, or foreign policy has each been in the ascendant at one time or another and controlled the other two. Meanwhile, the arms race became the obvious victor.

In the late 1950s and early 1960s, arms control was concerned primarily with the military aspect of the Cold War. Foreign policy aims took a back seat while basic superpower antagonisms persisted. Formal efforts at arms control and the development of negotiating procedures actually got their start when Defense Secretary Robert McNamara realized that without a formal U.S.-Soviet agreement, he would have to bow to political pressure and authorize the development and deployment of a nationwide *ballistic missile defense* system. The *SALT* talks and the *ABM* treaty, limiting the deployment of ABM systems, followed.

Then the SALT talks moved slowly toward a search for limits on offensive weapons, and the concept of *parity* was held up as the ideal state of superpower relationships. By 1977 West Germany's Chancellor Helmut Schmidt was saying that "No one can deny that the principle of parity is a sensible one. However, its fulfillment must be the aim of all arms-limitation and arms-control negotiations and it must apply to all categories of weapons."[28] But few people agreed with the chancellor, for the problem was, and is, one of definition. For example, when President Reagan took office in 1981, the U.S. had 2,500 more strategic nuclear warheads than did the Soviets. By 1986 the Soviets had a miniscule lead. The score broke down as the chart on top of the next page shows:[29]

To say that this is parity (10,174 vs 10,223) is meaningless without noting where the warheads are, their size, their location, missile *throw weights,* and other factors. What is more, during the 1970s, as now, arms control was complicated by NATO's dependence on nuclear arms for its defense against a conventional Soviet attack. There were no guidelines for determining the comparative weight

	United States	Russia
LAUNCHERS:		
ICBM	1018	1398
SLBM	616	979
Bombers	180	170
Totals	1814	2547
WARHEADS ON:		
ICBM	2118	6420
SLBM	5536	3123
Bombers	2520	680
Totals	10,174	10,223

of the 100-odd nuclear systems involved in that defense. This was the lack alluded to in Chancellor Schmidt's admonition, and the late 1970s brought a search for guidelines in the form of "options," as the defense secretaries for both Presidents Ford and Carter would phrase it. In short, there was an absence of doctrine with the natural result that arms procurement raced ahead of what the economy could afford, guided only by the military-industrial complex.[30]

Arms control is now at sixes and sevens. Its advocates have pushed it to the point where arms control negotiations have become a substitute for diplomacy; its detractors have yet to offer a viable alternative. But arms control cannot be substituted for foreign policy, especially in the face of the dramatic changes being engineered in the Soviet Union by Mikhail Gorbachev.

For Americans, understanding Soviet foreign policy has become increasingly difficult with time, as Oval Office attitudes have ranged from Kennedy's use of muscle in the Cuban Missile Crisis to Carter's naivete to Reagan's hostility, exemplified in his characterization of a basic "struggle between right and wrong and good and evil."[31] Moreover, according to the director of Columbia University's Reasearch Institute on International Change, "hopes for a radical change in the Soviet Union represent the wishful thinking of liberals, and expectations of the destabilization of the regime are the wishful thinking of conservatives."

"The Soviet Union is presently in the throes of a crisis of effectiveness. There is little reason to believe that the situation will change in the foreseeable future. But it is unlikely that the state is now, or will be in the late 1980s, in danger of social or political disintegration."[32]

For those who try to examine objectively a nation on which information is almost nonexistent, it is possible to detect a foreign policy that is more complex than a simple show of imperialism driven by nuclear strategy.[33] The formulation of foreign policy, however, does not come easily in the Soviet Union, as one might assume it would in a single-party system. First, there is a material and social decline indicated, in part, by the incidence of alcoholism and absenteeism, that eats at internal structures and drains the resources of policymakers. The USSR also faces the guns and/or butter dilemma. Nuclear arms cost money, and in an economy where resources are limited, the drive to maintain superpower status tightens a tourniquet that has slowed the flow of consumer goods for generations.[34]

Second, Soviet juggling of a rivalry with the U.S. and simultaneous engagements in foreign adventures is bound to injure international relations. Incursions in Africa, the Persian Gulf, and the Middle East make an easing of tensions between the superpowers more difficult.

Third, the Soviet stance in the Third World complicates its global position, as it tries to reduce its economic contribution to those nations, increase its military intervention, and maintain a certain control over the recipients of its largesse.

Finally, Soviet formulation of foreign policy is bedeviled by an indispensable need to remain successful in the eyes of its own citizens as well as 'the elites of client states. It is possible to assume that the current continuation of American Cold War attitudes under Reagan strengthens Gorbachev's hand. He is able to invoke patriotism and sacrifice at home and rally a cheering section of sorts in Eastern Europe. What exactly are Gorbachev's goals?

The Soviet premier does not want a new turn of the arms race. He does want arms control. The recent INF agreement is a turn in that direction. The emergence of breakthroughs in mobile-based ICBMs, space-based weapons, and ultrasonic *cruise missiles* will make *verification* more elusive. He is putting priority on domestic reforms over adventuresome foreign policy escapades. If he can improve relations with the United States, he may be able to gain access to Western technology and ultimately to financial credits.[35]

In short, Gorbachev wants to "get the country moving again." Simultaneously, his policy of *glasnost,* or openness, is having an effect. But the release of dissidents, the publication of a novel about the nightmares of Stalin's terror, the appearance of one tryst with free markets in one factory in Sumy, the promise of another candidate on the ballot (hand-picked by the party), even the demise of central planning—none of these "liberalizations" add up to what the West calls democracy. Vaulting the economic hurdles will be virtually impossible in a situation where uncontrollable inflation must result when prices kept unrealistically low are freed to follow market dictates.

Ultimately, a clearer understanding of Soviet foreign policy and Gorbachev's objectives will require the elimination of a number of misconceptions. Soviet foreign policy does not follow a master plan. Nothing like a master plan can be deduced from Soviet scriptures— the writings of Marx, Engels, Lenin, and Stalin. Similarly, there is no evidence that the Soviet world is actually divided into "hawks" and "doves," as ours is. Nor can Soviet foreign policy be pushed one way or the other by American policy; there is a complete divergence between the interests and values of the two nations. We have no ability at all to influence their domestic affairs or to cause significant change in Soviet social or political structures. But that is not to say these might not change as a result of domestic pressures and needs.

The Soviets are simply not like Americans. They see the world differently, they have different priorities, and they have a different way of valuing domestic and international affairs. As strange as their beliefs and values seem to us, ours are just as incomprehensible to them. As Sinologists have warned about the changes in China, "do not jump to the conclusion that *they* are becoming more like *us.*"[36] We are divided by opposed interests, and we are joined by the fear of nuclear war. This is where the two nations' policies meet.

In another view, the present American problem is not the total absence of a policy; rather, the policy that was put into place in the first decade of the Atomic Age is no longer suitable for a world only a decade away from the 21st century. The structure of that policy had four supports.

1. A system of deterrence to prevent war based on the stockpiling of nuclear weapons and the means to deliver them wherever we wanted them to go.

2. An international coalition directed at the *containment* of Soviet expansion and communist penetration of new spheres of influence.

3. A policy to intervene with military force if necessary anywhere in the Third World to prevent revolutionary change from the left.

4. A liberal international economic order stemming from the Bretton Woods Conference, calling for free trade, fixed currency rates, and freely convertible currencies.[37]

Today the supports are crumbling. What passes for policy is a speech that projects a "vision," undefined and misdirected in a world where each superpower has enough nuclear weapons to eliminate the other's society and knows it, where technology drives decisionmaking, and where what one side can do, the other can do too—regardless of who's ahead. What remains is the dubious supposition that a president mired in the backwash of the Iran-Contra affair, with barely a year left of his term at this writing, will spend the political capital necessary to educate the country to one simple fact: the use of nuclear weapons is not, and survival demands that it cannot remain, the sum-total U.S. foreign policy.

The words that follow comprise the language of nuclear confrontation. They appear in newspapers and magazines and are heard on television programs and speakers' platforms. People use them when they get excited about nuclear arms and policy. Definitions have been culled from the leading books and periodicals that have treated the subject of nuclear arms and strategy since Hiroshima. Entries are listed as they are spoken, and not as they would be found in an index. There is a listing, for example, for *Strategic Defense Initiative,* not for Initiative, Strategic Defense. Nor has scientific esoterica been included. To help the reader, ample cross-references have been provided, and all words or terms that appear as entries are italicized in the text. In short, *The ABCs of Armageddon* is a primer with a point of view: the busy reader and the voter ought to be able to find their ways through the frightening nonsense that is bankrupting the nation and shaping a future that "at this point in time" promises only Apocalypse.

The ABCs

A

Absentee Having nothing to do with a failure to report for work, this word is usually coupled with "problem" and signifies one of two things: some of our (or their) missiles are missing, or we do not have enough *satellites* in orbit to keep watch on all of the USSR all of the time.

Assume in the first instance that the U.S. (or vice versa) has received a warning that the Soviets have launched a *surprise attack*. Assume also that the U.S. is following a *launch on warning* policy, which means that it fires back without waiting to see what happens. Hence American silos will be empty when Soviet missiles arrive. American missiles will be "absent" and the attacker will, therefore, have an absentee problem.

The second use of absentee problem enters the arcane world of *ballistic missile defense (BMD)* and *Star Wars*. The goal of any such defense system is to hit Soviet missiles in their *boost phase*—when the *warheads* have not separated from boosters and are so close to the ground that they can only be detected by those satellites which, for technical reasons, must be stationed in relatively low orbits. These satellites are not stationary, but are constantly circling the earth. As a result, there are times when some of their missiles cannot be seen by our satellites and will escape our sensors and interceptors. That's our absentee problem.

Advantage Not to be confused with the game of international ballistic tennis, or *superiority*, advantage has to do with who strikes first in an intercontinental missile exchange. The concept grew out of all the "what if" discussions that surrounded the proposal for an MX *missile*. The thinking of experts like former secretary of defense Harold Brown, himself a physicist, went something like this:

The existence of an MX missile might easily lead the Soviets to assume that they would be targets for a *preemptive first strike*. They would then "calculate that a first strike would result in a missile ratio adverse to them, just as we calculate that a Soviet first strike would result in a ratio adverse to us. To the extent that this is so, either side will, during the next decade, have a so-called 'advantage' in firing first,"[1] the secretary said.

Since then, it has been pointed out that what Brown meant to say was: (1) the U. S. would be way ahead if it could shoot first, and (2) if we developed that capability, the Russians might fire first in desperation before they lost most of their missiles.

Alert   The message that goes out to the armed forces telling them to get ready for war. Alerts may be at many levels, and are sometimes used as a precaution, or as a deliberate "don't-tread-on-us" warning to the adversary. That seems to have been the case during the October (or Yom Kippur) War between Israel and Egypt in 1973. While this move was effective then, it has the potential for all kinds of mischief. For example, according to former Secretary of State Alexander Haig, "Secretary of Defense Weinberger raised the alert status of U.S. forces on the day that President Ronald Reagan was shot without knowing whether this move would affect U.S. strategic forces."[2]

Moreover, a recent study examined three nuclear alerts: one in 1960 at the time of the first U-2 incident, one during the 1962 Cuban missile crisis, and the one mentioned above during the Middle East war. In every case, the alert was ordered at the presidential level, and military commanders raised the ante, pushing the alert to a level closer to crisis conditions.

The joint chiefs issued their orders so that a higher level of alert than political authorities intended would result as the order went down the chain of command. Base commanders then went even higher, as they did what they thought was necessary to protect their forces. This seemed to confirm the comment of a former Pentagon official that while Sergeant Bilko can't start World War III today, General Bilko certainly can."[3]

Anti-ballistic missile (ABM)   Another attempt in the long search for a technological solution to a political problem. This is supposed to be a missile that can hit a missile, sometimes called a "weapon designed to hit a bullet with a bullet."[4] From the very beginning of the *arms race,* there was little expectation that such a weapon would ever be developed. Bernard Brodie, godfather of all of the nuclear dons, said at the outset that the ABM was "the old story of ingenuity in defense having to reckon with ingenuity in offense, with the latter having a large margin of the advantages."[5] The "beginning" was a boondoggle.

The Atomic Age was barely underway when the armed forces began to scrap about their respective turfs. So, in 1958, a ten-year-old squabble between the Army and the Air Force over control of *ballistic missile defense* was resolved by giving the Army the assignment to develop an ABM system. What began to take shape in 1960 was first called Nike-Zeus, with a price tag of $15 billion. It was dumped by President Eisenhower as "uneconomic." During the next administration, Secretary of Defense Robert McNamara also refused funds for a better reason: it didn't work.[6] In 1967 renewed pressure for the development of an ABM system prompted President Johnson to turn to his scientific advisors and the last three men who had served as directors of research for the Department of Defense. The question Johnson asked was "will it work?" The unanimous answer was "No."[7]

Nor were the Russians any more successful. Their ponderous Golosh interceptor system, deployed around Moscow, gave very little promise of hitting a bullet with a bullet. It was relatively easy, therefore, for both sides to start negotiating (the first *SALT* talks) toward an agreement to prohibit the deployment of ABM systems. In 1972 the ABM Treaty was signed, limiting each superpower to two ABM complexes, one to protect its capital and one to protect *ICBM* silos. Moreover, neither complex could have more than 100 interceptor missiles. In 1974 the number of permitted installations was reduced to one each.[8] Even so, toward the end of the 1970s, American strategists began to talk of an ABM defense as the answer to the defense of *NATO*. At the time, it seemed as if the Americans were looking for a technology that would protect vulnerable ICBMs rather than finding a political answer to the problem of European vulnerability.[9]

A decade later, the Pentagon began work on development of what it called an anti-tactical missile *(ATM)*. Whether this was ignoring the technical and political experience of the 1970s, or was another attempt at early deployment of some *Star Wars* system, was uncertain in 1987. (The Pentagon's *SDI* organization was supporting the research.)[10] What was certain was that another end run around the 1972 ABM treaty was in the making.

The treaty states specifically that the parties will not "develop, test or deploy an ABM system or components which are sea-based, air-based, space-based or mobile land-based." But the Pentagon under the Reagan administration has argued that there is an exemption for "ABM systems based on other physical principles." The air is filled with "broad," "revisionist," and "Legally Correct Interpretations." According to former Defense Secretary Weinberger, this is nonsense; he insisted that "right" is the only term for the new view and "wrong" for the old. But within other parts of the Reagan administration, some legal experts are saying that the right view is wrong, and vice versa.[11] Altogether, the search for a workable ABM seems to be just another fling, regardless of cost, at finding a weapon that will guarantee *superiority*. This time, however, the attempt is clearly prohibited by the terms of a treaty between the U.S. and the Soviet Union.[12] (See *BMD, Star Wars.*)

Anticipatory counterattack   Early Air Force jargon for a *preemptive* attack made by one side when it suspects that the other side is going to do the same thing. It comes from the days when the Pentagon was proposing schemes that went under the names of Pincher, Broiler, Grabber, and Sizzle.[13]

Paul Nitze, President Reagan's chief negotiator at the aborted Iceland summit meeting of 1986, was head of the State Department's policy planning staff in 1950, when he presented President Truman with National Security Council Memorandum No. 68 (NSC 68), the memo that would become a guide to the nation's nuclear policy for the 1950s and beyond. In it, Nitze characterized the *Cold War* as a struggle between free and slave nations. He wrote: If "we had objectives only for the purpose of repelling invasion and not to create a better world, the fight would be lessened."[14] Surely, it would. But from that day forth, the key words "create a better world" imparted a sense of crusading and enshrined the unsettling notion of preemption in national policy. However, the existence of such a policy has been denied officially ever since.

Arms control   "The last, best hope": that at least is how successive administrations over the past 40 years have looked at the problem of putting a cap on the *arms race* and perhaps reducing the superpower nuclear arsenals.

As Soviet Premier Mikhail Gorbachev's policy of *glasnost* entered its second year, those whose business it is to study and understand Soviet arms control positions felt that the Soviets had never been more interested in striking a deal.[15] Unfortunately, the Reagan administration had given every indication that it wanted nothing to do with arms control, as the president led the charge against what he called the "evil empire." Although the 1986 mini-summit between Reagan and Gorbachev at Reykjavik, Iceland, was a policy disaster, it opened the door to a Soviet offer to reactivate the original Reagan *zero-option* suggestion for scraping intermediate-range missiles in Europe. That is virtually the agreement Reagan and Gorbachev signed in December 1987. Over the years, the timetable of arms control negotiations looks like this:

August 1963—The Nuclear Test Ban Treaty signed by the U.S., USSR, and Great Britain outlawed the testing of nuclear weapons in space, above ground, and underwater.

1966—The *Outer Space Treaty* (signed in 1967) banned the introduction of nuclear weapons into space.

1968—The Non-proliferation of Nuclear Weapons Treaty. The U.S., USSR, and Great Britain were the major signatories, agreeing to limit the spread of nuclear weapons by not assisting nonnuclear countries to obtain or manufacture them.

May 1972—*SALT* I (Strategic arms limitation talks). Signed by the superpowers, the treaty limited *anti-ballistic missiles* to two sites each (reduced to one in 1974). The treaty also imposed a five-year *freeze* on the testing of intercontinental ballistic missiles and submarine-launched ballistic missiles. SALT I was in effect until October, 1977.

July 1974—The U.S. and the USSR signed a treaty and protocol limiting underground testing of nuclear weapons.

November 1974—The Vladivostok Agreement between the superpowers set the framework for a comprehensive agreement on offensive nuclear weapons and produced guidelines for a second SALT treaty.

September 1977—Despite its expiration date, the superpowers agreed to abide by SALT I.

June 1979—The superpowers signed SALT II, agreeing to limit *missile launchers* and heavy bombers as well as the the number of missiles with multiple warheads. President Jimmy Carter withdrew the treaty from consideration by the U.S. Senate when the Soviets invaded Afghanistan in December 1979.

November 1981—President Reagan suggested the zero option,

which offered to scrap the development of U.S. intermediate-range missiles for the elimination of Soviet missiles already in place, as Geneva talks started on limited intermediate-range missiles in Europe.

May 1982—Soviet president Leonid Brezhnev turned down the zero option but agreed to continue talks.

June 1982—*START* (Strategic arms reduction talks) began in Geneva.

March 1985—Disarmament talks began in Geneva.

October 1986—Reagan and Gorbachev met in Reykjavik without success.[16]

December 1987—Reagan and Gorbachev sign an agreement in Washington, D.C., to eliminate intermediate range missiles and ground-launched cruise missiles in Europe.

Arms race Just as it reads: because we think they have more and newer weapons than we have we develop even more and even newer weapons. Not wanting to be left behind, they follow suit. This is the process that has produced arsenals measurable in *trillions* of tons of TNT, trillion-dollar arms budgets, trillion-dollar budget deficits under the Reagan administration, a national debt in the trillions that has become commonplace in the U.S., and the ever present threat of total extinction for most of the peoples of the earth.

Since the bombing of Hiroshima in 1945, the U.S. has spent more than $750 billion to make 60,000 nuclear warheads. Among these are 71 different types that can be used in 116 separate weapons systems.[17] The race began when the Soviets turned down the postwar *Baruch Plan,* and when the U.S., after the Korean War and the French debacle in Indochina, decided to outbid the Soviets in military power. But behind this process is the possibility that the U.S. is racing with itself while the Soviets tag along, rarely getting out in front.

The Soviets do not publish figures on defense spending. Instead, we rely on the "educated" guesses of the CIA. It determines what arms the Russians have in numbers and then calculates what it would cost the U.S. to build that quantity of weapons. Consequently, big boosts in estimated Soviet defense spending occur when we raise pay rates in our armed forces. Since the Russians have much larger forces, their "spending" jumps spectacularly because we apply our higher wage rates to assess their costs.

Between 1945 and 1976, American nuclear forces were increased substantially twice, while the Soviets were involved in three armament pushes. On the American side, the reasons for the surge were technology, public and elite opinion, and some Soviet triggering moves. Except for public opinion, similar reasoning prompted the Russians to increase arms buildup. In both cases, no single reason weighed equally at any time.[18] And in all cases, the major U.S. problem has been the interpretation of information. For example, the incredible estimated inventory of Russian tanks is often given as a reason for increased defense appropriations. But if the Soviets could produce 3,000 tanks annually, which is doubtful, and not supply any of them to their allies, it would take some 15 years to replace their current stock.[19] In 1977 the United States had the capacity to produce some 2,600 tanks annually, and that was before the M-1 tank entered production.[20] In short, with the Soviets supplying tanks to their allies, and given the different national rates of production, the numbers given for the Soviets' tank roster have to be nonsense.

ASAT (Anti-satellite)   One of the more confusing—and dangerous—*acronyms,* because the development of weapons designed to knock down *satellites* threatens the heart of defense systems. And what we can do, they can do just as well. The U.S. relies heavily on satellites:

—an estimated two-thirds of armed forces' messages travel by satellite;
—early warning systems are tied directly to satellites;
—satellites carry sensors that detect Soviet military capabilities as well as eavesdrop;
—navigation satellites enable a soldier, a ship at sea, or an airplane to fix their locations anywhere in the world to within ten yards in three dimensions. This is possible under the U.S. Global Positioning System, which will be completely on line by the end of 1987.

Moreover, the U.S. Command, Communications, Control and Intelligence system (C^3I), which ties together all divisions of the armed forces and also keeps them in direct communication with the president wherever he is, depends entirely on satellite transmission.[21] More importantly, the design of an ASAT system is a step toward the militarization of space, extending not only the *arms race* but the arena of superpower confrontation as well.

Development of these weapons, first tested in the U.S. in the 1950s, has been underway in both the U.S. and the USSR since the early 1960s. Since 1967 the Soviets have been testing a missile-launched weapon that has been effective only about 50 percent of the time (observed and interpreted by U.S. satellites). U.S. experts say the Soviet system is of "dubious value."[22] In 1984 the U.S. began to test a homing system that was launched from an F15 fighter plane; the following year, it reached its target successfully, blowing an old American satellite to bits.

As the competition stands now, the Soviets would need several days to knock down all of America's low-orbit satellites, while the U.S. could accomplish the same goal in a few hours due to the mobility of its system. But because of the mix of low- and high-orbit satellites, "the superpowers' satellite networks are about equally vulnerable."[23] The real threat will come when both nations develop weapons that can be deployed from space platforms, especially as the U.S. moves into *Star Wars* technology.[24]

Astrodome   Also called an "umbrella in the sky," a "bubble," or a "bell jar."[25] Like the other words stolen to make pretty packages, this, too, is misused. Normally, it refers to the notion that an *ABM* defense, if and when incorporated into the *Star Wars* program, will provide an impermeable shield against missiles over the U.S.

Attack   In the world of nuclear warfare, the enormity of what the dictionary calls "setting upon another" has reached the point of incomprehension. The world stood disbelieving as Hitler hurled hundreds of bombers against Britain in the early days of World War II. It would do so again were the Soviets to attack Western Europe in a similar conventional fashion. But a nuclear attack?

According to some estimates, 80 percent of America's manufacturing capacity could be taken out by an attack of 435 one-megaton weapons and 264 100-kiloton weapons directed against specific targets like oil refineries and steel mills. This kind of attack is entirely possible, given existing weaponry.

The result? It would take 50 years for the economy to recover to its preattack level. Simultaneously, the loss of life would be staggering. Sixty-five percent of the urban population would be killed outright, or would die shortly after the attack. Altogether, about 100 million Americans would be killed. And some say that 45 percent of survivors would die within a year.[26] This is the immediate aftermath. The consequences of *nuclear winter* are a part of the frightening unknown.

Automated response The weapons are programmed to decide for themselves when to start shooting, without any interference from the president, the joint chiefs of the armed forces, or the secretary of defense. For example, the heart of the contemplated *Star Wars* program is an attack by weapons with automated response against Soviet missiles as they leave the ground, that is, in their *boost phase,* which lasts about 300 seconds until the *warhead* drops its booster. In those 300 seconds, here's what happens:

A U.S. *satellite* has to detect the Soviet firing and decide whether or not the missile is headed for a U.S. target. The system will then have to fix on the Soviet attacking missiles, spot the difference between missiles and decoys, fire its weapons, and then determine whether or not the target has been destroyed. All this has to be accomplished through a system of highly reliable computers and data links in just five minutes. In short, the system must be perfect. This scenario raises the question of whether we want the fate of the world to be decided by an inanimate system that has never been tested under less than ideal conditions, much less in battle.[27] Yet, this is what the designers and researchers of the Star Wars program are trying to achieve.

B

B-1   This offspring of the B-29 and B-52 intercontinental bombers is the latest contribution to the debate that asks whether the U.S. needs another, super-high-tech intercontinental bomber. The B-52 was scarcely off the drawing board before the Air Force proposed its successor, the B-70, which never got past the Kennedy administration. Next came the Advance Manned Strategic Aircraft, which eventually became the B-1. It first flew in 1974, but was cancelled by the Carter administration a few years later. Now another version resurrected by the Reagan administration, the B-1B, is coming into service with a price tag of $28 billion and a cover charge of $250,000,000 to fix defects. The plane's offensive and defensive electronics jam one another: for example, its terrain-following radar sees mountains where none exist.[1]

Still, according to some experts, there are several reasons why the U.S. ought to have an expanded intercontinental bomber fleet:

—Bombers represent the only intercontinental system with which we have had any experience.

—They can be recalled, as opposed to missiles, which cannot be brought back once they have been launched.

—There are human beings aboard who can make up their own minds about what to do and where to go, and when.

Since the B-1 will be unable to outwit Soviet air defenses by the end of the decade, it is generally believed that it should be kept only to ferry *cruise missiles* and leave it to the *Stealth bomber*—a newer version of tomorrow's bomber—to get through to Soviet targets. In most views, there is no reason to buy more B-1s.[2]

Balance   Another "who's ahead" word, sometimes used by itself, sometimes in the phrases "military balance" and "nuclear balance." Users of the term insist that the goal of U.S. policy should be to strike a balance with the Soviets at every level in every type of military system. A former deputy director of the Joint Strategic Planning Staff and four-star admiral in command of Pacific forces points out that a difference of 1,000 missiles makes very little sense. No matter what is figured—fusing, targeting, or other aspects—"you can hardly find a use for more than 1,000 weapons, more or less, on either side."[3]

But this is only one kind of question raised by the notion of balance. How does anyone balance the extreme accuracy of the Minuteman III against the heavy megatonnage of a Soviet SS-18 missile? The U.S. has more warheads on submarines; the Soviets have more warheads on land-based missiles. Where's the balance? Nevertheless, the concept persists, and there is considerable suspicion that many of the statements and statistics on balance that find their way into the media originate among special interests like the military and their suppliers. The respected British observer Lord Gladwyn says flatly: "Professional scientists on both sides seem to have only one object, which is to think up even more terrifying weapons and then to sell them to the governments on the grounds that, if they are not developed, the adversary will get there first."[4]

In "The Military Balance, 1986-87," Britain's prestigious International Institute of Strategic Studies upgraded its annual assessment of the superpower balance to say that the U.S. had 12,846 warheads on 1,910 launchers and the Soviet Union had 10,716 warheads on 2,502 launchers.[5] It has been pointed out, however, that such discrepancies are irrelevant. Only five percent of the U.S. arsenal, about 500 out of that total inventory of warheads, could destroy Soviet society, and military experts are confident that many times this number of nuclear warheads will safely survive any Soviet attack.[6] In short, each superpower is equipped to launch a *second strike,* come what may.

Balance of power The concept of checks and balances applied to the international scene. In effect, the balance of power is what happens when nations band together to make certain that no one power rules the others in a world that does not have a binding international government.

The Roman empire was the last instance in which one nation was able to rule the world. Since then, many attempts have been made, most recently by Adolf Hitler, who came all too close to achieving his goal. Although the balance-of-power system in international relations was workable throughout the 19th century and into the 20th, the conditions that nurtured it no longer apply. They have been replaced by nuclear armaments in the hands of two superpowers. Because of the destructive power of those weapons, their nearly instantaneous delivery systems, the likelihood that they will kill off an entire population before severly damaging military systems, all these and many more characteristics of nuclear weaponry have caused the substitution of *deterrence* for the historical balance-of-power approach to peacekeeping.[7]

Balance of terror   A new phrase for the old idea of the exchange of hostages,[8] which came into vogue in the late 1950s and early 1960s. It was, in effect, a euphemism for what was to become known—and derided—as *mutual assured destruction (MAD)*. As stalemate began to emerge between the superpowers, their respective intercontinental arsenals became useless, because their use by one side meant subjecting its forces and people to the utter destruction resulting from retaliation by the other. The populations of both countries were held hostage. Hence the balance of terror and the gradual development of new nuclear strategies such as *flexible response* or *graduated deterrence*.[9] By, 1963 it had become clear, as Secretary of Defense Robert McNamara observed bluntly, that "The Soviet Union could effectively destroy the United States even after absorbing the full weight of a U.S. first strike, and vice versa."[10] Essentially, this is the present situation.

Ballistic missile   A programmable skyrocket carrying nuclear explosives on its front end and produced in all sizes and with various capabilities. While the skyrocket was an ancient Chinese invention, the modern missile owes its conception to the American physicist Robert Goddard and its perversion to the Nazis, who used that basic model to develop the V1 and V2 "buzz bombs" fired on London during World War II. Flying in the face of a 1921 *New York Times* editorial that said his rocket wouldn't work, Goddard launched the prototype from his Aunt Effie's farm near Auburn, Massachusetts, in 1926. The Nazis, under the leadership of Wernher von Braun, developed the *Vergeltungswaffen* (weapons of reprisal) at Peenemünde in 1943.[11] After the war, von Braun led a group of his fellow scientists to the U.S., where they designed American missiles at the Redstone Arsenal in Alabama.

The V1s and V2s were essentially jet-propelled pilotless aircraft launched from sloping ramps that could reach a few hundred miles. Today, one type of ballistic missile has a range of over 7,000 miles, and several types carry as many as a dozen *warheads*. They can be launched from a truck, an underground cement tube called a silo, or a submarine. Another descendant of the V2s is the *cruise missile*.

Ballistic Missile Defense (BMD)   The heart of President Ronald Reagan's "vision," this is the architecture of the *Strategic Defense Initiative (SDI)* or *Star Wars*. Used interchangeably with *anti-ballistic missile* to describe a multilayered weapons system that might be used as a defense against the intercontinental ballistic missile. The weapons of such a system can be based on land, at sea, or in space. Located in space, their consideration immediately raises the question of the need to develop anti-satellite weapons (*ASAT*), which both superpowers have consistently shied away from.

It all began with *Bambi* (ballistic missile boost intercept), during the Eisenhower administration. Bambi was intended to destroy during the weapon's *boost phase* missiles aimed at cities. After millions were spent, the project was gutted during the 1960s because it wouldn't work. Simultaneously, the Nike-Zeus project, an interceptor with a one-megaton *warhead,* appeared. Its problem was guidance: about 30 percent of them missed. Nike-Zeus became Nike X and was sent back to the research labs. Then the Johnson administration started the Sentinel ABM program of interceptor rockets. The Navy and the Air Force also began their own anti-missile weapons projects. Finally, the Nixon administration turned from the defense of cities to the defense of missile silos, and the Sentinel program was reborn as the *Safeguard*.

In 1972 Nixon and Leonid Brezhnev signed the ABM treaty, which held each country to one ABM system. The Russians kept their interceptor system around Moscow. After $7 billion and a trail of test failures, Congress closed down the North-Dakota based Safeguard unit. But toward the end of the decade, the Pentagon began to fear for the vulnerability of silo-based ICBMs and to talk about growing interest and some successes in the development of exotica like *lasers, particle beams,* and other such technologies. The stage was set for SDI, although no plan describing the use of these technologies was prepared for the "speech" in which President Ronald Reagan first hinted at a Star Wars program.[12] Nor was any thought given to the role that the ABM treaty, which limits each superpower to a single ABM system, would play. However, the multilayered BMD system that evolved looks like this:

DEFENSE INTERCEPT PHASES

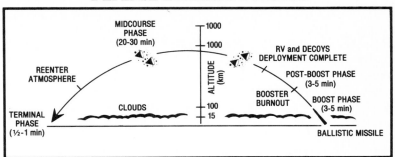

Boost phase

It takes most ICBMs up to 300 seconds to clear the atmosphere, which is exactly the time needed to release warheads. Soviet missiles, therefore, would still be over the USSR as they begin to release their warheads and, to have a clear shot at the Soviet missiles, a BMD system would have to be located in outer space. Positioned in outer space, sensors could detect the intense infrared radiation from boosters, which are easily damaged and vulnerable to *kinetic energy* projectiles. The advantage of attacking a missile in its *boost phase* is that it can be destroyed before it has released its warheads and while it is still carrying *decoy* material.

To improve defense in this phase, the Soviet Union could counter by reducing the boost phase of its missiles. With the 180-second boost phase of the MX missiles as a comparison, it has been suggested that the Soviets could reduce the boost phase even further, to 50 seconds, making it extremely difficult for a BMD system to lock onto targets.

Post-boost phase

In this phase, the boosters have fallen away from the "bus" that carries the warheads and decoys. This phase lasts from two to five minutes, during which a BMD system can also get a crack at warheads and decoys. The Soviets could defend themselves during this phase with "cluster release," *i.e.*, by releasing all warheads and decoys together, thereby shortening the post-boost phase.

Mid-Course Phase

After warheads and decoys have been released, they travel through space for about 20 minutes before returning to the atmosphere. Mid-course interception runs into the problem of locating the warheads. One solution proposed is birth-to-death tracking, in which a sensor would lock onto a warhead as it leaves the bus and follow it through to reentry.

Terminal Phase

This is the final phase of an ICBM attack, in which warheads and decoys reenter the atmosphere at an altitude of about 60 miles above the earth. The decoys burn up and the reentry vehicles *(RV)*, which are warheads plus heat shields, reach their targets in from 30 to 60 seconds after reentry, traveling at a very high velocity.

Advances in technology over the past 20 years, such as improved radar and other sensors, and refined computer processing and accuracy, have made terminal-phase defense a more likely possibility.[13] Still, the essence of BMD and, thus, of the Strategic Defense Initiative lies in a series of exotic devices that gave it the name Star Wars. A generation ago, SDI would have been called a "Buck Rogers" defense. Prominent features include:

Space-based weapons

Lasers could theoretically fire beams of concentrated energy through space, but they are receiving less attention due to the increasing vulnerability of space-based objects. Moreover, space-based sensors, which are the seeing eyes of SDI, telling the system what is where and when, are running into programming problems. There is considerable doubt that a computer system can ever be devised to take on the overwhelming communications and control problems that SDI would encounter in battle. Finally, railguns would use electromagnetic fields to accelerate *smart* projectiles to home in on enemy missiles. They have already been tested.

Ground-based weapons

Lasers fired from the ground would be reflected off space-based mirrors toward their targets. They would be cheaper than their space-based equivalents and safer, provided a mirror of the size needed can be hung in space. *X-ray lasers* could be fired into space *("popped up")* when needed, but testing problems are beginning to put them into limbo. The likeliest candidate for early use is probably a kind of interceptor that would be fired at Soviet warheads in the reentry phase and also located to protect missile sites.[14]

Such are the possibilities of a BMD system; the policy questions it raises are unending. In September 1985, the Office of Technology Assessment issued a study that it had made at the request of the House Armed Services Committee and the Senate Foreign Relations Committee. It found:

• The destructive power of nuclear weapons has given the advantage to the offense against the defense. "Unless this imbalance between the offense and the defense disappears, strategic defenses might be plausible for limited purposes, such as the defense of ICBM silos . . . but not for the more ambitious goal of assuring the survival of U.S. society."

• If the Soviets want to mount overwhelming missile attacks, no BMD could ensure the survival of the U.S. population.

• Much more has to be known about the effectiveness of BMD systems before the superpowers can formulate plans or negotiations to ease the transition from reliance on deterrent capabilities for the prevention of nuclear war to the use of an SDI system as a means of defense.

• No one seems to know what would happen to the strategic situation if BMD deployment took place without a superpower agreement to reduce offensive weapons as defensive forces grew.

• The technology is reasonably well in hand to build a terminal-phase defense system that would require the USSR to use considerably more nuclear warheads in a determined attack on U.S. silos, then under present circumstances. It is not clear, however, whether BMD is the way to go to protect U.S. ICBM silos, and there are doubts about whether this kind of approach would strengthen (by inhibiting a Soviet attack completely) or weaken the U.S. deterrent by forcing the Soviets to mount an attack so massive that some missiles would be bound to get through.

• It is impossible to say now what a BMD system would eventually cost. [Estimates run as high as $1 trillion.]

• SDI promises to increase the nation's safety if (1) the U.S. efforts are highly successful technically, and (2), the cooperation of the Soviets is obtained in reaching an agreement to limit the number of ICBMS employed by the superpowers. *There is, of course, absolutely no assurance that the Soviets would actually behave as we think they should.*

• The U.S. should avoid conducting its SDI research in a way that would impel the Soviets to break the ABM treaty.[15]

Still, there is no obstacle to a working SDI program more formidable than the development of the *software* that will tell computers what to do in battle. Its incredible complexity is only one hurdle. With the boost phase of a nuclear missile now running between 180 and 300 seconds, we face the prospect of a war in which there is no time for human decisionmaking. A president who needs even five minutes to get to the chopper that will take him to his command aircraft cannot possibly be in a position to make a timely decision. With SDI, we will have achieved automated war.

Bambi   A perversion of every child's delight, this acronym stands for ballistic missile boost intercept. The concept for such a system originated during the immediate post-*Sputnik* period when a frightened Congress was willing to spend virtually unlimited funds for any scheme that seemed to promise a technological advantage over the USSR.

Hatched by the nation's top scientists in what was called Project Defender, a multimillion-dollar research undertaking in 1958, Bambi was envisioned as hundreds of space-based battle stations. Using infrared sensors to track the exhaust of enemy missiles, the Bambi weapons propelled on rockets would simply smash into the rising enemy missiles. Components of the system were tested on Titan and Atlas rockets.[16] Additional studies cost millions more before the Department of Defense concluded that the scheme was an impossibility.

Now Bambi is alive again. This time its mission is the first step in *Star Wars'* projected "layered" defense scheme. (See *Anti-ballistic missile defense, BMD.*)

Bargaining chip   An element used in negotiating, based on the concept of devising particular weapons for the sole purpose of trading them away to improve our bargaining position. For example:

—In 1985 the Reagan administration, its *Scowcroft Commission,* and the Democratic chairman of the House Arms Committee all agreed that the threat to adopt the original *MX missile* program was an essential part of bringing the Russians back to the bargaining table in Geneva.

—A small *ASAT* (anti-satellite) weapon carried aloft on an F15 jet and launched from the plane was tested successfully in 1986. It was first conceived as a bargaining chip in 1976, during the Carter administration.

—What Kennedy's men called Sentinel and Nixon's, *Safeguard* (same system; more money), was proposed as a bargaining chip by Nixon, but was finally killed by the Senate.

This practice, by which scores of weapons have started as bargaining chips and ended as permanent parts of America's defense arsenal, led a prominent military analyst, Harvard's Professor Thomas C. Schelling, to observe: "Publically acknowledging that Soviet intransigence can oblige the United States to procure an expensive weapon of admittedly little or negative military utility is embarrassing."[17]

It has also been noted that the bargaining-chip approach to negotiations cranked up the *arms race* by forcing the Soviets to match us program for program. Neither side was willing to negotiate from an obviously inferior position.[18]

Baruch Plan   Submitted to the newly formed United Nations in 1946, this was the first American attempt to rein in the awful consequences of nuclear explosives. While the plan was named for Bernard Baruch, a perennial park-bench advisor to presidents who presented it to the UN, it was, in effect, the work of the Acheson-Lilienthal Commission appointed by President Truman.

The plan called for the creation of a supernational body that would (1) control "all phases of the development and use of Atomic Energy" and (2) have the power to mete out "immediate, swift and sure punishment" to those who violated its control.[19] Unfortunately, at almost the same time, the U.S. passed the McMahon Act, which prohibited the sharing of nuclear secrets with any foreign country, thereby making adoption of the plan unlikely. Within days, the Russians offered a counterproposal that called for immediate destruction of existing weapons, sharing of technical information, and creation of UN monitoring commissions—over which they would have a veto.

Realizing that introduction of the Soviet plan made a compromise virtually impossible, Great Britain decided to become an independent nuclear power. The ensuing arguments among the U.S.,

Great Britain, and the USSR continued for three years, until any possible consideration was terminated by the explosion of a Soviet atomic bomb on September 23, 1949. The *arms race* had begun.

Bean count   The numbers game, or "nuclear accountancy,"[20] by which unofficial guesstimates of the number of *warheads* allegedly possessed by each of the superpowers are converted to gospel. Current official estimates (CIA and Pentagon) assume arsenals of some 25,000 warheads apiece. It is generally agreed that 500 per side is enough to wipe any vestige of civilization from the face of the earth. The other 49,000 are the dividend from the *arms race.*

More important than numbers, however, is the nature of the delivery system, the accuracy of the system, and, most importantly, the degree to which it will work under battlefield conditions—about which we know absolutely nothing yet. Still bean counts, usually from unofficial sources, are said to be the basis of President Reagan's persistent assertions that the USSR leads the United States in every military category.[21]

Bolt from the blue   The ultimate in unforeseen events, not to be confused with a *preemptive attack* (one made before the enemy can mount an attack that is obviously being planned). For the past 20 years, discussion of a possible bolt from the blue has all but disappeared, except to emphasize that such an event is highly unlikely. The principal reason given for this assurance is that the Soviets know that the U.S. could always strike back, because its submarine fleet, which carries more long-range missiles than all those contained in its silos, cannot, within present technological restraints, be detected.

However, all the safeguards devised to prevent accidental firing have, in fact, made the system more susceptible to a surprise attack. Says Yale University political scientist Paul Bracken, "A highly centralized, tightly coupled system has very limited ability to respond to an unimaginable event whose occurrence is counted highly unlikely."[22] In short, whether or not the U.S. is able to respond to a bolt from the blue must ultimately depend on the state of its detection and communications system.(See *C³I.*)

Bonus   The ultimate "twofor": the extra destruction and deaths achieved by a missile attack on an installation located near a city. This formula for calculated mayhem had great appeal to the Air

Force during the 1950s before the emphasis in kill technology shifted to missiles and the notion of *deterrence*.[23]

Boost phase   The beginning of a missile's flight. This is the time span during which a defense strategy will try to eliminate a hostile missile. An interception of this kind has been compared to sacking the football quarterback before he can pass the ball.[24] "Star Warriors" speak of a multi-*layered defense* with at least three distinct layers: the boost phase; the mid-course phase, when the *warheads* are traveling through space; and the reentry phase, when the warhead has reentered the atmosphere and is virtually on top of its target. (See *BMD*.)

The boost phase lasts from three to five minutes. It starts when the missile leaves its silo, or some kind of mobile launcher, under power from the first-stage booster. When the first-stage booster is used up, it is dropped, and a second stage is ignited and takes over.

The boost phase lasts until the boosters stop burning and the missile is about 350 kilometers above the earth. At this point, the missile releases its warheads and *decoys* to foil defense measures. If the Soviets wanted to defeat boost-phase attacks on their missiles, they would only have to install fast-burn boosters (up to 50 seconds), thereby shortening the boost phase. Since sensors fasten onto the the heat of the burning boosters, shortening the burn time would defeat any conceivable boost-phase attack.[25]

Breakout   Another of the double-entendres that make understanding nuclear arms and strategy so difficult. In one meaning, a breakout occurs when one superpower sidesteps the provision of a treaty to add to its nuclear arsenal. The other meaning is that of "breakout capability": the ability to deploy an operational system quickly.[26] Today's techniques of *verification* make such a breakout unlikely. (See *Cheating*.)

Broken arrow   Pentagon terminology for a major nuclear accident. Between 1945 and 1975, there has been about one nuclear accident per year. Some estimates say there have been as many as 30 major accidents and 250 minor problems during this period.[27]

For example, in September 1980 someone accidentally dropped a wrench that punctured a Titan missile, causing it to ignite and explode. Two men were killed, and the missile's nine-megaton warhead was hurled two hundred yards from its silo. Other broken arrows have released radiated material that contaminated areas around the accident site. About 18 years after a nuclear-armed B-52 bomber crashed in Greenland, more than 500 workers who helped in the clean-up operation are sick, and 98 of them are suffering from cancer, despite an official report that there was no risk to human health.[28]

Broken back   A nuclear war fought like a conventional war, in which resources mobilized after hostilities begin will eventually turn the tide in the same way wartime production and supply made allied victory possible in World War II. The notion that a nuclear war could be fought and won first appeared in 1954 in Great Britain, where the phrase "broken backed war" described what would happen after an indecisive nuclear exchange. Indeed, the major premise had to be that the exchange, however devastating, was a draw, and that the war could go on from there. The flaw that invalidates this concept is that no one knows how to plan for such a war, or how to stop it once it has gotten underway.[29]

Build down   Used as a verb, noun, or adjective, this means "to reduce," or "a reduction." The term is widely used among nuclear strategists, from Star Warrior-scientist Robert Jastrow [30] to arms critic William P. Bundy, [31] who served in the state and defense departments during the Kennedy and Johnson administrations.

The idea of build down was devised to describe the Reagan administration's 1983 proposal to the Soviets during their Geneva arms-limitation negotiations. The proposal would allow either nation to introduce a new nuclear weapon in return for retiring old weapons. Even if the adoption of such an agreement were to slow down the *arms race* by substituting improved weapons for increased numbers, it would just as surely multiply the technological horror of future weapons.

Moreover, a considerable body of opinion sees the build-down proposal as one that the Soviets could not possibly accept because of their reliance on missile size and weight rather than on technological improvement. Hence U.S. intentions are likely to be suspect.

Before the *Reykjavik* meeting of November 1986, the U.S. was following a watered-down form of build down to keep the limits established under *SALT* II. Even though the U.S. never ratified Salt II, President Reagan had agreed to dismantle old *Trident* submarines as new Poseidons were introduced into service. Even these minimum measures have been subject to accusations of *cheating*, as each superpower introduces new missiles to replace older designs.

Burnout The term experts use for "complete destruction" or "millions dead or burned beyond recognition" around the site where a nuclear bomb has struck.

The one-megaton bomb is among the most destructive. It packs a force 80 times more powerful than the bomb used at Hiroshima. Dropped to explode at ground level, it leaves a burnout area—the area of total destruction—that extends at least 2.6 miles in all directions.[32] Total destruction includes not only all structures but every living thing as well. If the bomb is exploded high in the air over the target (an "airburst"), the burnout area is 60 square miles, more than three times greater than the ground burst.

Moreover, missiles can be targeted to have overlapping burnouts. The Russian medium-range missile, the SS-20, carries three separate *warheads,* each of which can be aimed separately. Western intelligence believes the warheads are 650 kiloton bombs (only 50 times greater than the Hiroshima bomb) with a burnout of 50 square miles. Three hundred missiles targeted on Europe would devastate *45,000* square miles, an area about the size of New York State and not much smaller than Florida or Illinois.

Burrowing One of technology's gifts to a safe-and-sane nuclear war, this refers to a *warhead* designed to burrow its way into the ground. It does not threaten the ozone layer. According to Carl Sagan, it minimizes "fire, soot, stratospheric dust and radioactive fallout."[33] A one-kiloton bomb will dig a crater about three-quarters of a football field in diameter and devaste everything in the way. A bomb the size of the Hiroshima bomb (about 13 kilotons) could destroy *hardened* missile silos and underground command posts.

Bus The front or business end of a missile, carrying the missile's guidance system, individual *warheads* (each of which can be targeted separately), and a good supply of decoys in case anyone is shooting back. Once the missile drops its rocket engines at the end of the *boost phase*, the bus releases its warheads in different trajectories aimed at different targets. By the time the bus has emptied its contents, the missile will be in mid-course.[34]

C

C³I (Command, Communication, Control and Intelligence) The heart of the matter. These are the wired and wireless electronic systems that connect command posts with the troops, wherever they may be, and use every possible device from walkie-talkies to satellites, to a special plane known as the E4B. It will serve as the president's command post in time of war. Formally called the National Emergency Airborne Command Post *(NEACP)*, it is familiarly known as *"Kneecap."* Journalists call it the "Doomsday" plane.

This very special plane has 50 antennas, 13 radio systems, *computers* that keep in touch with *satellites,* and two crews, so that, with air-refueling, it can stay aloft indefinitely. However, in reality, with all its Buck Rogers equipment, the plane can stay in the air for only 48 hours, because engine oil will break down in that length of time.[1] In another part of the communications network are satellites with sensors that collect intelligence about enemy activities and serve as a navigation aid.

Despite C³I's intricacies, as President John Kennedy said, "there is always some son-of-a-bitch who doesn't get the word."[2] The frailties of the system raise the question, "who's in charge?" Certainly not the president, for there doesn't seem to have been much improvement in the system since the *Mayaguez* rescue of 1975, when U.S. forces conducted raids 30 minutes after President Ford ordered them to cease.[3]

In the U.S. "grounding" of an Egyptian plane carrying the four terrorists who were involved in the *Achille Lauro* incident in October 1985, it came to light that the planes used by the president and the secretary of defense are literally on different wavelengths.[4] They were able to talk to each other only through Italian-troop ground stations. And should the president be able to get into the act, he may find only chaos. In the Iranian rescue operation of April 1980, troops waiting for incoming helicopters talked to the White House, but they couldn't talk to the helicopters or to the Rangers guarding the site.[5]

Even though the deficiencies are glaring, Reagan budget figures indicate clearly that command systems have gotten short shrift, at least through the president's first term.[6] Moreover, recent experiments and the country's experience with *EMF* have shown that communications during a nuclear *attack* may be impossible.[7]

Because communications problems make it difficult for higher levels of command to stay in touch with lower levels, it has become necessary to delegate the "nuclear choice" further and further down the line. But according to Lord Zuckerman, the British scientific advisor to many of his governments, such delegation is why "every nuclear war game that has been played out realistically on the basis of actual military dispositions in the European theater has shown that the result would be mutual military disaster."[8] Still, military leaders who are fully aware of the C^3I system's deficiencies remain all set to "go first" during a growing crisis, for fear that they won't be able to get their missiles off. One of the Reagan administration's leading strategic advisors puts it bluntly: to "cut off the head of the Soviet chicken."[9]

Given the present state of the U.S. command and communication system, there is little likelihood that the military forces will get a go-ahead command within minutes after the detection of a Soviet attack. Nor is there any promise of much change in the near term, even though the weaknesses in the command systems of both superpowers confirms that there is a strong incentive for either side to begin an attack before damage has been suffered.

Catalytic war   A war between the U.S. and the Soviet Union that would be started by a third country firing off a missile which one superpower believes has been fired by the other superpower.

According to the Harvard Nuclear Study Group, three conditions are necessary for a catalytic war to occur:

—The third party must have *nuclear weapons* and a *delivery* capacity.

—The third party must have a motive.

—The superpower's forces must be susceptible to being triggered by such an attack.[10]

These conditions are not that difficult to satisfy. As long as a college undergraduate physics student can design a bomb from descriptions in a textbook, third party availability is ensured. And third-world motives are a dime a dozen. In short, the abilitiy of "crazies" like Libya's Colonel Muammar al-Qaddafi or Iran's Ayatollah Khomeini to trigger a nuclear holocaust is altogether possible as long as they have the technology. Pakistan, India, North Korea, and Israel are also likely candidates for the role of catalysts.

In August 1980 President Carter brought his senior advisors to the White House to discuss the buildup of Soviet forces that had been in progress in Afghanistan, just north of Iran, since the Soviet invasion of that country in December 1979 and the aborted attempt to rescue American hostages in Iran in April 1980. The U.S. did not have sufficient conventional forces in the area to stop the Russians. Hence the principal question was whether the U.S. should resort to the use of nuclear weapons. Here was the textbook condition for the intervention of a Khomeini. Fortunately, the crisis situation aborted.[11] (See also *Horizontal escalation*.)

Celestial snooker   Still another descriptive title for President Reagan's *Special Defense Initiative (SDI)*, popularly known as *Star Wars*. In England, where the synonym originated, snooker is a game of pool. Being snookered means ending up behind the eight ball. [12]

CEP (Circular error probable)   The ultimate measure of how good a missile really is is its accuracy. CEP is the radius of a circle whose center is directly on the target, within which half the bombs from a missile are expected to fall. The other half will land outside the circle. Presently, the Minuteman III missile has a CEP of 600 feet (a tenth of a mile). The best Soviet missiles have a CEP of 1,200 feet (a fifth of a mile).

Such measurements highlight the battle between sheer size of *warheads* and their accuracy. The Minuteman III, for example, has been given a 55 percent chance of destroying a *hardened* Soviet missile silo while the most accurate, weightier Soviet missiles are given only a 40 percent chance of taking out an American missile silo in one shot.[13] Indeed, it has been pointed out that ever since the missile became a military weapon, claims of Soviet leadership in accuracy have ultimately been proven wrong.

Cheating   What the other side (U.S. or USSR) is accused of doing when it violates a treaty condition in one way or another. Whether or not there is cheating depends completely on who defines the original provisions and who interprets the cheating. The Soviet radar installation currently under construction at Krasnoyarsk is probably the most notorious example of alleged cheating and the most illustrative of the commanding role of interpretation.

The *SALT* I Treaty of 1972 forbids the construction of phased-array radars "for early warning of strategic missile attack except along the periphery of its national territory and oriented outward."[14] The Krasnoyarsk radar is located 500 miles from the Soviet-Mongolian border and faces outward. Because of its location, the U.S. says that this is clearly cheating. Not so, say the Soviets because the radar can be used only for space tracking and is not capable of battle management. The accusation of cheating comes from the U.S. Defense Department,[15] but the CIA and British intelligence sources both claim that there is no cheating, on the grounds that:

The radar is not sufficiently well designed to serve as *ABM* radar;

Operates at the wrong frequency to provide *early warning;*

Is not *hardened,* as most battle management radars are;

Is not defended by interceptor missiles;

Does not cover the path of incoming U.S. missiles.

Nevertheless, the Krasnoyarsk radar has been a cheating *cause célèbre* for over a decade. But in 1985 and again in 1986, the Soviets offered to stop building the radar at Krasnoyarsk if the U.S. would stop the modernization program on its radar installations at Fylingdales in Great Britain and at Thule in Greenland. According to the Russians, the Fylingdales-Thule radars are much more of a breach of the 1972 ABM treaty than the Krasnoyarsk project.[16] And Raymond J. Garthoff, one of the principal U.S. negotiators of the ABM Treaty, agrees.[17] Most other allegations of cheating follow a similar pattern.

Cheating was the reason President Reagan gave in early 1986 for abandoning adherence to the 1979 SALT II treaty. The U.S. did not ratify the treaty but each superpower agreed to adhere to its provisions as long as the other did.

In making the announcement, the president outlined a new policy of "proportionate response" (*i.e.*, because you cheat, we'll cheat). Still, Secretary of State George P. Shultz, General Richard H. Ellis, U.S. delegate to the Soviet-American panel in Geneva that handles such disputes, and the joint chiefs of staff agree that if there is any cheating, it doesn't, in the words of Representative Les Aspin, Chairman of the House Armed Services Committee, "amount to a hill of beans."[18] Indeed, the chiefs made public a report stating that the Soviets continue to comply with the treaty by dismantling strategic systems.[19] State Department officials said the same thing in private Congressional testimony made public in January 1986.[20]

Long after he had left the White House, President Carter would say: "My impression was that the Soviets were, indeed, observing the agreements previously reached. That fact was confirmed to me by Secretary Kissinger when he came down here to Plains, Georgia to brief me even before I was sworn in as president. And so I had the sense, first of all, that the Soviets negotiated in good faith; secondly, that they did carry out the terms of an agreement once reached (with some small violations on both sides), and thirdly, that my restraints were just as much with the Senate as they were at the bargaining table with the Soviets."[21]

Chicken   Who flinches first? A "game" in which the consequences are not just the death of one driver, but possibly hundreds of millions of deaths. Thermonuclear poker may be an even better description for this Pentagon game. By its rules, the U.S. must be able to raise the stakes (escalate the conflict) in a way that is believable to the Soviets. This means being able to escalate again and again to more destructive levels of nuclear exchange, to the point where the Soviets will be afraid to match the U.S.[22] One major fallacy in this kind of idiotic thinking is the simple fact that the Russians don't play poker. They play chess.

The other major fallacy is what Harvard professor Thomas A. Schelling called the ubiquity of uncertainty: "Not everybody is always in his right mind. . . . Violence, especially in war, is a confused and uncertain activity, highly unpredictable depending on decisions made by fallible human beings organized into imperfect governments depending on fallible communications and warning systems and on the untested performance of people and equipment. It is, furthermore, a hotheaded activity, in which committments and reputations can develop a momentum of their own."[23]

Civil Defense   A program to provide the population with shelters of various kinds in the event of enemy *attack,* ensure the continuity of effective government during and after attack, and improve the prospects for postwar recovery. The growing interest in fighting and "winning" a nuclear war has stimulated efforts to improve population protection; indeed, the U.S. program is immense, despite some of its questionable assumptions. For example, according to Thomas K. Jones, deputy undersecretary of defense for strategic and nuclear forces until 1985, "If there are enough shovels to go around, everybody's going to make it."[24]

The program is widespread. Low and high risk areas have been designated; relocation plans have been drawn for cities. Plans have also been prepared for the protection of factories and for shelters to house important government documents. Fifty percent of some 3,000 localities selected for evacuation have complete "crisis relocation plans." Current plans call for nearly 9,000 emergency operation centers, some of which are already stocked for extended occupation. There are some 600 "protected" commercial broadcast stations, with plans to have nearly 3,000 by 1989. But the enormity of this program is rarely mentioned when anyone discusses the Soviet civil defense program, simply because the U.S. program pales by comparison.[25]

There is little doubt that Soviet civil defense efforts have far outstripped those of the U.S. But for civil defense to have any impact on the results of nuclear war, both superpowers will have to devote far greater resources than they are committing now. However, "no amount of effort would [ensure] the ability of either nation to continue as a functioning society" after a nuclear exchange, according to William P. Bundy,[26] former undersecretary of defense under President Kennedy and assistant secretary of state under President Johnson. What proponents of civil defense have failed to realize is the enormity of the evacuation problem and the virtual impossibility of providing adequate medical help. Soviet authorities have pointed out that the single disaster at Chernobyl compelled them to call upon medical resources throughout the country.

Cocked pistol   The ultimate of the five phases of *alert,* which begin with "fade-out."

Cold war   A phrase coined by perennial presidential advisor Bernard Baruch in 1948 to describe the state of affairs between the superpowers. Winston Churchill had noted in vivid terms the previous year in his speech at Fulton, Missouri, "From Stettin in the

Baltic to Trieste in the Adriatic, an Iron Curtain has descended across the continent." In the ensuing years, the Soviets' European allies would be referred to as the "iron curtain" countries. Since 1947 the tension between the superpowers has risen (with the Berlin Blockade) and fallen (with *detente*). No troops have moved; no shots have been fired, but, all the while, the *arms race* continues.

What the future holds is unclear, but surely it lies somewhere between the liberals' dream of a democratized Soviet state and the conservatives' certain prediction of the complete collapse of the Soviet Union. There have, of course, been enormous differences in Soviet attitudes from Stalin to Khrushchev to Andropov and now Gorbachev, with his policy of *glasnost.* Gorbachev's priorities differ from those of his predecessors, and the results to which his policies are likely to lead, and the degree to which his compatriots will allow him to lead, are still open questions.[27]

Cold-launch   A way to get intercontinental missiles to where they're going without damaging the *launcher.* Most land-based missiles are currently housed in concrete silos within the ground, from which they are fired when the booster engine is ignited. The silo is damaged beyond reuse. The Russian SS-18, however, is popped out of the silo mechanically before its booster is ignited. This system is similar to launching from submarines. The older Poseiden submarines popped their missiles out of the launch tubes with steam pressure. Once the missile cleared the surface, its rocket engines ignited.[28]

Collateral damage   A relative of *bonus.* If the Soviets mount a *first strike* (attack the U.S. first) aimed at the missile silos in the Midwest, those who live too near the bases will die "collaterally." Interestingly, the Soviets do not have a word for collateral damage.[29]

Compellence   Beyond a policy of *deterrence,* which maintains things the way they are, compellence seeks to force an adversary to do something specific, "such as pursuing a desired policy, cooperating with the threatener, changing an activity or ceasing a line of action already begun."[30] For example, once hostilities have started at a low, probing level, compellence would seek to convince an enemy that he ought to cease hostilities because every move he makes will be matched. In short, compellence recognizes that both superpowers are operating under a "diplomacy of violence"[31] and that, in the nuclear age, diplomacy has become poker with six-shooters on the table.

Computer   The incredible devices that foul up your checking accounts, send you the wrong store bills, run factories, help your doctor tap into diagnostic information, direct—and misdirect—modern weapons systems, and possibly start nuclear wars.

Technically speaking:

> A digital computer is an electronic machine that performs high-speed calculations. It also assembles, stores, correlates, or otherwise accepts, processes, and prints information. It does this according to programs, which are written instructions that tell the computer what to do.
>
> A computer system consists of hardware and *software*. The hardware includes a central processing unit that performs mathematical and logical operations, a memory unit for data and instructions, and devices for input and output. The software consists of the various programs that make the system do what the operator wants it to do.
>
> The digital computer carries out its computations by counting. An analog computer, on the other hand, computes on the basis of measurements of physical or electrical quantities. Some instruments like compasses and speed indicators use analog techniques to get their values and then convert to digital formats for easier reading and further use.

Obviously, computers may serve many purposes. A scientist at the Livermore Laboratory in California, where much of the *Star Wars* experimenting is underway, calls computers "as much a weapon as nuclear *warheads* are."[32] Other scientists would say computers are incredibly adept aids. But because humans must tell computers what to do, they can be very uncertain aids, as, for example they were at Cape Canaveral, where numerous space shuttle missions were cancelled due to computer glitches (malfunctions).

In a Star Wars battle-management system, computers would have to detect and count missiles in an *attack,* discriminate between *decoys* and warheads, calculate flight paths and track intended targets, aim *BMD* weapons, take note of hits and misses, and reaim weapons—all in an environment of thousands of attacking warheads and innumerable decoys.

But "because of the extreme demands on the system and our inability to test it, we will never be able to believe, with any confidence, that we have succeeded. Most of the money spent will be wasted," stated Canadian scientist David L. Parnas, who resigned from an *SDI* advisory panel on computing in support of battle management for the Office of Naval Research in Washington.[33]

The necessity for advanced testing of any battle-management system that SDI will use is illustrated by experiences with the Aegis air-defense system. The battle-management system for Aegis is designed to track hundreds of airborne objects within a 50-mile radius of the U.S.S. *Ticonderoga,* a cruiser on which Aegis had been installed. In its first test, the weapons system missed 6 out of 16 targets because of mistakes in *software.* (Earlier small-scale and simulation tests had not uncovered the errors).[34]

The reliability of computers is often measured, not by whether they will fail, but by how long they will operate between failures, called the mean time between failures.[35] For a computer used in an *ABM* system, the measure would be about eight days. But there will be blips, for a computer rarely works on the first try after a program has been written. Repeated trials are needed to get the bugs out.

Yet, the computers directing modern nuclear arms on the ground or in space will never have been tested under realistic conditions. The world's largest computer program is the one that supports the U.S. Social Security system. It has 4,000,000 lines of instructions and, after 20 years, bugs still appear. Some Star Wars computers will require well over 10,000,000 lines and will never be tested. Recently, American Telephone and Telegraph conducted a study of 200 major corporate computer users. For every 1,000 lines of computer code, there were 300 serious errors.[36]

Put another way, the average programmer can write about 3,000 lines of bug-free instructions annually. It would take 1,000 programmers about three years to produce the 10,000,000 lines that SDI needs. But these programmers would have to cooperate as closely as the crew of an eight-oared shell, not for minutes but for years. This feat has probably not been achieved in human history.[37]

In the Falkland Islands War between Great Britain and Argentina, the H.M.S. *Sheffield* was sunk by an Exocet missile, which the ship's computer picked up and then recognized as a friendly missile. Obviously, someone forgot to tell the computer that Argentina was not friendly, or that because the Exocet is a French-made missile, it is not necessarily friendly.[38]

A similar kind of human error occurred on June 19, 1985, in a simple SDI experiment. The crew of the space shuttle was ordered to position the craft so that a mirror fixed to its side could reflect a laser beam fired from the top of a mountain 10,023 feet above sea level. The experiment failed because the shuttle's computer read the information it received on the laser's location as an elevation in nautical miles instead of feet!

Containment A policy for U.S. relations with the Soviet Union developed by George Kennan, a student of Soviet affairs, diplomat, and one-time head of the State Department policy planning staff. It was first enunciated in 1947, in an article signed "X" in *Foreign Affairs*.[39] Kennan would admit later that he had not edited the article carefully enough, and that this lapse stimulated a continuing debate over "what Kennan meant to say." Writing two decades later, Kennan said that the article was a plea for the belief that "ugly as was the problem of Soviet power, war was not inevitable. . . . there was a middle ground of political resistance on which we could stand with reasonable prospect of success. We were in fact already standing on that ground [the Marshall Plan] quite successfully."[40]

Containment urged the U.S. to stop making unilateral concessions to the Soviets, to support resistance to Soviet attempts to expand its political influence, and to await the weakening of Soviet power as it dealt with frustrations abroad. Essentially, it was a policy that aimed at eventual negotiation to alter the status quo. Although the number of nations dominated by Soviet influence had diminished a decade later, Kennan admitted that, in the end, containment failed. The enormous pull exerted by technology-dominated foreign policy, left little, if any, room for negotiation.

Containment has not been allowed a place in the world of *Star Wars (SDI)*. Attemps to wrap the SDI concept in containment to make it less revolutionary and, by inference, to line up Kennan on the Star Wars side, were quickly disavowed. He said, "I emphatically deny the paternity of any efforts to invoke that doctrine today in situations to which it has, and can have, no proper relevance."[41]

Controlled escalation The little boys' game of who flinches first, as played by superpowers with all the destructive paraphernalia of nuclear armaments. Sometimes called controlled reprisal, this notion, which originated in the late 1950s to describe the intensification of warfare, could be called step-by-step war. The word *escalation* has become part of the language and was used to describe the growing war in Vietnam. Escalation, or controlled escalation, is often associated today with the defense of *NATO* countries. (See *escalation dominance*.)

The most common *scenario* is one in which the Soviets overwhelm NATO conventional forces in Western Europe. NATO fires a *nuclear weapon* at Soviet forces, which retaliate. NATO strikes back a bit harder. Then it's the Soviets' turn, and so on and on. The idea behind this gradual escalation is that hostilities can be stopped at any of these stages, provided, of course, that communications between the superpowers are kept open at all times. About this, however, there are doubts.

In its worst form, proponents of controlled escalation see it as a tit-for-tat city-trading scheme,[42] in which levels of destruction are ratcheted until one side calls "uncle." Although the notion has persisted to the present day, it has been pointed out repeatedly that "escalation is impervious to intricate control."[43] More importantly, the Soviets do not recognize any such strategic approach.

Correlation of forces   The Soviet expression used to measure the balance between East and West. But the Soviets go beyond the Western notion of measuring comparative forces, which is usually confined to numerical comparisons of military forces. (See *bean count, balance*) The Kremlin includes in the correlation of forces the state of the economy, social cohesion, national unity, and the worth of alliances. When the Soviets speak about the "correct" correlation of forces, they say they are ahead in the superpower race. When it is unfavorable, they talk about irrelevancies in negotiations and follow Lenin's dictum of throwing dust in the enemy's eyes to give themselves time to regroup and change the correlation.[44]

Consequently, during the Brezhnev era, the nonmilitary components in the correlation of forces were running in the Soviets' favor. Their economy was improving. The USSR had benefited from the jump in oil prices. U.S. prestige in Asia had diminished as the Vietnam War wound down in a U.S. defeat. As Gorbachev came to power, these elements were running against the Soviets. Where his reforms and *glasnost* will take the USSR is still to be determined.[45]

Counterforce   A policy of using nuclear forces to destroy an enemy's armed forces rather than cities and population centers, i.e., using your arms to destroy his arms. At the very beginning of the *arms race* it was questioned whether any such targeting distinctions could be made. According to Bernard Brodie, one of the most respected early nuclear commentators: "The distinction in priority could turn out to be an academic one. It is idle to talk about strategies being counter-force strategies, as distinct from counter-economy or counter-population strategies."[46] Too many people live near defense establishments and air fields to escape. During the Nixon administration, a policy guideline memo signed by the president called for the destruction of 70 percent of the Soviet industrial base if a war ever started. This would amount to attacks on some 200 Soviet cities inhabited by one-third of the nation's population.[47]

As technology progressed, the targeting debate became ever mushier. MIRVed missiles were called counterforce weapons, as if they couldn't be fired at cities or factories. Since they could do exactly that, the whole idea looked too much like the rationale for a *first strike*. This was the problem that bothered Robert McNamara, defense secretary to both Kennedy and Johnson, who had given counterforce its big push and then dropped it. Still, there are many adherents of counterforce today, despite the large number of "ifs" associated with it: will weapons work the way they are supposed to?; will both sides understand what they are supposed to do?; will both sides refrain from playing *chicken*?[48]

Countervailing strategy   Articulated most recently by Harold Brown, President Carter's secretary of defense, countervailing strategy is "a strategy that denies the other side any possibility that it could win—but it doesn't say that our side would win."[49] He elaborated in his Annual Report to the Congress for 1982; countervailing strategy proposes "to convince the Soviets that they will be successfully opposed at any level of aggression they choose, and that no plausible outcome at any level of conflict could represent 'success' for them by any reasonable definition of success."[50]

The idea of countervailing strategy actually began with President Ford's secretary of defense, James Schlesinger, who enshrined the concept of levels of aggression by proposing the notion of nuclear options to give greater flexibility in targeting and to change targets in a "prolonged nuclear war." Still, the idea that step-by-step escalation is possible, and that the U.S. could prevail, has become a part of the Reagan administration strategy.[51]

Countervalue targeting   A *strategy* of aiming *nuclear weapons* at places like cities and factories, where there are high concentrations of population. The opposite notion is *counterforce* targeting, which

aims at military installations. Each strategy has legions of proponents. The superpowers' targeting plans, designed to eliminate as
much of the other nations' economic infrastructure as possible, run
hard up against the frightening fact that there are 2,500 cities in
the world with populations of more than 100,000 persons which
are, in one way or another, close to nuclear installations. Obviously,
they are all on each nation's targeting plans .

Coupling   The promise by the U.S. to use its nuclear capabilities to
meet *NATO* defensive requirements, as a threat to deter Soviet conventional forces from attacking NATO. The assumption is that if
NATO forces are losing a conventional battle, the U.S. will counter
with short-range nuclear weapons and step up to the use of intercontinental missiles. The Russians know this, and, therefore, will
refrain from initiating hostilities.

However, by resorting to nuclear arms to protect its European
allies, the U.S. would be putting its large cities at risk. This, it has
been said, is not a very believable threat. On the other hand, there
are questions about who's ahead in European conventional forces.
Given the poor quality of troops among Soviet Eastern European
allies, and the clear NATO lead in technology, the answer seems to
tip the balance toward the West.

Credibility   The belief that a promise made is a promise kept. For
example, Saudi Arabian rebels blow up oil wells. The Saudi king
asks the U.S. (his ally) to send rapid deployment forces to squash
what is obviously a rebellion. The U.S. agrees. The plane carrying
U.S. forces is downed in Saudi Arabia by missiles that are obviously
of Soviet origin. The U.S. strikes back by sending in better armed
reinforcements. It has "credibility." The USSR is not about to let
down the rebels, its clients, and sends in help. It has "credibility."
In fulfilling their promises, the superpowers have risked the possibility of starting World War III.

The same kind of situation could occur in Europe if Eastern bloc
conventional forces tangled with *NATO* forces. To maintain credibility, the superpowers would feel obligated to assist their clients.
Here, too, the superpowers would be risking World War III, not to
save face, but to do what they had said they would. Credibility lies
at the heart of the notion of *deterrence* and creates what has been
called the *usability paradox*. Given credibility, nuclear weapons
can prevent aggression, because there is always a certainty that

they will be used. But the easier they are to use, the greater the temptation to use them.[52]

Crisis Center   Not where the trouble starts, but where it might stop. As originally proposed by Senator Sam Nunn, chairman of the Senate Armed Services Committee, the Crisis Center was to be a joint undertaking of the U.S. and Soviet Russia.[53] Jointly staffed, it would provide a platform for continuing discussions of common interests. Senator John Warner joined Nunn in urging the administration to negotiate such an agreement. President Reagan and Secretary Gorbachev discussed it at their meeting in 1985, and, in May 1987, an accord was reached. Though not as extensive as Senators Nunn and Warner had suggested, the agreement was nevertheless signed on September 15, 1987 in the White House Rose Garden by Soviet Foreign Minister Eduard A. Shevardnazde and Secretary of State George P. Shultz with President Reagan.

The pact calls for the establishment of "risk reduction centers" in Moscow and Washington. The centers will exchange the kind of information that could be misinterpreted, such as the movement of troops or weapons systems. Overall, the idea is to reduce misinformation and misperceptions to a minimum, and, it is hoped, to supplement the so-called hot line that has run between the Oval Office and the Kremlin since 1963.

Communications equipment between the two centers will be of the highest order. For example, until 1984, there was no improvement to the original hot-line system. It consisted of 20-year-old teletype machines printing at 30 words per minute (personal computers with laser printers print eight pages per minute).

Providing more current information in greater depth can help crisis management immeasurably. For example, a crisis between the superpowers might occur when (1) the leaders see a vital interest threatened; (2) both leaders believe that relations are close to the breaking point; and (3) one thinks the other is about to strike, so the pressure mounts for him to strike first. This is the broad view. But crisis management is more likely to be concerned with minute-by-minute developments. The stakes are high, and there is very little time to make a decision. The decisionmakers simply don't have all the information they need, and the choices they face may well be at the ends of the spectrum, where extremes prevail.[54] The Crisis Center would provide some of the information needed to make the decisions.

Cruise missile   Essentially, a small, slow, highly maneuverable pilotless aircraft that can be launched from the ground, the air, or at sea and guided to hug the terrain to avoid enemy radar. As originally conceived, it was to provide a long arm for the B-52 bomber, which could launch a cruise missile as it approached enemy borders, then turn around and go home, thereby foxing air defenses. The cruise missile can carry a *warhead* the same size as one carried by a *ballistic missile* fifteen times its size.

Technically, the cruise missile is a marvel: it flies low, invisible to enemy radar detection screens. Its *computers* are fed maps obtained from *satellites* that show the terrain over which it flies. Any deviations from the flight plan are corrected automatically.

Politically, the cruise missile is a monster. It figured importantly in the *SALT* I negotiations, was given up by the Air Force for economic reasons, then reembraced to become a pawn of interservice rivalry, as each branch fought for its own version. It drove Henry Kissinger to declare that "Those geniuses [in the Defense Department] think the goddamn thing is a cure for cancer and the common cold."[55] Because of its small size, a cruise missile is easily hidden, making the process of *verification* and *arms control* infinitely more difficult. In mid-1986, the issue of submarine-launched versions became a football tossed between the superpowers in the arms control talks, because of the difficulty of distinguishing between nuclear and conventionally armed cruise missiles.[56]

Still, there is very little that the cruise missile can do better than a ballistic missile, and, consequently, a good deal of suspicion that it is a classic instance of the military's inability to resist a "sweet technology." The cruise missile is cheap, very accurate, very hard to shoot down, and a marvel of navigational control. Although it is not indispensable to a nuclear weapons arsenal because it does nothing more than the ballistic missiles that are already in place, but there was undoubtedly a great temptation to produce it and then find a mission for it.[57] Indeed, it has been reported that work is already underway on development of a supersonic version. It has been said in testimony before the Senate Armed Services Committee that the Tomahawk nuclear cruise missile, which can be launched from a submarine, "is well suited for a post-attack reserve role, to provide a wider range of *escalation* control options to the national command authority"[58]—assuming that such a national authority still exists!

Damage limitation   Prevention, insofar as possible, of the ultimate horror. Under current targeting and strategic plans, an all-out nuclear exchange between the superpowers, aimed at military and economic targets, would kill 155-165 million people in the U.S. and 64-100 million in the Soviet Union. Over the years, two approaches to damage limitation have evolved in U.S. policymaking. One is to have enough nuclear arms to destroy Soviet weapons before they can be launched, thereby deterring *attack*. The other would apply in an accident situation. For example, misread warnings could impel the U.S. to launch strategic missiles toward Soviet targets. The U.S., learning of its mistake, would assume that any warning beamed to the Soviets would be ignored and lead to Soviet retaliation. Hence to "limit damage" to its forces, the U.S. would launch an all-out attack and begin a nuclear holocaust that could not be turned around.[1]

Davy Crocket   The weapon that should never have been made. Conceived as a "nuclear bazooka," it was to have a *warhead* of less than one kiloton and to be carried by an individual soldier. The weapon was already in production before the realization dawned among defense officials who had ordered it that there was no way of controlling its use once it had been issued to troops. The high command withdrew it.[2]

Decapitate   "Off with their heads." This is the quick, all-or-none *strategy*. If we can obliterate the other side's command and decisionmaking structure, *i.e.*, decapitate, we win. Every administration of the past 40 years has toyed with this "final solution," as surely as the Soviets have, for the command structures of both nations are highly susceptible to neatly directed nuclear *attacks*.

In May 1982 the *New York Times* printed the gist of the Reagan administration's first "defense guidance" plan—the one that sets forth what targets will be hit with what missiles from what sources in the event of hostilities. It describes two possible strategies, one for fighting a "protracted" nuclear war and another that would attempt to win a short war through decapitation.[3] Not long thereafter, in December 1983, the Pershing missile was deployed in West Germany. This missile, President Reagan said, was built to "advance the cause of peace and disarmament,"[4] even though decapitation was its principal purpose. This presented no great change from the Carter administration policy, whose defense guidance plan projected "a brief, spasmic and apocalyptic conflict" based on decapitation.[5]

Throughout its history, decapitation has been interpreted as a sign of a *first strike* policy, typical of both the Carter and Reagan administrations. Thus, decapitation is seen as the way to a quick victory.[6] However, many analysts think it is a disastrous policy, because rather than preventing retaliation, it might induce an hysterical, last-ditch counterattack. The loss of a command structure could also instigate attacks ordered by lower-level commands that suddenly found themselves on their own. Finally, decapitation eliminates anyone with whom either of the superpowers can settle differences and negotiate a peace.

Decoupling   Used in discussions of *NATO* defensive policy; a way of breaking the chain that leads from "the man in the foxhole to the man in the Minuteman hole."[7]

According to the theory developed in the late 1950s and early 1960s, if the USSR launched a conventional attack against Western Europe, NATO forces would respond with nuclear battlefield weapons. If things went badly, the U.S. would launch intercontinental missiles (strategic) against the USSR. Any attempt by the U.S. to do less, by negotiation or through abandonment of its obligations, was termed decoupling. (See also *Coupling*.)

There were two questions involved, one the obvious question of whether an American president would take a step that led to the destruction of Chicago or New York because Hamburg or Paris had been obliterated. According to one European observer, the step was not likely to be taken because the "Americans are not, after all, completely crazy."[8] For this reason, the threat to take such action was not very believable, especially to the Soviets. The second question had to do with what some jargonists have called the "condominium" *strategy*. It asks just how much decoupling would result from superpower diplomatic negotiations toward more peaceful relations. For example, the negotiations to eliminate intermediate range missiles from Europe raised originally just that question.

Decoy A piece of equipment that is carried in a missile along with actual *warheads* and is released with those warheads. The decoy looks like a missile to an attacking warhead, which therefore may be diverted from its target. New kinds of decoys are now being developed to confuse the attacking warhead instead of diverting it. The big *ICBMs* and *SLBMs* may carry as many as 100 decoys.

Deep cuts Along with *nuclear freeze* and *build down,* this is one of three prominent proposals for reducing nuclear arsenals and reversing the *arms race.* Originally proposed by Sovietologist, diplomat, and historian George Kennan, deep cuts are vaguely related to some of the proposals that developed in the 1986 mini-summit at *Reykjavik.* This proposal suggests a halving of the superpower arsenals in a relatively short time and the surrender of their nuclear triggers to a binational or multinational authority.[9]

Defense A word with two major classes of use—one military and one financial.

In military terms, defenses can be active or passive. Passive defense protects targets (military installations, factories, or cities) against enemy attack. Active defense involves detecting, tracking, and shooting down incoming offensive forces. When active defense becomes active offense is a moot question.[10] This is what bothers the Soviets about *Star Wars.*

Financially, the many uses of the word defense are opaque. In submitting figures for the 1986 defense budget, the Reagan administration said it could get by with defense outlays of $277.5 billion and national defense outlays of $285.7 billion. Neither the president nor Secretary of Defense Weinberger explained the important difference between "defense" and "national defense."[11] The defense budget covers the military functions of the Department of Defense. But other expenses, like those for the independent Atomic Energy Commission, which manufactures all the nuclear *warheads,* are lumped together into what is called national defense.

Defense-dominated The phrase the strategists use to describe a nation that puts all its chips on defensive systems; for example, reliance on the *Star Wars* program would indicate a defense-dominated nation. From the Soviet point of view, however, Star Wars is an offensive approach because it would allow the U.S. to virtually ignore the possibility of a Soviet *attack* and strike first at any time.

If the Soviets developed such a system first, American thinking would change, probably toward the Soviet viewpoint. Since no defensive systems of the kind that Star Wars envisions have ever been built—and may never be built by either superpower—most strategic thinking is in a "what if?" mode, leading one observer to speculate that the offense-defense argument produces a series of successive cycles: "He thinks we think he thinks we think . . . he thinks we think he'll attack; so he thinks we shall; so he will; so we must."[12]

Delivery system   This term describes how a nuclear *warhead* gets to where it's going. With the exception of the missile, which is essentially a skyrocket carrying a warhead, bombs get to their targets the way they always have, via aircraft, artillery, depth charges, torpedoes and, of course, in suitcases. The scary part is the incredible means of targeting common today, primarily automatic or automated, *computer* and radar directed. Applied to missiles, this technology produces systems like "fire-and-forget" or "launch-and-leave," whereyby the pilot of an aircraft fires the missile and goes home.

Dense pak   A concept whose time never came. Because of the increasing vulnerability of missile silos in the Midwest to enemy *attack*, the Carter Administration proposed the Multiple Protective Shelter System. About 200 missiles on moveable *launchers* would be shuttled continually at random among 4,600 concrete shelters, thereby completely fooling the Soviets, who would have to fire at all 4,600 shelters to hit the missiles. Based on the expection that the *SALT* II treaty which placed limitations on the number of *warheads,* was about to be ratified, the Carter administration believed this system would strain the Soviet missile inventory. The Reagan administration killed the program as soon as it took office, because it believed that the system was not justified economically and was unworkable. Nevertheless, in its first term the Reagan administration proposed a similar system of its own called dense pak.

Under the Reagan plan, 100 missiles were to be installed in super-protected silos, each less than half a mile apart. The theory was that any Soviet attack on the silos would do more harm to its own missiles than to the silos. The missiles that arrived first would create such a cloud of dust and debris that the later missiles would be put out of commission. Congress promptly vetoed the scheme because it was too expensive as well as ludicrous, but it is mentioned from time to time. (See *MX missile, fraticide.*)

Destabilizing   Used to describe whatever upsets the *balance* between the superpowers in weapons or in attitudes. For example, the introduction of newer, faster, more accurate *counterforce* nuclear weapons into Europe would be destabilizing, because weapons designed to be used against "their" weapons must be fired first to destroy them before they can be activated. The Reagan administration's insistence on proceeding with *Star Wars* is destabilizing. So is the increasing use of cruise missiles, since it is presently impossible to determine whether they are carrying conventional or nuclear *warheads*.

On the political side, the Soviet invasion of Afghanistan and the Reagan administration's decision to break out of the confines of *SALT* II treaty restrictions are both examples of destabilizing moves.

Detente   In Russian, *"razryadka"* the word given by the superpowers to the management of their relations in a way that would avoid the pitfalls induced by the *arms race*. It was their acknowledged response, in the late 1960s and early 1970s, to the fact that a state of strategic *parity* existed between them; *i.e.,* if either country were attacked, it could destroy the other. Basically, detente called for:

—Negotiations for *arms control* agreements;

—Taking steps that would build mutual confidence, such as notification of troop movements and maneuvers;

—Regular communications to establish a system that could be used in times of special tension;

—Expansion of relations in such areas as trade, credit, and consumer technology.

Unfortunately, the joint U.S.-USSR statement of "Basic Principles of Mutual Relations" that became the Nixon-Brezhnev declaration of 1972 did little good. The two countries were experiencing diametrically opposite domestic circumstances, which created different expectations and performances.

For the USSR, the decade 1965-75 was the best economic period it had ever had. The Soviets had achieved parity with the U.S. militarily. Internationally, they were sailing high. Relations with Egypt, Iraq, and India were growing closer, and Iran was a peaceful neighbor. In Western Europe, trade and credits flowed through the Iron Curtain; West Germany seemed to be accepting the division of the German nation between East and West.

For the United States, those years were times of trouble. The Vietnam War had created more internal dissent than any foreign war in American history, and Watergate had deeply shaken the government and the nation. America was a country in disarray. Especially because of Watergate, detente created exaggerated hopes that simply could not be fulfilled. It has been noted that detente failed less because of what the Russians may have done and more because of what the U.S. failed to do.[13] An increase in U.S. and *NATO* military expenditures did not occur; the U.S. made no attempt to confront Soviet moves in Angola, Ethiopia, and the socialist states in Africa.

In a sense, detente never had a chance. Starting with the Middle East conflict in October 1973, a certain disillusionment set into the Oval Office and accelerated during the Ford and Carter administrations, creating an atmosphere in which any undertaking with the Soviets was suspect. The Angolan conflict, the Ogaden War, and the "discovery" of the Soviet brigade in Cuba all added to the feeling of despair.[14]

Detente finally collapsed with the Soviet invasion of Afghanistan in 1979 and the destruction of the Solidarity movement in Poland in 1981. Nevertheless, detente may well remain essential to the future avoidance of mutual destruction, for its failure did not invalidate its basic premises: the urgent need for arms control and the mangement of relations so as to avoid military confrontation. In short, there are no technological solutions to political problems, a fact that detente recognizes.

Deterrence The policy that has kept us out of nuclear war, according to Queen Elizabeth II of Great Britain who exclaimed at the end of the 1970s: "Their *[nuclear weapons]* awesome destructive power has preserved the world from major war for the past 35 years." Secretary of Defense Harold Brown did not agree; he declared at about the same time that "a reasonable degree of nuclear *stability* in a crisis is probably assured ... Unfortunately, longer term stability is not fully assured." What they were talking about is simply the process of using the threat of force to convince an enemy that he is better off if he does not use military force against you. The Romans said it this way: "If you want peace, then prepare for war." Thomas Jefferson said it another way: "How can we prevent those wars produced by the wrongs of other nations? By putting ourselves in a condition to punish them. Weakness produces insult and injury, while a condition to punish often prevents it."[15]

In short, the enemy's fear of retaliation keeps him from starting a war, because the incredibly destructive consequences would far outweigh any possible gain. This is deterrence, which Lord Zuckerman, a leading scientific advisor to British governments, has called little more than "a verbal rationalization of a prevailing situation."[16] Its effectiveness, however, does not depend simply on having lots of weapons; they must be weapons that cannot be destroyed before they are used.

The enemy has to believe that the weapons will be used and that a threat is not a bluff. Each superpower must assume that the other is rational, which, under some circumstances, may be very hard to do. This, perhaps, is why Bernard Brodie, one of the country's first nuclear strategists, pointed out: "One of the foremost factors making deterrence really work and work well is the lurking fear that in some massive confrontation crisis, it might fail. Under these circumstances one does not tempt fate."[17] Nevertheless, in the late 1950s, when the Soviets marched brazenly into Hungary and America stood all but tongue-tied, the U.S. had a clear nuclear superiority over the USSR. Deterrence had not stopped the Soviets.

There are variations on deterrence, which is essentially a theme of punishment. Since the 1960s, both superpowers have been developing a war-fighting deterrence, which assumes the ability to fight a nuclear war and prevail. *NATO* looks at deterrence as the right to counter conventional attacks with nuclear weapons, and, if necessary, to start a nuclear war. During the 1950s and the 1970s, and again today, the American idea of deterrence includes a possible *first strike*. Says a strategist close to the Reagan administration, "The West needs to devise ways in which it can employ strategic nuclear forces coercively while minimizing the potentially paralyzing impact of *self-deterrence*."[18] And President Reagan himself defines deterrence this way: "U.S. Defense policies ensure our preparedness to respond to and, if necessary, successfully fight either conventional or nuclear war."[19] This, say most observers, is a dangerous perversion of deterrence, because a successful policy of deterrence implies that the war will not be fought.

Deterrence gap   Like the *window of vulnerability* and the *missile gap*, the deterrence gap was all propaganda. The term was used in an attempt to defeat early *arms control* efforts during the Eisenhower administration, and alleged that America's nuclear forces were insufficient to the task of protecting the nation and that more weapons were needed to reach *parity* with the USSR.[20] Since then, the notion of a deterrence gap has usually been raised by those who oppose arms control and favor gaining superiority in nuclear arsenals over the Soviets.

Directed energy   The ultimate in *anti-ballistic missiles (ABM)*, "the bullet that can hit a bullet." Unfortunately, the missile that has to hit another missile is traveling at the same speed as its target. Consequently, the chances of a direct hit are infinitesimal and so, some scientists have turned to the dream of directed-energy weapons. They would be the backbone of any future *Star Wars* system and, in one way or another, would all be space-based weapons. Generally, three types are discussed:

1. *Laser* weapons—an intense beam of electromagnetic radiation, aimed with a device similar to a telescope. They would vaporize the surface of the target.
2. Radio-frequency weapons—electromagnetic radiation aimed with an antenna. They would damage a missile's electronic circuits.
3. *Particle-beam* weapons—intense beams of subatomic particles aimed with a high-energy accelerator. They would strike deep into the innards of an oncoming missile.

A number of scientists cite many reasons why the construction of these weapons is an impossibility. According to the British Star Wars champion Lord Chalfont, "Whatever technology is eventually used, even by the most optimistic assessment, it would not be possible to construct a *multilayered defense* system" using directed energy weapons with today's technology.[21]

Disinformation   The bane of public relations, with which it has been confused, disinformation is the ultimate in packaging nuclear arms and strategic policy in a way that may run a gamut from outright fabrication and mendacity to the studied use of deceptive euphemisms. The word itself came into general use suddenly in 1986 to describe the stories that were purposefully leaked out to mislead (disinform) Libya's Colonel Muammar al-Qaddafi. Then came the news that the U.S. had been disinforming both sides in the Iran-Iraq war. Indeed, in 1987, Iraq would claim that a major defeat had been caused by U.S. disinformation.[22] This non-word was not simply disingenuous, its use reflected a tendency that has persisted throughout the Atomic Age, confusing not only Americans, but U.S. allies and enemies as well. Moreover, that use has become increasingly dangerous, as the forces of the U.S. and the USSR operate more and more on high-tech hair triggers. *Crisis centers* such as the superpowers agreed to in June 1987 were created, in effect, to produce understanding by eliminating the misinterpretation of either verbal statements or actions that range from troop movements to irrelevant television productions.

The verbal creation of false scents has been a scam since a cave man held the first press conference. They have clouded not only international relations, but national understanding of what successive administrations have been up to. President Eisenhower understood the art of disinformation well. In the 1950s, atomic tests were conducted in the Nevada desert, and ranchers complained that *radiation* was killing off the cattle and endangering the health of their families. When the Atomic Energy Commission asked Eisenhower whether it should stop the tests, his answer was to continue, but to play down the radiation hazards. "Keep them confused," he said.[23] In a sense, he was only following the example that the AEC had already set. Under its project for monitoring the worldwide dispersal of Strontium 90 from radioactive fallout, the AEC had named a specified amount of the isotope a "sunshine" unit.[24]

But it was not only presidents who were adept in the art of confusion. In attempting to wiggle out of the morass that concepts like *superiority, balance* and *parity* had created, Defense Secretary Robert McNamara simply changed the rules. As an indicator of "who's ahead," he shifted from the number of *delivery* vehicles, in which the Soviet Union was ahead, to the number of *warheads*, in which the U.S. was about to move ahead.[25]

What is new in the disinformation industry is the growing extent of deception and the unthinkable consequences that it can stimulate. To say that a summit is not a summit *(Reykjavik)*, or that the swap of a captured journalist for a convicted spy is not a swap (Daniloff), is comparatively innocent in a world of insiders. And if the *Midgetman* missile suddenly falls from favor, it is referred to as the "small" *ICBM* and renamed the SICBM.[26]

Serious consequences become possible, however, when tests are conducted that look good on television but have very little to do with testing the components involved in Star Wars.[27] Or when we are not trying to win a nuclear war, we simply want to "prevail"; or we are not planning to win, but "we certainly are planning not to be defeated," according to the secretary of defense.[28] A quarter of a century earlier, Herman Kahn wrote prophetically, "The word 'prevail' is much used in official statements . . . because its use is ambiguous. The reader does not know whether the author is serious about his goal . . . it probably does more harm than good to set it up as a goal."[29]

Too many of these goals, however, are affected by what the CIA has to say, and there is no reason to suppose it has a special immunity from the practice of disinformation. For example, until 1983, the CIA reported year after year that Soviet defense spending was growing at the rate of 4-5 percent annually. But that year, the CIA changed its mind. No, expenditures hadn't been growing that fast after all, especially during the late 1970s and early 1980s. Between 1976 and 1981, the rate was more likely 2 percent, and spending for weapons didn't grow at all. But, ironically, 1976 was the year of anxiety, as CIA estimates resulted in a sudden increase in Carter administration defense expenditures.[30]

The outright lie is also prevalent. During the summer of 1987, newspapers across the country carried front-page stories of troubles with the *MX program,* as revealed in Congressional hearings. Six missiles already emplaced in silos did not have guidance systems, and those that had been delivered didn't work. A spokesman for the Northrop Corporation, the manufacturer of the systems, admitted the errors in a TV news interview. The federal government filed suit for $1,000,000 in damages while an Air Force general said on the same TV program that there was nothing wrong with the MX.[31]

Finally, a whole new generation of disinformers can be found among the young scientists who are doing the major work in the nation's top research centers. Their leader at California's Livermore Laboratories, where much of the leading-edge weapons design is being done, is 42-year-old Lowell Wood. He said it all in the early 1980s:

"If it can be believed that offensive ICBMs—which have never flown over the Pole, or over Soviet, U.S. or Canadian territory, or out of a real operational silo, or in any type of nuclear war environment—are going to throw warheads which have never been fired under acceleration or in the atmosphere onto Soviet targets whose details are quite unknown, then surely the same people can believe in the validity of defensive exercises that I've sketched. It's simply a matter of getting used to a new idea."[32]

Only a few years later, however, Mr. Wood would take a different tack. In a debate in October 1986, he would say that he had not come "to assert the technical *feasibility* of strategic defense. To do so, I believe, would be intellectually dishonest. Whether or not strategic defense will be technically feasible a half-dozen years hence will become generally known only a half-dozen years hence. And anyone who presumes to tell you now what will be true that far away in this complicated area is, frankly, a confidence man. If he isn't reaching for your wallet, he probably wants your vote or your contribution, which is a more popular form of theft against which the law provides no protection."[33]

This is the stuff of Kafka. As the pace of disinformation and manipulative communications accelerates, the pressure to comprehend it all could make a cult hero of Joseph K, the protagonist in Kafka's novel *The Trial*. In the novel, Joseph K is pulled out of bed in the middle of the night, hauled off to a court he never heard of, charged with a crime he doesn't understand, convicted on the evidence of witnesses he can't cross-examine, returned to his home to await imposition of the death sentence, and, finally, one night, is marched off into a lonely quarry and quietly knifed. Yet, he continues to insist to the end that "It is only a trial if I recognize it as such."

Doomsday machine   The ultimate weapon: the one that kills everyone on earth. It is used as a threat behind which one side or the other hides. Fortunately, so far as is known, this weapon has remained a notion of some nuclear war theorists. Doomsday machine has become a phrase that describes the ultimate in destruction. For example, Carl Sagan, professor of astronomy and space sciences at Cornell University, believes that the *nuclear winter* resulting from a nuclear exchange is, in fact, the dreaded doomsday machine.[34]

Early Warning   The first signal from *satellites* and sensors on land and sea telling command authorities as far up as the White House that missiles have been launched against the U.S. or its armed forces anywhere at any time. The longest leeway this allows is 30 minutes—the time required for a Soviet missile launched in the USSR to reach the continental U.S. The lead is reduced to about eight minutes for a missile launched from a Soviet submarine off U.S. shores.

Assuming he survives *decapitation* and the early warning reaches the president (the only one who can authorize the use of *nuclear weapons*), he can do one of three things:

—*launch on warning,* that is, "press the button" giving the signal to launch U.S. nuclear weapons immediately;

—wait for confirmation that missiles have actually exploded on U.S. territory or positions (primarily to avoid an accidental exchange), the theory being that targets and retaliatory weapons can be selected better by knowing the true nature of the enemy attack;

—surrender.

EMF (Electro magnetic force)   An important key to whether or not there will ever be a nuclear war. The phenomenon of electromagnetic force, an end-product of a nuclear explosion, did not spring full blown from the mind of some scientific super genius. It was discovered by accident in atmospheric nuclear tests conducted in 1958 and confirmed by the so-called Fishbowl tests of 1962. In these tests, which took place hundreds of miles from Hawaii and 250 miles above the earth, an EMF made most of the island's power and communications systems inoperable.[1]

Today, the magnetic pulse from a single one-megaton warhead exploded 300 miles above Nebraska would put out all the communications and power systems in the country. But it doesn't hurt people. Someone standing in an open field during an EMF "attack" would not feel any sensation at all. EMF passes through the human body, wood, glass, and plastic without causing any harm, but as it passes through electronic equipment, it wrecks it. And it is inconceivable that either superpower, contemplating an attack upon the other, would not first fire a missile to explode above the enemy's country, creating an EMF disaster that would render its communications systems inoperative.

Endurance   The ability of command and control networks to persist unscathed during a "protracted nuclear war." This is what the Pentagon is demanding of communications devices that it orders, making them more expensive and, in some instances, more difficult to operate.[3] The key "enduring" system on which the Pentagon is betting is *GWEN* (ground wave emergency network), a nationwide grid of 300-foot unmanned towers. However, every small town selected as a building site is resisting the towers. For a time, Castine, Maine, has stopped its GWEN installation dead in the water.[4] The resistance arises from the fear that the town will become a target and from environmental aspects, i.e., the towers will be unsightly.

The goal of endurance, however, may be a futile one. First, as Henry Kissinger might have asked, as he did of the concept of nuclear *superiority,* "What in the name of God is a 'protracted nuclear war' and who will be alive to terminate the war with whom?" Second, why endurance when the nation may well be left leaderless in a nuclear attack. With 30 minutes as the maximum time between warning of attack and missile landings, the president must get the word within minutes. If he's in Washington (a big "if"), he may have less than ten minutes to reach a helicopter, fly to Andrews Air Force Base, board *Kneecap*, and get as far from Washington as he can. Numerous exercises have shown that this is impossible. And, finally, the notion that 300-foot towers will ride out a nuclear attack is somewhat fanciful.

Equivalent megatonnage (EMT)   An index of destruction, this is another way of measuring who's ahead in the *arms race.* EMT moves analysis from the size of a weapon to the estimated area that a weapon would destroy. In the early 1980s, Soviet forces had about 6,000 EMT to the U.S.'s 4,000. But the picture is quite different when the three components of national nuclear forces are compared (see *Triad*). The Soviets have 75 percent of their destructive force in ICBMs, 20 percent on submarines, and only 5 percent on bombers. The U.S. force potential is much more evenly divided.[5]

Escalation   The little boys' shoving match, this is the process by which, a war becomes increasingly violent, either purposefully or unintentionally. Since the Soviets began to build a nuclear arsenal, defense planners and strategists have been concerned about the escalation of fighting from conventional hostilities to nuclear war and have questioned whether the process could be controlled once the nuclear "fat" was in the fire.

Theorists have hypothesized a vast collection of incremental moves, resulting in a *scenario* of step-by-step war. The strategists began to speak of an *escalation ladder,* on which every rung presented a chance to stop short of all-out nuclear war. From this, it was not far to a concept of limited nuclear war, which has been debated repeatedly during the past two decades. Despite such scenarios, most informed observers of every political and ideological persuasion have pointed out that the *first use* of nuclear weapons, however limited, against the Soviets or their allies, would probably bring on a cataclysmic attack against North America.[6]

Trouble has almost been guaranteed. Former Secretary of the Navy John Lehman said that even if the Soviet Union used only conventional weapons in an attack, American nuclear submarines would *attack* "in the first five minutes of the war" in an effort to eliminate the Soviets *strategic nuclear reserve!*[7] Since then, the Pentagon has confirmed that policy.

Escalation ladder   See *Escalation, Limited War.*

Exotic kill mechanism   A weapon that employs intricate technologies. These are the Buck-Rogers weapons of the *Star Wars* program, some of which literally depend upon mirrors in space for their effectiveness. Whether they will ever be perfected is a subject of debate in the scientific community. (See *Directed-energy weapons, Laser, Strategic Defense Initiative.*)

Extended deterrence   "Touch my friend and I'll hit you with everything I've got." This policy means opening the *nuclear umbrella* over our allies from *NATO* to the Middle East and beyond and threatening a nuclear response to a conventional move against any of them. This theory is as old as the *nuclear weapon,* and has been ridiculed equally as long as simply unbelievable. Moreover, its credibility diminishes in reverse proportion to the distance of a U.S.

ally from Washington, D.C. If it is hard to believe that any president would sacrifice American cities to save a European city, it is even harder to believe when the ally is in the sands of the Middle East or the rice paddies of the Far East.

Nevertheless, every president from Truman to Reagan has flirted with the notion of extended deterrence. Carter's national security advisor, Zbigniew Brzezinski, said: "With an integrated strategy, combining mutual strategic security with conventional global flexibility, the United States should be able to maintain extended deterrence to deny the Soviets a quick conventional victory in any Eurasian theater, and to insure a conventional Soviet miliatry defeat in the event of a non-Eurasian clash."[8]

In the early 1980s, the Reagan Administration created a special cabinet level group, chaired by the national security advisor, to coordinate the public relations of nuclear deterrence abroad. This group spawned a special planning team directed by a former advertising executive to develop a public relations strategy to sell "the deployment of Pershing II and Cruise missiles in Europe"[9] To what end? Extended deterrence, of course.

Escalation dominance Son of *escalation* and the *escalation ladder,* this means a nation has superiority at every successive level of combat, not only to fight but to win a nuclear war. This notion, which originated in the late 1950s and early 1960s, fell into disrepute in the following decade. Now it's back in favor, but has been widely judged as nonsensical now as it was then. For the suggestions that have been offered over the past 40 years to compensate for a failure of *deterrence* are no closer to common sense than they have ever been.[10]

F

Fail safe   A signal suggested by Albert Wohlstetter in the early days of Strategic Air Command control of the nation's nuclear forces, whereby bombers would return to their bases after an alert unless they recieved a positive, coded signal to proceed toward their targets. Wohlstetter, one of the original theoreticians of nuclear war, said that he got the idea from his childhood, when he was fascinated with the way that train accidents were avoided by "dead man's" controls.[1]

Fallibilism   A notion borrowed by the nuclear war strategists from the philosophers; *i.e.,* the unexpected and the uncertain are the most important element in any inquiry or analysis. Fallibilism has probably led to the Pentagon's penchant for *worst-case* (belt-and-suspenders) analysis and the attendant geometric increase in defense costs.

Fast burn   This describes the kind of booster the Soviets could use on their missiles to defeat *Star Wars* easily. The Reagan program contemplates hitting Soviet missiles in their *boost phase* (the time between blastoff and the moment when boosters are jettisoned) when the end of the missile that carries the *warheads* is proceeding through the stratosphere. This lasts from 180 to 300 seconds. But through the fast-burn approach, the boost phase can be reduced to 50 seconds. The device proposed in the *SDI* program to home in on the missile during its boost phase is an X-ray laser which would be *"popped up"* (lofted) into space, taking 100 seconds to reach its required altitude. Say Star Warriors like Lowell Wood at the Livermore Labs, where the advanced Star Wars work is being done, "If fast-burn boosters eventually do become available, pop-up systems will eventually be unable to cope with them."[2]

Finlandization   Under the influence of the bully on the block, this term came into use to describe what happened to the policy of an independent country that had to accommodate itself continually to the wishes of a stronger nation, which it could not afford to offend if it hoped to maintain its autonomy. The original case, obviously, was the relationship between the USSR and Finland. With the 1970s growth of the concept that the real Soviet threat to Western Europe was political rather than military, it was not long before "self-finlandization" was employed to describe the same process in the absence of active pressure from the dominant country. In short, a country might act in a particular way simply because it knew that any other conduct would cause its adversary to exert military pressure. And a case can be made that *NATO's* political decisions have certainly been influenced by the Soviets' conventional strength and their growing nuclear arsenal.

Nevertheless, the rush to use "shorthand" terms like these in the hope of achieving a measure of analytical certainty illustrates the crudity of political concepts used in most strategic studies. Finlandization, in its applied use, seemed to neglect altogether the fact that Finland still enjoys a large degree of autonomy despite its smaller size and its history of difficulties with the USSR.[3]

Firebreak   A term borrowed from forest-fire fighting to describe the gap between conventional and nuclear war. It has been applied most often to the possibility of war between Soviet forces and *NATO* and the attempt to keep any such conflict conventional. The firebreak in this instance would, in effect, be the decisionmaker's hesitation to use *nuclear weapons* to prevent defeat by conventional arms in the recognition that nuclear weapons are a thing apart, as President Johnson pointed out: "Make no mistake. There is no such thing as a conventional nuclear weapon."[4]

First strike   Hitting first, not simply to wound an enemy, but to ensure that the stake has been driven into the vampire's heart. A first strike is suicidal unless it can guarantee the elimination of the enemy's retaliatory forces. Hence the notion of a "credible first-strike capability," which each of the superpowers has accused the other of setting as its primary goal.

Opposed to the first-strike capability is the *second-strike* capability—the ability to absorb a first strike and return a devastating counterattack. Such was the alleged purpose of the *MX missile,* for which lobbying had begun in the mid-1970s. But the physicist

Richard Garwin pointed out that when the MX arrived at its target, it would find Soviet missiles and bombers gone (see *absentee problem*). He told Secretary of Defense James Schlesinger, "What you really want—but are not willing to say" is a first-strike capability.[5]

First-strike bonus   The surrealistic little "extra" that one superpower might get for striking first in a crisis: the possibility of suffering less damage from retaliation. But there may not be a "bonus" even if both sides are evenly matched quantitatively. For example, if there are qualitative differences, it could take 90 percent of U.S. forces to wipe out 50 percent of Soviet forces (leaving the U.S. 10 percent of its forces), and the Soviets would have five times as many forces as the U.S. going into the next round of a nuclear exchange.[6]

First use   The first use of nuclear weapons, usually as part of *NATO* defense policy. Under this policy, NATO and the U.S. are pledged to resort to the use of nuclear arms the moment that the Soviet Union or its Iron Curtain allies attack the West with conventional weapons and seem to be winning. Indeed, first use has been a consistent element in U.S. policy throughout the atomic age, and every president since Truman has refused to pledge *no first use* even though the Soviets had offered to do so in the early 1950s.

The reason for this intransigence is the persistent use of the nuclear threat. Every president from Truman to Carter has, at some point, considered resorting to nuclear weapons, for instance, in Korea, Berlin, Taiwan, Suez, Lebanon and Jordan, Cuba, Vietnam, Iran, and the Yom Kippur War.[7] Despite this evidence, the American public has no idea of the extent to which first use is an ingrained part of U.S. defense policy. According to a survey conducted in 1984, 81 percent of Americans who were polled believe that it is part of U.S. policy to use nuclear weapons "if and only if the Soviets attack the United States first with nuclear weapons."[8]

Flexible response   One more example of what some critics have called the "misplaced abstractions" with which nuclear strategy has been conceived, this describes *escalation* in the use of *nuclear weapons* from itty-bitty ones to great big ones, and, especially in the case of *NATO*, to the final bang from the continental U.S. to Soviet Russia.

Under a flexible response strategy, with each step up the *escalation ladder,* decisionmakers would face a wholly new, unplanned situation with wholly new, unplanned possibilities from which to choose. And as they inched their way toward the ultimate response of massive, intercontinental retaliation, the European battlefields on which these flexible responses occurred would be totally obliterated along with millions of civilians.

For example, the United States has tested only once a nuclear-armed artillery shell, which would probably be one of the first weapons used in an escalation from conventional to nuclear arms. The shell was detonated six miles from its firing point. The fireball mounted thousands of feet into the air and the shock wave was felt 90 miles away. A participant wrote: "The first flash would sear the eyeballs off anyone looking in that direction, friend or foe, for miles around . . . The electromagnetic pulse would knock out all communications systems, the life blood of a battle plan. . . . Anyone for 50 miles in any direction who lived through it would realize that it was a nuclear explosion. It would seem like the end of the world, and probably would be, for any man who had a similar weapon under his control, who had a button to push or a lanyard to pull, would do so instinctively."[9]

Despite the fact that the strategy is hardly viable, flexible response was first presented to President Kennedy, to give him a whole new menu of options from which to choose his responses to a hypothetical Soviet move. Eugene Rostow, one-time head of the Arms Control and Disarmament Agency, pointed out that "The President of the United States must never be put in a position where he would have to choose between abandoning a vital American interest and launching a nuclear war." That's precisely where every president has been since 1945.[10] And still is. According to Secretary of Defense Caspar Weinberger, "Our policy of flexible response" is a proud ingredient of the Reagan administration's policy planning.[11]

Fog of war   Nuclear strategy's version of World War II's "Snafu" (situation normal, all fouled up). This is the atmosphere of indecision and confusion that occurs when communications break down and decision-making goes astray during hostilities. In a review of Henry Kissinger's work, Harvard analyst and consultant to the Brookings Institution William Kaufmann noted: "In his version of warfare, airmen do not get panicky and jettison their bombs, or hit the wrong targets, missiles do not go astray, and heavily populated areas—whether rural or urban—do not suffer thereby. Surely this is wishful thinking."[12]

Football The stuff that movies are made of, this is the attaché case containing war plans that is carried by an aide who goes wherever the president goes. It is widely known that most presidents have treated prepared war plans and the football with benign neglect. A former director of the White House Military Office, who served under every president from Johnson to Carter, said of the football:

> No new president in my time ever had more than one briefing on the contents of the Football, and that was before each one took office, when it was one briefing among dozens. Not one president to my knowledge, and I know because it was in my care, ever got an update on the contents of the Football, although material in it is changed constantly. Not one president could open the Football—only the warrant officer, the military aides and the Director of the Military Office have the combination. If the guy with the Football had a heart attack or got shot on the way to the president, they'd have to blow the goddam thing open.[13]

No command that the president issues is valid unless he follows the procedures outlined in the documents contained in the football.

Footprint Much more insidious than Bigfoot, this is the area over which a *MIRV*ed missile can spread its *warheads*. Conceptually, it is not very different from the pattern of a shotgun. Thus the footprint of a typical MIRVed missile is about 90 miles along the missile's trajectory (150 kilometers) and 30 miles (50 kilometers) wide.[14]

Force multiplier Whatever adds to the effectiveness of existing nuclear weapons. For example, *MIRV*ing increases the effectiveness of missiles ten times. However, ironically, something that can act as a force multiplier in one instance can become a force destroyer. For example, electronic technology may make troops more efficient and effective but because it is more vulnerable and perishable than weapons, it may end up as a force destroyer. The destruction of electronic components will be more important than the destruction of weapons, for as electronics go, so goes the loss of command and control capabilities.[15]

Fratricide   In nuclear terms, the "brothers" killed in fratricide are missiles. When a missile explodes, it sends up a mushroom cloud of rock, dust, and other debris. If a second missile following the first runs into that cloud, it will be put out of action. Fratricide not only presents real problems for targeting policy, but has encouraged some unbelievable strategic thinking. For example, the Reagan administration came up with a new method of deploying the *MX missile,* which the president named the Peacekeeper. This was called *dense pak,* whereby 100 MX missiles would be placed in cheek-by-jowl silos over a relatively small area. Then, if the Russians attempted a *first strike* at the silo fields, they would come in so close together that they would destroy each other (fratricide). Experts didn't think the idea would work; Congress didn't like it because it was not only expensive, but ludicrous. And so dense pak was jettisoned to await a second coming, like so many schemes that have appeared and reappeared over the past five decades.[16]

Freeze   See *Nuclear freeze.*

G

Game theory   Applied in the nuclear field, another futile attempt to make the imprecise precise. Invented by mathematicians John von Neuman and Oskar Morgenstern in 1944, game theory applies the logic of statistics to the choice of strategies in a game. A game involves a set of rules applied to a situation in which two or more players try to win as much as they can, or to minimize their opponents winnings. "Nuclear strategists" borrowed the techniques of game theory at the beginning of the atomic age as a way to make strategic problems manageable.

Any number can play, but, among the strategists, there are only the superpowers. Two assumptions of the theory made the game especially attractive to situations in which the superpowers confronted each other: one player's move depended upon what his adversary did. There was complete interdependence. Furthermore, each player would act rationally and try to get the most he could out of the game. Since certain values were assigned to certain outcomes; "getting the most" meant getting as large a "payoff" as possible, while knowing that the adversary was trying to do the same thing.

There are also different types of games, two of which are among the best known: zero-sum games, in which one player's gain is another player's loss, and non-zero sum or variable-sum games, in which gains do not equal losses. In the latter, both players can win or lose, or win and lose. This is the game played by nuclear strategists.

Its attraction was the appearance of definition; its disadvantages are immense. The assumptions made by the players are often unrealistic. There is no assurance that the outcome of a game will in any sense be matched in an actual confrontation. The theory seems to work only if the players would, in practice, be "rational, calculating and 'utility-maximizing'." All the pressures that make people involved in crisis situations behave unpredictably and illogically were omitted.[1]

Other games no less unrealistic have attracted attention. One is the auction game invented by Dr. Martin Schubik of Yale University. Schubik auctions off a dollar bill. The highest bidder buys the dollar for his bid; the second highest bidder pays what he bid but doesn't get a dollar in return. Inexperienced bidders, the good doctor guessed, would end up bidding more than a dollar for the dollar. And he was right. This, he says, is the *arms race* in miniature. Each side spends more and more money without getting ahead of the other.[2]

In short, superpower reactions and decision-making involve value judgments and political behavior. Their outcomes can't be analyzed accurately through such devices as auction games or the game of *chicken*. And surely, analysis can't be structured with devices that were designed, like game theory, to manipulate the neat precisions of scientific theory.[3]

Garage A *satellite* in low earth orbit, in which from 6 to 24 "kinetic kill vehicles" (to a rabbit, a slingshot is a kinetic kill vehicle) would be parked. Such satellites would represent the first defensive layer of an accelerated, modified *Star Wars* program, which requires enough garages to park some 10,000 weapons. Probably 400 garages would be needed, and they would be deployed in orbits[4] that are most vulnerable because of their proximity to Earth. Moreover, designers would face the horrendous task of sweating the kill vehicles down to 250 pounds to make them economical. This is not yet in sight.

This garage configuration would be in the first defense layer, wherein Soviet missiles lifting off from their *launchers* would be shot down by weapons in the garages before they shed their boosters. Weapons in two additional, ground-based layers would attack Soviet missiles in mid-course flight and as they reentered the atmosphere.

Assuming all technological problems in constructing them can be solved, there would still be the hurdle of getting the garages and kill vehicles into space. Conservative estimates say that about 8 million pounds of gear would have to be orbited; others estimate double the poundage. Eight million pounds alone would require about 125 space shuttle flights, five times the number launched before the *Challenger* disaster. If the Pentagon could get a "heavy lift vehicle," which isn't even on the drawing boards, only about 55 flights would be needed.[5] (See *Star Wars*.)

Altogether, according to Ashton B. Carter, a Harvard physicist and Pentagon consultant, "It may be possible to put a system like this in place, but it is not clear that it has any military value."[6] This in view of the fact that the Soviets are unlikely to agree to the *ICBM* limitations that are necessary to make the Star Wars program viable.

Geosynchronous orbit   An orbit about 35,800 kilometers (21,500 miles) above the earth. A *satellite* placed in this orbit revolves around the earth once a day and maintains the same position relative to the earth. It could be placed to hang over Washington—or Moscow. It appears to be stationary and is therefore extremely useful as a "spy" or a communications relay.[7]

This orbit may not have a great role to play in any *Star Wars* defense system simply because of its distance from the earth. It's too far away to place the kind of mirrors needed to redirect *laser* weapons in it because such mirrors would have to be precision "instrument" the length of a football field. (See *BMD*.) But a lower orbit can't be used for this, because weapons, mirrors, or anything else located in lower orbits would run into the *absentee* problem.[8]

Glasnost   The word to watch, this is the Soviet equivalent of letting it all hang out. This Russian word has no exact counterpart, but its interpretation in English is usually "speaking boldly and openly."

There is evidence in the press, in figures revealed for the first time on public attitudes in the Soviet Union, that a veneer of *glasnost* is evident even at the top of the Soviet hierarchy.[9] But whether or not Gorbachev's *glasnost* policy is successful, one thing is certain: neither the liberal's notion that in time the USSR will democratize itself, nor the conservative's assumption that the USSR will fall apart under its own totalitarian weight, are reasonable guides to assessing the Soviet destiny. Neither will happen. (See also *Perestroika*.)

Global unilateralism   A variant of isolationism that envisions the United States acting on its own. Global unilateralism was concocted largely by those who want to withdraw U.S. forces from Europe and "bring the boys home." The idea is to retract international agreements with allies and clients to permit the U.S. to pick and choose its foreign policy objectives minus the constraints of "entangling alliances." Alliances would be allowed, but they would be made on an ad hoc basis, and U.S. foreign policy would undoubtedly take on a "pragmatic" tone.[10] The *NATO* alliance would surely be a casualty of global unilateralism.

Graduated deterrence　The first in a long line of "buzz words," equally zany, describing policies of which the latest is *flexible response*. And whenever graduated deterrence came into the discussion of *NATO* defenses, the concept of *extended deterrence* was not far behind, saying essentially that the protective *nuclear umbrella* that the U.S. held over its head could be opened wider to include some of its allies.

All these variations of the same basic policy had three premises. In a time of crisis, the president of the United States should be able to decide on a course somewhere between suicide and surrender (the war plans given to Kennedy gave him five possibilities.) Second, it was possible to approach hostilities on a step-by-step basis. Third, the nuclear umbrella that America held over its own head could be "extended" elsewhere to protect our allies by warding off conventional as well as nuclear assaults. These are, at best, confusing abstractions.

Henry Kissinger reportedly told our European allies not to ask the U.S. "to multiply strategic assurances that we cannot possibly mean, or if we do mean, we should not want to execute, because if we execute, we risk the destruction of civilization."[11] Yet, Kissinger would reverse his position as a member of the Reagan administration's Commission on Integrated Long-Term Strategy. Formed without public notice to advise Reagan's sixth national security advisor, Frank Carlucci; Secretary of Defense Caspar Weinberger; and the president, the commission was advised that the strategy it was seeking "must provide credible responses to a wide range of possible attacks."[12]

Hardening The process of reinforcing targets with steel and concrete to protect them against pressures measured in thousands of pounds per square inch caused by a nuclear blast. Silos in which intercontinental ballistic missiles are readied for launching are hardened. Now, with the advent of *Star Wars,* hardness is also "measured by the power needed per unit area to destroy the target by means of a *directed-energy* weapon[1]—a *laser* or a *particle-beam* weapon.

Hard-point defense A conception that is supposed to promise the defense of *ICBMs* (intercontinental ballistic missile), thereby providing an answer to the supposed vulnerability of American ICBMs. (See *window of vulnerabilty*). Instead of putting more missiles into more concrete silos, hard-point defense envisions a missile that will shoot down the enemy missile before it can hit the silo.

The U.S. talks about a hard-point defense, but has done nothing about it for two reasons. One is that the *ABM* treaty stands in its way. And second, there are real questions about the vulnerability of U.S. ICBMs and the nature of the U.S. *deterrrent.* Two-thirds of America's nuclear forces are in undetectable submarines and in bombers equipped with *cruise missiles;* only one-third (33%) is in silos. Soviet ICBMs, however, account for 70 percent of their nation's deterrent forces. In short, as things stand now, the Soviets would have to spend 70 percent to get 33 percent. Such is the what-if nature of the games "strategic analysts" play. From here it is only a short step to "preferential defense" and something called "shoot-look-shoot."

A variant of hard-point defense, preferential defense says that defense forces could be located secretly around a limited number of launch sites. Since the attacker doesn't know which silos are defended, he has to fire more missiles than he would normally fire.

But it's possible, under another *scenario,* that the attacker might fire a small number of missiles to ascertain which silos the defender is protecting, then follow with an all-out attack on the undefended ICBMs (look-shoot-look).[2]

Hibakusha One of the few, nonpackaged words, which means precisely what it says: the "explosion-affected persons," as the survivors of Hiroshima and Nagasaki are described in Japanese. Seventeen years after Hiroshima, the psychiatrist Robert J. Lifton visited Japan to study the psychological effects of the bombing on survivors. He found that the terror of the bombing was unforgettable, as Hiroshima survivors recalled that "for acres and acres, the city was like a desert except for scattered piles of brick and roof tile. I had to revise my meaning of the word destruction." And, "the feeling I had was that everyone was dead. The whole city was destroyed. I thought that all my family must be dead. It doesn't matter if I die. I thought this was the end of Hiroshima, of Japan, of humankind."[3]

High Frontier The defensive zone that the *Star Wars* program envisions in space. After President Reagan made his surprise speech outlining the *Strategic Defense Initiative* (Star Wars) that would protect all America and make nuclear missiles obsolete, a rationale was written by General Daniel O. Graham, former director of the Defense Intelligence Agency. The report, called "The High Frontier," was published by the conservative Heritage Foundation.

Horizontal escalation A Reagan administration concept that ties an increase in hostilities in one area to an increase in another area. For example, should the USSR invade Iran through Turkey, *NATO* would probably begin hostilities in Europe. And it is quite possible that a conflict in the Middle East would set the stage for compensating action elsewhere in the world. Horizontal escalation, it is said, applies particularly to naval forces, and, as the Reagan administration sees it, activity is less likely to be in the European theater and more likely to be in the Persian Gulf and the Indian Ocean.[4]

In all this, according to Brookings Institution analyst Joshua Epstein, one question never seems to be answered: "What Soviet behavior (capitulation, redeployment of forces, negotiation) is the horizontal counteroffensive supposed to elicit?"[5]

Horizontal proliferation One of the nuances used to describe where the new bombs are; *i.e.,* who else besides the superpowers has acquired nuclear arms. The "club" now includes England, France, India, and China; Israel is also thought to have a nuclear arsenal and Pakistan may very well be in the group. "Vertical" proliferation, on the other hand, describes the increase in nuclear arms in an existing arsenal. (See *Proliferation.*)

House address What you say when you're ashamed to say target. This euphemism is usually employed in discussions of missile accuracy: is a missile accurate enough to hit its house address—say, a hardened silo—and demolish it? Indeed, U.S. policy seems to be concentrating on accuracy rather than on increasing explosive force. Talk among the current crop of Strangeloves, runs to such statements as this: "It is extreme accuracy that permits the U.S. to credibly threaten nuclear *attacks* at various levels of conflict and the ability to dominate at each level if the nuclear exchange is escalated."[6]

Hugging A tactic devised by the Soviets to reduce the threat of battlefield *nuclear weapons.* It holds that the best way to prevent a possible shift from the use of conventional weapons to battlefield nuclear weapons is to engage the enemy as closely as possible. Then he cannot use any kind of nuclear weapon without endangering his own troops.[7]

Inadvertent use   The "Iran-Contra defense" applied to the use of *nuclear weapons:* "I didn't do it, he did, and I didn't know about it." A nuclear war can start in Europe in one of two ways: either one of the Warsaw Pact countries or *NATO* deliberately begins to use of nuclear weapons, however small; or they are used without the advance knowledge of responsible political authorities because someone in the chain of command panics. The latter is inadvertent use.

ICBM (Intercontinental ballistic missile)   The land-based missile that can span continents, it travels at speeds that enable it to go from

	Weapon	*Kilotons*	*Kill probability**
CLASS I			
U.S.	*MX missile*	300	.93
	Trident II (Mark 5)	475	.79
Soviets	None		
CLASS II:			
U.S.	Minuteman III	335	.57
Soviets	SS-25	550	.69
	SS-18	500	.54
CLASS III:			
U.S.	Minuteman III (Mark 12)	170	.39
	Trident II (Mark 4)	100	.37
Soviets	SS-24	100	.27
	SS-17	500	.24
	SS-19	550	.22
*The ability to destroy a target, 1.0 being perfect.			

the U.S. to the Soviet Union in about 30 minutes, or vice versa. Such missiles launched from submarines are called *SLBMs.*

The 1986 superpower lineup ballistic missile warheads that can blow up hardened targets is shown on the chart on previous page.

In addition, each superpower stocks a number of *soft*-target warheads with *kill probabilities* ranging from .03 to .17 for the U.S., and from .02 to .06 for the Soviets.[2]

Inspection The ability to look at the other fellow's turf to ascertain that he isn't doing something prohibited by treaty. On May 10, 1955, the Soviet delegation to the London *arms control* talks announced substantial acceptance of American disarmament proposals, including on-site inspection. It had taken a decade to get to that point. But suddenly, in an abrupt turnaround whose affects are still felt, President Eisenhower turned down the Russian offer. "Are we ready," Eisenhower asked, "to open up every one of our factories, every place where something might be going on that could be inimical to the interests of somebody else?" Recently, on-site inspection was included in the INF agreement signed by Reagan and Gorbachev in December 1987. (See *Verification*).

Intimidation Not *"compellence,"* or *"persuasion,"* but, according to the French political analyst Ramond Aron, "the attempt by vague threats to obtain from someone a change of conduct."[2] This is what Khrushchev tried to do in the U-2 incident and, by implication, in the Cuban Missile crisis, but these attempts were basically bluffs. Neither worked; for one of many reasons, Russians are not poker players, and they are not practiced in being "called."

K

Kill probability The results of a "game" anyone can play, providing he has a "bomb damage computer," which is a special circular slide rule that was once available, like some promotional souvenir, from the Rand Corporation, or any number of other *think tanks.*

In this game, assuming the explosive power of an incoming missile, its *CEP,* and the blast resistance of a silo, you line up the right arrows on the slide rule and a decimal figure appears in the window. This is the kill probability. It means that if the figure is say, .5, a Soviet *first strike* would "kill" 50 percent of the Minuteman ICBMs in the silos.[1] This kind of calculation is one of many attempts to lend strategic analysis an aura of precision that it simply does not have.

Kiloton The basic measure of nuclear destruction, equivalent to 1,000 tons of TNT. The bomb dropped on Hiroshima was 12 kilotons (equivalent to 12,000 tons of TNT) and killed over 100,000 people immediately, another 100,000 died a lingering death. Today's typical bomb has a yield of about 500 kilotons or .5 megatons, a megaton being the explosive equivalent of *1 million tons of TNT.* Several weapons in both superpower arsenals are between 9 and 20 kilotons.

Kinetic energy weapon A baseball pitcher who beans a batter transforms the baseball into a kinetic energy weapon, putting it into the category of slingshots, rocks, boomerangs, cars in the hands of drinking adolescents, guns of all kinds, and other assorted articles of mayhem. All of these weapons are using the energy of motion to destroy inanimate objects or to terminate life.

Now, with the advent of *Star Wars,* kinetic energy weapons are simply called "kinetic kill" weapons. Said former Secretary of Defense Caspar Weinberger, "Technologies relating to precision rocket interceptors and hypervelocity guns will be explored to provide potential nonnuclear kill of *ballistic missiles* in all phases of flight."[2] It should be noted that "kill" now means destroy, so that magazines can carry headlines like "SDI Delta Space Experiment to Aid Kill-vehicle Design."[3]

Kneecap (*NEACP:* National Emergency Airborne Post) A special aircraft from which the president and his advisors can direct the course of a nuclear conflict. Similar aircraft, all of which are equipped with the latest communications and computerized aids, are available to lesser commands. For example, the Strategic Air Command post, called "Looking Glass," has been kept in the air continuously since Feb 3, 1962, always on the alert for an attack.[4] These command planes are alternated every eight hours.

The airborne command posts have appalling liabilities, three of which are obvious:

1. An assault from Soviet submarines stationed offshore would take about *eight minutes* to hit US targets. In that time span, the president has to be located and a helicopter ordered. Until recently, Kneecap was kept at Andrews Air Force Base, ten miles from Washington. Obviously, the president would have missed his rendezvous. Now that the plane has been was moved to an Air Force base in Indiana, the whole exercise has become impossible.

2. Electromagnetic forces *(EMP)* created by a nuclear explosion would make communications virtually impossible.

3. The basic assumption behind all airborne command posts is that they will stay aloft for indeterminate periods by refueling in the air. Refueling? During and after a nuclear attack?[5]

Krasnoyarsk A Soviet radar installation that has raised U.S. cries of *cheating*.

Ladder down According to the Congressional Office of Technology Assessment, this is a hypothetical technique, by which to foil the terminal (target-point) defense of *nuclear weapons* using *ABMs*. (See *BMD.*) It is envisioned that an attacker will explode a *warhead* far above a *launcher,* creating a fireball that will "blind" the ground radars upon which a terminal defense depends. The attacker follows this up with successively lower firings that clear the way for more attacking missiles. So on and on, until an attacking missile finally gets through the defenses.[1]

Laser *(Light Amplification by Stimulated Emission of Radiation)* Applied to nuclear strategy, this is the "death ray" idea from old magazines like *True Amazing Stories*: an intense beam of visible or invisible light, which apparently can be used as a weapon that reaches its target with the speed of light. In the laboratory, a laser can burn holes in metal or disrupt whatever is inside a container—a missile, for example. Research began on such weapons in the early 1960s. It should be noted that Russian and American scientists shared a Nobel Prize for the development of the laser.

Currently, four types of lasers are under consideration for *Ballistic Missile Defense* (BMD): infrared chemical lasers, electrically driven ultraviolet lasers, free-electron lasers, and *X-ray lasers* produced by nuclear explosions.[2] They either burn holes in the target missile or hit them head on, disrupting electronic equipment in the missile or a *satellite* target. The X-ray laser can be *"popped up"* into space on a missile and then fired once it's aloft. The other three (also called optical lasers) need a mirror in space to redirect them and a space-based source of energy.

Aside from needing such equipment, an effective optical laser weapon would have to be able to find the target, make sure the target isn't a *decoy*, point the laser at the target, and fire. Then it would have to determine damage or miss-distance—find out how much damage was done if the target was hit; if not, figure out how

95

much the shot was off target—fire again until the target is destroyed, and report the results to a command post. It is expected that by the early 1990s, researchers will have some idea whether a laser weapon operating in space can be produced.

However, by the spring of 1987, Edward Teller had agreed with some of the young scientists at the Livermore Laboratories, who were beginning to doubt the ability of the X-ray laser to destroy missiles.[3] It could, they contended, knock out battle stations, satellites and sensors, but it would not be the wonder weapon that inspired President Reagan's 1983 *Star Wars* speech ("I have a vision").[4]

Launcher Also called launch vehicles: the devices from which weapons are fired. *SALT* II (Strategic Arms Limitation Treaty) was written primarily to limit the number of launchers; the figure agreed upon was 2,250 for each side. Under the treaty, launchers could be fixed underground missile silos, transportation vehicles for mobile missiles, launching tubes aboard nuclear submarines, or intercontinental bombers with or without *cruise missiles*.[5] The treaty was signed by President Carter but was not ratified by the Senate. However, both the Carter and Reagan administrations, adhered to its limitations until the Reagan administration started its "on-off" policy by mentioning nonadherence at a White House press conference on November 25, 1986.[6]

Launch on warning The ultimate "use 'em or lose' em" decision to retaliate on *early warning* that a nuclear *attack* has been launched. Assuming that the early warning has been verified and is not just a flock of geese somewhere in northern Canada,[7] the president has three possible courses of action. First, he can launch immediately (launch on warning). Theoretically, by the time Soviet missiles reach their targets, U.S. missiles will have flown the coop. Second, he can wait for confirmation that Soviet missiles have landed. Third, he can surrender. Congress has forbidden the use of funds for any study of surrender or its consequences.[8]

As the survivability of U.S. silo-based missiles becomes increasingly problematic, the merits of a launch-on-warning policy are being considered again, even though it is believed that a Soviet attack would also include missiles launched from submarines.[9] In the latter case, assuming that the USSR had launched a preemptive strike there would be about eight minutes in which to evaluate all possibilities and get the president onto *Kneecap*. In the final analysis, launch on warning, according to strategist John Steinbruner, should be seen "as a symptom of perilous security conditions that demand more thought than they have yet recieved."[10]

Laydown The word to use if you're ashamed to say "nuclear *attack*." For example, as used in the Pentagon's description of the *GWEN* network of some 300 to 500 relay stations, which is supposed to ensure that "there is a communications backbone even after a nuclear laydown.[11]

Layered defense The heart—and soul—of *Star Wars,* not to be confused with *Multilayered Deterrence,* a theoretical construct of the Defense Department. An *ICBM* flies a distinct trajectory that looks something like the path of the "bomb" thrown by football quarterbacks, very often on a hope and a prayer. Star Wars divides the trajectory—with as much hope and prayer—into four distinct phases. (See *BMD.*)

The Star Wars program says, in effect, that the exotic weapons we're working on will get the hostile missiles, if not in the first layer, then in one of the subsequent layers. But there won't be 100 percent accuracy. If half the attacking missiles get through the *bus* layer, and half again through each succeeding layer, only one in 16, or just over 6 percent, would make it to their targets. In terms of numbers, the prospect is frightening, because in a medium Soviet attack of 600 ICBMs carrying 6,000 *warheads,* 375 warheads would still reach their targets. If the targets were factories and infrastructure, American society would be devastated because of the proximity of those targets to cities, and the damage "only" 375 warheads can inflict.(See *Leakage.*)

Leakage A measure of the ones that got away; *i.e.,* the number of enemy missiles that penetrate *Star Wars' layered defense.* Even if the 4 defense layers were 99 percent effective, the leakage would cause tremendous destruction. If 10 Soviet missiles got through the defense screen (one-tenth of 1 percent of the entire Soviet arsenal), would cause the kind of destruction that McGeorge Bundy called "a disaster beyond history."[13] If the leakage rate were, for the sake of speculation, 5 percent (Star Wars is 95 percent effective), Soviet *warheads* falling on U.S. cities would cause 30,000,000 American deaths.

Star Wars proponents admit that defenses without leakage are impossible and are beginning to speak of "acceptable" failure rates. "Acceptable" translates into "approximately 20 million" casualties, according to a member of the Defense Department's General Advisory Committee.[14]

Leakout Not to be confused with *leakage,* or with a crack or hole that allows something to escape, accidentally, leakout in nuclear parlance, means the deliberate evasion or abrogation of a treaty provision. The Reagan decision to continue work on some exotic *Star Wars* weapons is considered a leakout of the *ABM* Treaty.

Lethality "Bang, it's dead!" Combining accuracy and yield, this term measures a weapon's ability to destroy *hardened* (cement-reinforced) targets such as silos and command posts. Measurements are very precise. According to experts, "Lethality is defined in terms of double-shot *kill probability* (two *warheads* per silo) against a 6000-psi [pounds per square inch] silo: Low=less than .3; moderate = .3 to .6 high = .6 to .9; very high = more than. 9"[15]

Likely A not-very-nuclear sounding word that is as close as an expert will ever get to saying "maybe." It also appears as "chances," "odds," and "probable" or "probably." Any one of these alternatives is used to win arguments in the worlds of budgets, weapons, strategic decisions and *disinformation* by creating an atmosphere of precision that simply doesn't exist.

During President John Kennedy's consideration of early plans for the 1961 Bay of Pigs invasion, he asked the joint chiefs for an estimate of success. A "fair chance" was the answer. The man responsible for that estimate would say later that he had meant the odds were "three to one against."[16] This is no more misleading than the newspaper which editorializes that "the Soviets are *unlikely* to respond to U.S. defense by stockpiling more missiles . . . a *likely* Soviet defense is to slowly deemphasize nuclear weapons— investing in areas *likely* to yield some return [italics added]."[17] "Likely" has a scientific cousin, called probability—a branch of mathematics that measures the likelihood that an event will occur. (See *probability.*)

Limited war A war fought with limited resources for limited ends. Early in the Atomic Age, some analysts of nuclear strategy, including Bernard Brodie, were beginning to realize that "the prospects of a large-scale mutual exchange of *nuclear weapons* on cities reduces war to a suicidal absurdity."[18] Hence the almost immediate search for a war-fighting strategy that would nibble at the enemy to achieve limited objectives and reduce the pressure for an all-out nuclear exchange.

In one of its earliest and most persistent versions, limited war was designed to match the arsenals of *deterrence* with the goals of a particular action.[19] Would either superpower launch a nuclear *attack* that would incinerate its homeland simply to settle a border dispute? But the notion of limited war overlooked the fact that such a war might not remain limited. This lack of guarantee looked even more threatening with the development of battlefield nuclear weapons. Two military exercises showed clearly that the concept of limited war would not work out in reality. The results would be catastrophic simply because nuclear explosives do not produce limited results. One exercise, Operation Sage Brush, was conducted in Louisiana, where some 70 "small" bombs (less than 40 kilotons) were dropped on military targets. The umpire ruled that all life in the state had ceased to exist.

In another game, conducted in West Germany, *tactical* nuclear weapons were used only by *NATO* forces. During a 2-day period, 355 nuclear devices were exploded, primarily over West German territory. This action would have left nearly 1,700,000 dead and 3,500,000 wounded.

Even so, there is intermittent pressure for a limited war policy, despite the fact that, as the "Gang of Four" (McGeorge Bundy, George F. Kennan, Robert S. McNamara, and Gerard Smith) has pointed out, "no one has ever succeeded in advancing any persuasive reason to believe that any use of nuclear weapons, even on the smallest scale, could reliably be expected to remain limited." For there is, as they point out, "the total impossibility for both sides of any guarantee against unlimited escalation."[20] This is also the Soviet view. According to former Defense Minister Marshal Ustinov, "to count on victory in the arms race and in nuclear war is madness . . . there can simply be no such thing as a limited nuclear war."[21]

LOAD (Low Altitude Defense) Not what it sounds like, a *ballistic* *missile defense* system that is still on the drawing boards but has already created considerable controversy and chewed up millions. If approved, LOAD is probably the only such system the U.S. could put into place by 1990. As a last-ditch defense of *ICBMs* against enemy *attack,* it uses very small radars and small missiles with small *warheads* to be detonated near incoming ICBMs. However, there are doubts. For one, it can be overwhelmed relatively easily. And, two, it may very well flag the location of the very missiles it is intended to defend.[22]

Look-down-shoot-down One of the very few Pentagon euphemisms that makes some sense. For 20 years, experts have been predicting the perfection of a Soviet air defense system that would use large numbers of high-speed interceptor aircraft equipped with radar. The aircraft could detect any low-flying planes underneath and shoot them down. *Cruise missiles* would be vulnerable to this kind of attack. Now, according to *Aviation Week & Space Technology,* both superpowers have this ability.[23]

m

MAD (Mutual assured destruction) The state of the nuclear art, otherwise known as the *balance of terror*. Not a policy or even a theory, but the way things have been for the last 25 years in a world where each of the superpowers has been vulnerable to a devastating nuclear *attack*. This U.S. position was, in effect, acknowledged by the Soviet Union when it agreed to the *ABM* Treaty of 1972,[1] in which the mutual policy of offensive dominance was recognized. What that means is that both superpowers maintain nuclear forces sufficient to ride out a *first strike* and retaliate with an attack that the enemy could not tolerate; that is, both sides would suffer incalculable destruction. It is "mad," it is a fact of life, but it works, *i.e.,* it keeps the peace.

This is the case because, as Secretary of Defense Robert S. McNamara pointed out, "No meaningful victory is even conceivable in a third unlimited world war, for no nation can possibly win a full-scale thermonuclear exchange. The two world powers that have now achieved a mutual assured destruction capability fully realize that.[2] To counter the inevitability of mutual assured destruction, we have developed the defensive posture and assumed capabilities of *Star Wars*.[3] Yet, William L. Shirer reports, "the overwhelming preponderance among scientists here and in Europe is that we have no such key [to the technology that assures America's nuclear shield] and most probably never will."[4]

MARV (Maneuvering reentry vehicle) The *warhead* that can change targets in flight, primarily to avoid hostile action. MARVs are being used to correct the poor accuracy of submarine-launched missiles. The MARV concept is also a factor in *cruise missiles* equipped with "map guidance" systems. And if MARVs are tied into the *NAVSTAR* navigation system of 24 *satellites,* they will be accurate within 30 feet in three dimensions.[5] It has also been suggested that MARVed warheads could outwit the tactics of *Star Wars* defenses. (See *MIRV.*)

101

Massive retaliation "Nuclear lightning": the John Foster Dulles doctrine that if anyone attacked the U.S., the nation would, in the former secretary of state's words, "retaliate instantly, by means and at places of our own choosing." Eisenhower called it a "fundamental truth."[6] But like President Reagan's open-ended *Star Wars* speech, the Dulles announcement of 1955 was an invitation to different interpretations and debate.

James Reston, in the *New York Times*, said at the time that massive retaliation meant an immediate U.S. nuclear attack on China or the USSR in the event of another Korea, Dulles himself backed off that extreme view in an article published by *Foreign Affairs,* but retained the right to reply to aggression with nuclear arms. And although criticism continued to mount, massive retaliation was U.S. policy throughout the Eisenhower administrations,[7] and has remained U.S. policy to this day. The fact was that the U.S. was relying on nuclear arms as a substitute for deficiencies in conventional arms.

Present *NATO* policy, under which *tactical* nuclear arms would be used if conventional forces appeared to be losing, is nothing less than a kind of high-tech massive retaliation.

Means of delivery Whether by suitcase or submarine; the way a nuclear warhead gets to its destination. Combining the nature of nuclear explosives with means of delivery presents a problem for the defense. The fact that the British in World War II were able to stop 97 out of 101 V-2 "buzz bombs" (4 percent got through) is irrelevant in the nuclear age. What was a laudable record of damage control then would mean the end of London now.

Today, nothing less than 100 percent of incoming warheads would have to be eliminated and this, say even the most avid proponents of Star Wars, is impossible. Indeed, *Star Wars* has imparted a high-tech ring to the old saw that the military is inclined more often than not to fight the last war. (See *Leakage.*)

Megaton The measure of nuclear destruction; the force of one million tons of T.N.T. A kiloton is the equivalent of 1,000 tons of T.N.T.

It has been estimated that the superpower's combined arsenals contain an aggregate yield of approximately 10,000 megatons or 10 billion tons of T.N.T. The Hiroshima bomb that killed between

100,000 and 200,000 people was a 12 kiloton bomb of the type that is now used as the trigger in a nuclear warhead.

MHV (Minature homing vehicle) A "kinetic-kill" weapon designed to knock down low-altitude enemy *satellites*. It would hit the satellite directly rather than depending upon explosives to gain its effect. This infrared guided missile will be able to destroy low-altitude Soviet satellites that perform reconnaissance and targeting functions. It will have no effect, however, on satellites that provide missile attack warning, navigation, and advanced communication functions because of the distant orbits in which these satellites are placed.[8]

The weapon has already been tested successfully, according to the Air Force. On August 22, 1986, an F-15 plane took off from Edwards Air Force Base, California, flew to a high altitude, and fired a rocket at the light emitted by a distant star. The test was judged a success. But, said Congressman Les AuCoin even before the firing, "Testing against a point in space is like doing batting practice without a ball."[9]

Midgetman missile The missile the Pentagon doesn't want: a proposed single-*warhead ICBM* of high accuracy that can be based on a mobile launching vehicle, as opposed to the more deadly MX missiles.[10] The idea behind the Minuteman was that an ICBM on a mobile launching platform could be moved from one location to another, making it harder for an enemy to hit it. Proponents argue that it would solve the problem of ICBM vulnerability. Whether or not Midgetman is ever built will depend not so much on technology as on disentangling it from the political constraints that have overwhelmed it since its inception.

To gain Congressional support for the ten-warhead MX missile, the Reagan administration agreed to back the Midgetman, which had been recommended by the *Scowcroft Commission,* headed by Lieutenant General Brent Scowcroft, a retired Air Force officer who had been President Ford's national security advisor. An important part of the Scowcroft recommendation was that employment of a small ICBM should be tied to an *arms control* strategy that would encourage the USSR to adopt a similar weapon. Thus both superpowers would move away from the use of highly *MIRV*ed (multiple warhead) ICBMs, and the U.S. would gain restrictions on the multiplication of Soviet warheads.[11] In October 1986, the administration proposed a ban on mobile missiles, then rescinded it in January 1987.

Neither the Midgetman's ability to survive enemy action, nor its possible contribution to easing the *arms race,* are at all certain. These two factors depend upon such variables as the missile's basing mode, its relation to other U.S. nuclear forces, what happens to Soviet forces, and the future of arms control. This may be why the Midgetman has been called "a missile in search of a mission."[12]

Military-industrial complex   Ike's phrase for the alliance of interests between the Pentagon and its suppliers. On the evening of January 17, 1961, President Eisenhower went on national radio and television to deliver a farewell address to the American people. He spoke of the Cold War and warned of the incessant search for a technological solution to the nation's international problems. But as he warmed up, he came to the point for which the speech is remembered.

Eisenhower pointed out, first, that the emergence of *nuclear weapons* and enhanced technologies had shifted the defense complex from cranking up the economy on demand, as the country did in World War II, to the creation of a "permanent armaments industry of vast proportions." Then he spoke the words that expressed his deepest feelings: "This conjunction of an immense military establishment and a large arms industry is new in the American experience . . . The total influence . . . economic, political, even spiritual . . . is felt in every city, every state house, every office of the federal government." Then came the warning: "In the councils of government, we must guard against the acquisition of unwarranted influence, whether sought or unsought, by the military-industrial complex." But there was another warning not so well remembered. "The prospect of domination of the nation's scholars by federal employment, project allocations, and the power of money is ever present, and is gravely to be regarded." Tieing it all together, he said in Jeffersonian tones, "it is only a citizenry, an alert and informed citizenry, which can keep these abuses from coming about."[13]

MIRV (Multiple independently-targetable reentry vehicle)   Refers to a missile that has more than 1 warhead and could house as many as 16, each of which can be aimed separately. One observer called it, "multiple independent butchery." It works like this: What's left after the missile drops its booster is called the *bus*. It carries guidance equipment and an IRV (independently-targeted reentry vehicle), which is the nuclear *warhead*. A MIRVed missile has more than one IRV on board. And if the IRV can navigate itself to a target, it becomes a *MARV*. Hence MARVed MIRVs, believe it or not.[14] The MIRV was the technological development that squeezed aconfession out of Secretary of State Henry Kissinger. He wished that he "had thought through the implications of a MIRVed world more thoroughly."[15]

Because of that "oversight," we now face Soviet missiles, all MIRVed with ten warheads (limited by *arms control* agreements). Moreover, MIRVing not only made destruction more accurate, it reduced the cost of missile procurement and at the time was a way to counter the Air Force desire for *ABM* systems. MIRVing, in short, was all things to all people when it was developed; today, it has accelerated the *arms race* and created problems with the basing of *ICBMs*.

Missile launchers   See *Launcher*.

Missile gap   The missile deficiency that was never there. In 1959, Kennedy ran for the presidency on the alleged existence of a "missile gap" between the U.S. and the USSR, and accused the Eisenhower administration of letting the nation's security get rusty. Once in office, Kennedy and McNamara, his Secretary of Defense, found that they had inherited 5,000 aircraft capable of delivering nuclear warheads together with 1,100 ICBM's either deployed or under construction. At the time of Kennedy's inauguration, the intelligence community had been able to find only two Soviet missiles, and they were at test sites. [16] No one has so far explained why Eisenhower didn't blow the whistle during the campaign: the first U.S. reconnaisance (spy) satellites were launched in 1959.[17]

Still, the Kennedy Administration felt compelled to redeem campaign pledges, and doubled the Minuteman force and upped the Polaris submarine fleet from 19 to 41 boats, thereby escalating the arms race drastically.

Model   A "shooting script" for Apocalypse. In Webster's terms, a description or analogy used to help visualize something that cannot be directly observed, or a mathematical description of a state of affairs. At the beginning of the Atomic Age, models became the tools of analysts who were trying to describe what would happen in situations where nuclear arms might be employed. They are still used despite the early lesson learned in the Korean War. In that conflict, models neglected the fact that it was one thing to deal with a nuclear-armed adversary and quite another thing to deal with his client.

The decision to adopt the *MIRV*ed missile was helped along by the Pentagon's long-standing insistence that the country that struck first in a nuclear war would "win." *Computers* confirmed it. Repeatedly, with their models of what would happen, they produced the same answer: the side that launched a *preemptive attack* would suffer less damage, have fewer casualties, and end up with the larger reserve.[18] From findings like these came the technological "improvement" everyone wishes had never been adopted—the MIRVed missile.

In short, what the model cannot possibly incorporate is judgement, which Royal Air Force Marshal Sir John Slessor seems to have in abundance:

> I have perhaps the somewhat unenviable advantage of an experience, which fortunately has been denied to most people, of being in a city which was literally wiped out with most of its inhabitants, in 55 seconds, by the great earthquake in Baluchistan in 1935, a far more effective blitz than anything laid on by either side in the late war, except Hiroshima and Nagasaki. When people talk light-heartedly about that sort of thing on a widespread scale not being decisive, I have to tell them with respect that they do not know what they are talking about. No country could survive a month of Quetta earthquakes on all its main centers of population and remain capable of organized resistance.[19]

Molink   The Moscow-Washington hot line, established immediately after the Cuban Missile Crisis of 1962, during which Soviet Chairman Nikita Khrushchev and President Kennedy were forced to communicate through diplomatic channels. Originally a teletype tieup, the line has since been improved, and messages now go via *satellite*.

Molink's real value was demonstrated during the 1967 Israeli war, which began on June 5. That morning, Soviet Premier Aleksei Kosygin called President Johnson to indicate his strong interest in having the superpowers use their influence to end hostilities. On June 8th, Johnson called Kosygin to say that U.S. forces were aware that the Israelis were responsible for an attack on the USS *Liberty* and that carrier-based aircraft in the area were scrambling only to help survivors. Two days later, Johnson used Molink to tell Kosygin that the Israeli counterattack against Syria would stop short of Damascus.

The line was also used in the India-Pakistani War in 1971 and during the Yom Kippur War of 1973. However, it was not designed to survive a direct confrontation between the superpowers.[20]

Multilayered deterrence *Deterrence* sliced finely and thinly, but still deterrence, which, according to the Pentagon, consists of three components.

Defense—if the USSR thinks that nuclear aggression won't work, it won't attack.

Escalation—The USSR must know that if it attacks first, it faces escalation to hostilities that would exact a higher cost than it is willing to pay.

Retaliation—Says the Pentagon, "if the adversary confronts a credible threat that aggression will trigger attacks by a surviving U.S. retaliatory capability against the attacker's vital interests, which will result in losses exceeding any possible gains, he will not attack."

What escalation and retaliation seem to indicate is that even if the attacker wins at first, he can't win later on, and, if the U.S. retaliatory capability is great enough, an adversary won't attack in the first place.

Of these three layers, "defense" is the most reassuring, said former Sectretary of Defense Caspar Weinberger, because what was talking about was a "war-fighting capability" that can defeat an attack and restore the peace. This, he maintains, "forms the foundation of effective deterrence."[21]

MX missile The Peacekeeper, as President Reagan, calls it: a missile that carries 10 warheads, each with a destructive force of 335 kilotons (30 times that of the Hiroshima bomb) and independently targetable to an accuracy of 100 meters. It is supposed to have a *boost phase* of 180 seconds, and to release its *warheads* just beyond the atmosphere at 200 kilometers (about 63,000 feet).

Shorter boost phases of 50 seconds and 90 kilometers are believed possible for this missile[22], thus confounding a Soviet *Star Wars* program because it would be unable to destroy U.S. missiles in their boost phase. And, assuming what we can do, they can do, the MX raises the question, why build Star Wars? The MX is not going away, however: the first ten missiles went "operational" in Wyoming silos just before Christmas 1986, as the Soviets were readying their version (SS-24), which is rail-mounted and also carries 10 missiles.[23] Indeed, the MX is America's answer to the large Soviet *ICBM,* and it has a long history.

First approved by President Nixon, the MX became the centerpiece of Carter and Reagan administration plans to upgrade U.S. ICBM forces and to face the problem of survivabilty created by Soviet *MIRV*ing. It is also designed to destroy Soviet "hard targets" like ICBM silos and command centers.

After a study of 35 different schemes, Carter proposed to shuttle 200 missiles among 4,600 shelters (a plan known as "Racetrack").[24] Reagan poohpoohed the idea and cancelled it upon taking office. Instead, he supported a system called *dense pak,* which would put the MX into silos so close to each other that incoming Soviet missiles would blow each other up *(fratricide).* Then it was the turn of Congress to poohpooh, which it promptly did.

In desperation, the administration turned to a bipartisan presidential commisssion on strategic forces, the *Scowcroft Commission.* It scoffed at the MX, proposed the small, accurate *Midgetman* missile, and dismissed the vulnerability problem by pointing out that the Soviets would not attack ICBM silos because U.S. submarine-based missiles and bombers provided an overwhelming retaliatory force. Three years later, however, the Reagan administration proposed a rail-basing system for the MX.

Designed to solve the so-called "vulnerability" problem (see *Window of vulnerability),* the MX still runs into questions about its purpose. Is it a *first-strike* weapon? If not, it is pointless as a retaliatory weapon, because after a Soviet first strike, Soviet silos will be largely empty. If it *is* a first-strike weapon, it flies in the face of U.S. strategic policy of not striking first, as enunciated by every administration since Truman, and, more vehemently than most, by the Reagan administration.

N, O

NATO (North Atlantic Treaty Organization) Formed by a treaty signed in Washington, D.C., on April 4, 1949, as though in anticipation of the successful testing of the Soviet atomic bomb barely five months later.*

The original signers were the United States, Canada, Iceland, Great Britain, France, Denmark, Norway, Belgium, the Netherlands, Luxembourg, Italy and Portugal. NATO's original purpose, as one of its founding fathers, Secretary of State Dean Acheson said, was *"deterrence* of aggression in whatever form."[1] Its goal has remained deterrence especially of a possible Soviet attack with covential forces on any of the NATO countries with the threat of nuclear "first use." (See *No first use.*)

The U.S. maintains substantial conventional and nuclear forces in Europe and keeps its hands on the nuclear trigger. With the retirement of U.S. General Bernard Rodgers as the NATO comander-in-chief in 1987, command passed for the first time to a NATO member. The cost of the U.S. commitment depends on who is asking and when. In 1978 President Carter asked the Pentagon to provide the percentage of the defense budget that was allocated for NATO. Within a period of six months, Pentagon estimates had gone from 40 to 85 percent.[2]

Since 1949 four nations have joined NATO; the Federal Republic of West Germany, Greece, Spain and Turkey. In a fit of pique, President Charles De Gaulle took France out of NATO's integrated command in 1966 and asked the alliance to remove its bases and headquarters from French territory. Today, the French are cooperating with NATO strategy but they have not rejoined the alliance.

Neutron bomb The bomb that turns a tank into a microwave oven.

---

* It is interesting to note that the leading physicist in the group that developed the bomb was 28-year old Andrei Sakharov, who would be among the first dissidents freed by Mikhail Gorbachev in 1986.

Popularly known as the bomb that kills people and spares property, and sometimes called "this revolting weapon," the neutron bomb (enhanced-radiation weapon) was designed as an anti-tank weapon, which destroys tank operators. It is a minature H-bomb (one kiloton) designed to release its energy as radiation rather than as blast. In fact, its radiation dispersal is virtually equivalent to that of the bomb that was dropped on Hiroshima. The intense radiation penetrates armor plate, causing tank crews to collapse a few minutes later and to die within 48 hours.

Opposition to the neutron bomb has come from those who claim its use will lower the *nuclear threshold* by making it easier to resort to *nuclear weapons*. Opponents believe that the primary hurdle in warding off nuclear war is the shift from conventional to nuclear arms, not the incremental shift from weaker to more powerful nuclear weapons.[3]

No first use The policy that stemmed from a memo sent to President Truman by Dean Acheson after Hiroshima, urging the president to declare to the world that the United States would not be the first nation to use nuclear arms. "No first use" has surfaced intermittently, but a first-use policy has been part of *NATO* policy since 1968. That year's NSC (National Security Council) directive refers to the failure of "direct defense" (NATO troops are being pushed back) and "deliberate *escalation*" (use nuclear weapons).[4] Assuming, therefore, that Russian conventional forces break through defenses, NATO armies have been trained to depend on the use of nuclear weapons. However there is now:

—strong opinion that NATO conventional forces could hold in the face of a Soviet conventional attack;[5]

—growing belief, according to McGeorge Bundy, that "fear of convulsion in Eastern Europe and respect for the internal political strength of the NATO nations . . . make a Soviet decision to attack Western Europe exceedingly unlikely under any present or foreseeable conditions";[6]

—serious consideration of the fact that senior military officials on both sides of the Atlantic have long held that nuclear explosives have no utility whatever as battlefield weapons.[7]

Thus there is considerable interest in the idea of no first use—a policy to reduce the likelihood that nuclear arms will be used—as opposed to *arms control,* which would keep nuclear arms but limit their numbers. Expectedly, questions of adding to conventional forces in Western Europe create concern among the NATO nations and budgetary apprehensions in the U.S. Nonetheless, it could be said that no first use moves mankind, for the first time since Hiroshima, away from the choice between peace and complete destruction toward a choice between peace and war.[8]

Nuclear bullet The Pentagon's dream of making the world safe for *nuclear weapons*: a missile that would eliminate *collateral damage* and approach the effect of a conventional bullet, which damages only its target. Such a weapon—allegedly, an enormously accurate *ICBM*—would help to make a *surgical strike* possible. Then, on a second go-around, ICBMs that create more collateral damage could be used if necessary.[9]

Nuclear dilemma The question of what to do when *deterrence* fails. Early on, there was some recognition that nuclear explosives had altered the nature of war beyond recognition. They existed not to be used, but to deter an opponent from making a move, even one that employed conventional forces. The requirement, therefore, is for another system of deterrence that can be applied at lower levels and keep the confrontation within bounds if nuclear deterrence fails. In short, "the bomb" exists: it will not go away, and it is far too frightful to be used; some other form of frightfulness is needed to guard against the initiation of hostilities. Such is the absurdity of the nuclear dilemma.[10]

Nuclear freeze An answer initiated by the public to *arms-control* footdragging and the *arms race;* this is a simple message that says "stop now." In November 1982, nuclear freeze referendums passed in 8 out of 9 states, and, the following spring, the U.S. House of Representatives voted 278 to 149 to endorse the freeze concept. At that time, 75 percent of the public supported a verifiable freeze, according to surveys conducted by the major broadcasting networks.

Unfortunately, Congressional support for the freeze was a mixed bag. Nearly all the House Democrats who supported the freeze also supported appropriations for the *MX missile* at almost the same time. The resolution to support the freeze eventually died in the Republican Senate.[11]

The freeze calls for a verifiable agreement between the superpowers to ban testing, production, and employment of all new missiles and aircraft designed to transport such missiles. Earlier versions suggested by Presidents Johnson and Carter lacked public support at the time. Although public support has increased, the obstacles to negotiating a freeze are horrendous, involving the need to arrive at *verification* procedures for development and production of nearly 100 different kinds of weapons. However, there seems to be sufficient support for a partial freeze,[12] if it can get by the lobbying of the *military-industrial complex.*

Nuclear guarantee   America's implied promise to its allies around the world to use its nuclear capability to protect them against any major attacker. This alliance system, which has persisted through all presidencies from Truman to Reagan, has kept the peace between East and West, apparently on the basis of nuclear *deterrence.* So it is with *NATO,* which depends on a nuclear deterrence provided by the U.S. The *credibility* of this American guarantee is now being questioned. What does the *Strategic Defense Initiative (Star Wars)* do for U.S. allies? There are still no answers.[13]

Nuclear umbrella   See *Extended deterrence.*

Nuclear threshold   The point at which nuclear arms are used. How a country reaches the threshold is still a matter of intense debate. In the early Sixties, one strategist developed an "escalation ladder" that had 16 rungs running from Subcrisis Disagreement to the Aftermath of an "all-out" War. A few years later, the ladder was lengthened to 44 rungs with the nuclear threshold at rung fifteen.

However helpful the ladder concept might prove to national decision makers, four questions remain unanswered: Are the Soviets looking at the same kind of ladder? Would either of the superpowers be able to recognize a rung if they saw one? Would the steps from rung to rung be deliberate? And finally, can control be exercised from step to step? In each case, the answer would inevitably be "no."

Nuclear weapons   Throughout the Atomic Age, these words have encompassed all "bombs," *cruise missiles,* or other devices (except aircraft) that carry nuclear explosives. The term is used synonymously with *warhead* (the "bomb" on the business end of the vehicle carrying the explosive.) Currently, the Los Alamos and Livermore Laboratories are the "Detroit" of warhead production.

The confusing practice of altering nomenclature is followed whenever the subject of "nuclear weapons" comes up. For example: "In the United States, the development, production, storage and planning for the use of nuclear weapons involves well over 200,000 people and an annual budget of more than $35 billion."[14] Here, nuclear weapons mean warheads. But in the same source, "Every working day, about eight new *warheads* roll off ther assembly line. Old *weapons* (italics added) are also retired . . . There are currently some 26,000 warheads in the American nuclear arsenal."

Nuclear winter   The secondary effects of nuclear war. Introduced by Dr. Carl Sagan in 1983, and revised in 1986, the theory of nuclear winter says simply that the debris and smoke from fires caused by nuclear explosions and hurled into the atmosphere can alter climatic and temperature patterns sufficiently to produce catastrophic effects upon living patterns.

Tests and *computer* simulations conducted by the National Center for Atmospheric Research, the Los Alamos National Laboratory, and the Lawrence Livermore National Laboratory reduced the original estimates of temperature drops. But the scientists involved still maintain that the indirect aftereffects of nuclear war would cause human misery on a scale without precedent.[15]

What should be noted is that drastic temperature drops are not needed to produce devastation. One degree will do the job, according to Dr. Sagan: "A single day in which the temperature dips below zero can destroy a rice crop. A local temperature decline of three or four degrees is enough to destroy all wheat and barley growth in Canada."[16] This is no flight of the imagination.

Dr. Sagan also points out that "the explosion of the Tambora Volcano in Indonesia in 1815 led to an average global temperature decline of only one degree C, due to the obscuration of sunlight by the fine dust propelled into the atmosphere; yet the hard freezes the following year were so severe that 1816 has been known in Europe and America as "the year without a summer."[17]

Pentagon officials are now worried about the consequences of nuclear winter, especially as it affects a decision to make a first or *preemptive strike*. Views within the Pentagon run a gamut of guilt: "a wistful hope that more study will make the nuclear winter problem go away; embarrassment at having overlooked it for 40 years; resentment that the peacenik doom-mongers might have been right all these years, even if they didn't know why they were."[18]

What's more, forest fires in Oregon and Northern California that occurred in the fall of 1987 provided additional substantiation for the nuclear winter thesis. Smoke coulds were chased some 400 miles out over the Pacific, demonstrating that they would not disappear and measurements within the burn area indicated temperatures of 50 degrees in areas where 80 degrees had been forecast.[19]

Nuke As a noun, a *nuclear weapon;* as a verb, to *attack* with nuclear weapons, as in, "nuke 'em." This slang expression has been used since the development of the first generation of nuclear weapons, the atomic bomb; through the second generation, the present hydrogen bomb; and into the third generation, now under development secretly. Named Prometheus, this version of the hydrogen bomb is a weapon designed for use in the *Star Wars* program and emphasizes pinpoint targeting.[20] It should be noted that President Reagan has promised that nuclear weapons will not be used in the Star Wars program. (See *Disinformation.*)

NUTS (Nuclear Utilization Target Selection) One more approach to the concept of *escalation, escalation dominance, escalation ladder, horizontal escalation,* and even *limited war*—all variants of the same thing. NUTS is at least aptly and honestly named. It says that the notion that *nuclear weapons* can be employed step by step to keep hostilities just short of all-out war is impossible. Indeed, President Carter's secretary of defense, Harold Brown, who originated the term, pointed out that it was "very *likely*" that the use of nuclear weapons at any level would immediately escalate to general nuclear war.[21] Some analysts have cautioned against confusing this concept with "nuclear use theorists" (also NUTS): "As these nuclear use theorists (NUTS) increase their influence at the expense of those who believe in mutual assured destruction, (MAD), one can truly say that the world is going from MAD to NUTS."[22]

Outer Space Treaty of 1967 A multilateral treaty signed and ratified by both the U.S. and the Soviet Union. Article IV of the treaty forbids basing *nuclear weapons,* or other weapons of mass destruction, in space. The treaty also forbids using weapons that require a nuclear detonation to provide power, such as the *X-ray laser,* on which the *Star Wars* system depends so heavily. (See *Cheating.*)

P

PAL *(Permissive action link)* A friend indeed: an electronic combination lock that requires at least two people to open it, installed on all *ICBMs* except the very oldest. PAL prevents the accidental or unauthorized firing of ICBMs. So far, it has not been installed on submarine-based missiles, which can be launched without the express orders of the president or his successors.

Parity The great "what is it?" in the nuclear debate—overall military equality between the superpowers. The *nuclear freeze* groups believe in parity between the U.S. and the Soviet Union; so does the Reagan administration. Their problem, and everyone's, is with definitions.

At this writing, parity could be said to exist between the superpowers: each side can withstand a *first strike* and hit back to inflict unacceptable damage. This, in fact, is *MAD* (mutual assured destruction), according to the specialists, some of whom have called parity the *balance of terror*.

Attempts to measure parity grew out of the talks leading to the *SALT* I treaty of 1972 and have continued ever since. Now, we have more bombers, better technologies, more missiles on undetectable submarines. They have more *ICBMs* and, with *MIRV*ing, more deliverable *warheads* on those ICBMs.

Looking at parity from another viewpoint, 70 percent of their offensive weapons are ICBMs, 20 percent submarines, 10 percent bombers. We have a third in ICBMs, a third in bombers, a third in submarines. We have 66 percent survivable against their 30 percent. The size of the warheads has to be considered: in what weapons are the big ones and the small ones installed, and where are their *launchers* located?

All these comparisons revert to the fact that the only parity between the superpowers lies in mutual assured destruction, and, as long as the *arms race* continues, that is where it is expected to stay. Indeed, according to Harvard history professor Stanley Hoffman, "It is impossible to prove that the outcome of political conflict in the last 30 years has been determined by the exact ratio of strategic nuclear forces. It is the relative importance of the stake to each side in every crisis which has been decisive."[1] (See *Superiority.*)

Particle beam   One of a number of *directed-energy* weapons being considered for the *Star Wars* program, this uses a nuclear explosion to accelerate subatomic particles toward a target. The obstacles to developing such a weapon are formidable.

If the technology for providing a space-based source of power could be attained, there would still be a need for systems of target detection, tracking, aiming, and assessment. All this would be operated from nearly 100 *satellites* placed in orbit 1,000 kilometers above the earth. Moreover, a 10-meter target 1,000 kilometers away would require a weapon that was accurate to one part in 1,000,000.

If all these problems could be solved, the weapon system would still be vulnerable to enemy destruction via presently available technologies. An adversary could, for example, destroy the particle-beam weapons, jam the link between the weapon and ground control, and use *decoys* to throw off the system's sensors. Here, in short, are some of the shortcomings of the Star Wars program in microcosm.[2] (See *Strategic Defense Initiative.*)

Payload   Another who's-ahead concept: a measure of the weight per weapon that one superpower can throw at the other. Payload includes the weight of the *warhead* and the missile's "guidance system." The value of this measurement is uncertain, since U.S. and Soviet warheads of equal yields have different weights. The U.S. is ahead in overall payload because of its bomber forces; the Soviets are ahead in ICBM payload.[3] (See *bean count, equivalent megatonnage, launchers.*)

Penetrance   A measure in percent of the missiles that get through a ballistic missile defence: sometimes called "porosity." Penetrance can be increased with "penetration" aids which are aimed at confusing the defense system. And if a balloon could be used as a decoy, so could additional warheads. This lead to the development of the MIRVed missile in the early Seventies.

Perception   It's not what you see, but what you think you see, that matters in the race for *superiority* between the superpowers. In the face of general recognition that the superpowers are deterred from war by their ability to blow each other to smithereens, the incredible notion has been advanced that the world must percieve an "essential equivalence" between their forces.

Enshrining the notion of "perception" in his 1975 Report to Congress, Secretary of Defense James Schlesinger said bluntly, "to the degree that we wish to influence the perception of others, we must take appropriate steps (by their lights) in the design of the strategic forces."[4] Later in the decade, Carter's defense secretary, Harold Brown, concurred: "It [perception] guards against any danger that the Soviets might be seen as superior—even if the perception is not technically justified."[5] Then came Reagan.

The Report of the President's Commission on Strategic Forces (the *Scowcroft Commission*), assembled to decide on the viability of building the *MX missile,* said that it could not be protected. Still, the Commission gave a weak go-ahead, pointing out that "The overall perception of strategic imbalance . . . has been reasonably regarded as destabilizing and as a weakness in the overall fabric of deterrence."[6]

All this has persisted in the face of worldwide opinion surveys (including one in 1978 sponsored by the Pentagon, no less) that have given a verdict of "nonsense" to perception theory.[7] Finally, a poll conducted by the Public Agenda Foundation in September 1984 found that 90 percent of the public believed that "we and the Soviets now have enough nuclear weapons to blow each other up many times over."

Perestroika The Russian word for "the great reconstruction" that Mikhail Gorbachev is trying to achieve in the Soviet Union. (See *Glasnost.*)

Pop-up Another first from the fertile mind of Edward Teller, "father" of the H-bomb and, arguably, of *Star Wars,* this is the capability of sending or "popping up" *X-ray lasers* into space from submarines cruising relatively close to Soviet installations. Once in space, the weapons would lock onto the heat of the booster flames of Soviet missiles and destroy them while they were in their *boost phase* (from three to five minutes long). This was Teller's way of circumventing the placement of battle stations in space, which is outlawed by several treaties. As he put it: "The time available to act, if you take into account the amount of time you consume in accelerating these objects to high altitudes, is counted in seconds—perhaps 100 seconds."[8] And there's the rub.

However challenging, the pop-up system needs breakthroughs in rocketry, communications, and *computers.* If the breakthroughs are achieved, the demand for decisions made with incredible speed replaces the president with a computer, and war becomes a matter of our computers against theirs. Finally, the most telling objection of all is that there is a positive countermeasure: a time reduction in the boost phase of Soviet rockets. According to the Pentagon's Fletcher Committee, established in 1983 to evaluate Star Wars for the president, it is possible to build *ICBMs* with a 60-second boost phase. And we know that anything we can do, the Soviets can do too.[9]

Positive release   The Soviet system for authorizing the use of *nuclear weapons,* under which only the highest political authority can give a go-ahead. The general staff acts only under this system and then, as an implementing agent, gives authority wherever it is needed.

In cases of military action with conventional weapons, control is negative, as it was in 1983, when the Soviets shot down a Korean airliner. In such situations, Soviet air commands have standing orders to shoot down intruder aircraft unless specifically ordered not to.[10]

Post-attack era   After the war is over: a favorite topic of conversation among proponents of fighting a nuclear war limiting American casualties to 20 million. Nowhere in those conversations is there any recognition of how much that figure would be increased by the destruction of medical, transportation, and food-delivery systems, to name just a few essential services. Yet, as State Department consultant Colin S. Gray puts it: "The United States should plan to defeat the Soviet Union and do so at a cost that would not prohibit U.S. recovery. Washington should identify war aims that in the last resort would contemplate the destruction of Soviet political authority and the emergence of a post-war world order compatible with Western values."[11]

Preemptive strike   Get him before he gets you. This policy calls for striking first when you believe that the enemy is about to *attack* with the object of destroying as many of his *ICBMs* as possible. It is alleged that preemption is Soviet policy. According to the Pentagon, the Soviets will fire their missiles first if a crisis has reached the stage where a nuclear exchange seems inevitable. With the advent of *MIRV*ing and the development of missiles with vastly improved accuracy, the Soviets were assumed to be capable of destroying most of the U.S. force of *Minuteman ICBMs* in their silos. Hence the *window of vulnerability.*

What seems to be emerging, however, is the view that the idealized picture of a flawless Soviet attack, as presented to the public and to Congress, is sufficiently blurred around the edges to be dangerously misleading. A number of uncertainties indicate that an all-out attack on Minuteman silos would eliminate barely 50 percent of the missiles, leaving 500 Minutemen intact and 70 percent of the U.S. retaliatory force ready to go. There are several reasons for this estimate.

Neither the Soviet Union nor the U.S. has ever fired a missile from a silo. The U.S. tests its Minutemen by periodically removing one from its silo and shipping it to Vandenberg Air Force Base in California, where the missile is fired out over the Pacific.

Both the U.S. and the Soviets test on East-West ranges. In war, those missiles would fly on North-South trajectories, where gravitational forces are different. There is no way of knowing what the effects on guidance systems will be.

The covers of Minuteman silos are built to withstand overpressures caused by nuclear explosions of 2,000 pounds per square inch (psi) There is little test data even for forces of 200 psi and almost none for 500 psi Obviously, neither U.S. nor Soviet silos have ever been subjected to a nuclear blast of any magnitude.

Any attack on the silos would have consider the effects of *fratricide.* If two missiles are aimed at each silo, which is likely, radiation from the first explosion would destroy the second rentry vehicle. If, instead, one enemy missile were fired and then the second to avoid fratricide, the Minuteman would probably have been fired in the interval.[12]

In short, it seems reasonable to suppose that the attempt at a preemptive strike by either superpower would lead to all-out nuclear exchanges, with their dreadful, incalculable consequences. It is worth remembering that even the bellicose Prussian prime minister Otto von Bismarck told Emperor Wilhelm I of Prussia, "I would . . . never advise your Majesty to declare war forthwith, simply because it appeared that our opponent would begin hostilities in the near future. One can never anticipate the ways of divine providence securely enough for that."[13]

Prevail The word that's used when the Pentagon would rather not say "win" a nuclear war. Thus former Secretary of Defense Caspar Weinberger asserted that neither side can prevail in a nuclear war but, he added, "we are not planning to be defeated." Then, with President Reagan's approval, a senior White House advisor proclaimed that "prevailing with pride is the principal new ingredient of American security policy."[14] If there were any doubts that the Pentagon intends to prepare to fight and prevail in a protracted nuclear war, they should have been eliminated by its announcement of the plan to acquire hundreds of small nuclear reactors "that would generate electrical power in a protracted nuclear war." Transportable by air, these reactors would cost some $20 billion, and negotiations are already underway for developmental work.[15]

For the past 40 years, most responsible observers have insisted that in the event of a nuclear war, there will be no "prevailing," no "winning" of any kind. Even so, some have dallied with the thought that after a nuclear exchange, survivors could pick up the pieces and resume their normal lives. Prominent among these was the late strategic analyst Herman Kahn, who asked us to "consider the possiblity—both menacing and perversely comforting—that even if 300 million people were killed in a nuclear war, there would still be more than four billion left alive."

Kahn went on to advise that "one of the most important continuities of the nuclear era is that wars can still be fought, terminated and survived ... Reconstruction will begin, life will continue, and most survivors will not envy the dead." It is important, he added, "for national leaders to recognize that they will be judged by how well they exercise their responsibility to help their country prevail,"[16] all of which is not a far from former Defense Secretary Caspar Weinberger's stance.

Preventive war See *Preemptive strike*

Probability A branch of mathematics that measures the likelihood that an event will occur. Today, unfortunately, probability, which plays an indispensable role in such widely separated fields as medicine, public opinion analysis and nuclear physics, is all the experts have to predict the performance of nuclear weapons. Except for Hiroshima and Nagasaki, those weapons have never been used. But in an ongoing attempt to quantify what is not quantifiable, probability produces the kind of gibberish that permeates the whole vocabulary of nuclear *strategy*. To give an example, "The harm done by risk is equal to the probability of the bad event times its disutility," says Harvard's Joseph Nye.[17] Another example from a Pentagon consultant: "The probability of the success of a first strike is the probability that all of them do perform as expected. The first of these is the kill probability; the second is commonly called the reliability."[18]

In pointing out that "chance must be something more than the name we give to our ignorance," the economist John Maynard Keynes, another pioneer in probability theory, warned that "no knowledge of probabilities, less in degree than certainty, helps us to know what conclusions are true, and that *there is no direct relation between the truth of a proposition and its probability.*"[19]

Project Kiwi The nuclear-fueled aircraft that stirred little boys' imaginations, Congressional appropriations, and little else for a long, long time.

Shortly before the end of World War II, a curious Air Force officer, Donald J. Keirn, tried to join the Manhattan Project to find out whether nuclear energy could be used to power aircraft. By 1946 a long-lived, well-financed project was underway. The project was known officially as NEPA (Nuclear Energy for Propulsion of Aircraft). However, designers were never able to solve the obvious twin problems caused by the weight of reactor shielding needed to protect a crew from radioactivity and the danger from dispersion of radioactive material in a crash. Finally, after years of expensive, high-tech boondoggling, the Kennedy administration killed the project in 1961.[20]

Proliferation The slow but steady enlargement of the "club" of potential nuclear bombardiers. The timetable of nuclear bomb acquisition is as follows:

1945: United States
1949: Soviet Union
1952: Great Britain
1960: France
1964: People's Republic of China
1974: India

Until 1974 the five member "nuclear club" was apprehensive about the spread of nuclear explosives to the world's leading industrial countries. They had signed the Nuclear Non-proliferation Treaty, which went into effect in 1970, and continued to support the International Atomic Energy Agency (a United Nations unit), which sends inspectors to nuclear power facilities to make certain that fuel is not being diverted to military uses.

But with the Indian explosion (a breach of India's agreement with Canada, which supplied the technology ostensibly for development of a nuclear power plant), the club's concern shifted to Third World countries where nuclear prestige could obliterate the stain of poverty. The problem is, as the strategist Albert Wohlstetter put it, that "There are not two atoms, one peaceful and one military. They are the same atom."

The so-called "nuclear fuel cycle," which lies at the heart of nuclear power generation, produces plutonium, the material that's essential in the production of nuclear explosives. The purchaser of a nuclear power plant from any of the world's suppliers is getting a bonus. He has only to separate the plutonium from the waste, and he's in business. In short, the power-plant salesmen of the Western world are today's version of the fabled arms salesmen of old. However, the Soviet salesmen don't give up the trigger. Whenever the Soviet Union has exported power and research reactors to nations within its sphere of influence, it has insisted upon control. The Soviets own the fuel elements. They reprocess and manufacture the fuel cells. Soviet technicians transport and install the fuel elements, and, when the time comes, take them away to repeat the process. So far, no one has been able to convince the salesmen of nuclear reactors to make the Soviet approach the basis for an international agreement.

Meanwhile, proliferation seems to continue apace. It is suspected that Iraq, Libya, Pakistan, and South Africa are hard at work on development of a nuclear bomb. There could be interest in Argentina, Brazil, Chile, South Korea, and Taiwan. No one knows, and everyone fears what a terrorist somewhere is up to. This fear is heightened by the fact that students at Princeton University and the Massachusetts Institute of Technology, using unclassified documents, have designed very respectable, workable nuclear *warheads.*[21]

Prompt Nuclear wartalk for "Bang! You're dead." The analysts who play war games on computers to guess at the outcome of nuclear exchanges usually project their findings in terms of "prompt" and *"soft"* fatalities. The prompt fatalities die immediately; the soft take a little longer. Nigel Calder, a critic of the idiocy of wargaming, described prompt fatalities as the "men, women and children punctual enough at doomsday to escape a lingering death.[22]

An altogether different use of prompt measures the speed with which one superpower or the other can strike back. A background paper prepared by the Congressional Budget Office refers to the "prompt *counterforce* capability" of the *MX missile:* "The *MX* ICBM and the *Trident*-2 submarine launched missiles, both highly accurate ballistic missiles planned for future development in survivable basing systems, would provide a prompt counterforce capability, one that would provide the means to retaliate against reserve Soviet ICBM's within minutes of a Soviet first strike. Such prompt counterforce capability would give the Soviets little time to launch a second-round attack before the arrival of counterattacking U.S. missiles."[23]

R

Radiation One of the horrifying effects of a nuclear explosion, which has unalterably changed the face of modern warfare and made the possibility of war between superpowers the conjectures of madmen. Unfortunately for mankind, the appeal of the "bomb" lies in its economics and in its awesome destructive forces.

Dynamite (chemical explosion) takes about a thousandth of a second to blow up. A nuclear explosion releases about 99 percent of its energy *one million* times faster. A one-megaton bomb, equivalent to one million tons of TNT, weighs about 2,000 pounds and can fit into a container about 20 inches by 40 inches. But one million tons of TNT would fill a freight train 300 miles long. At a speed of 50 mph, it would take 6 hours to pass a reviewing stand. And with an average market price of 84¢ per pound, the trainload would cost about $1,680,000,000. So much for the economics. There is no comparison of destructive powers.

The United States Strategic Bombing Survey of Allied bombing in World War II reported that "The major cities of Germany present a spectacle of destruction so appalling as to suggest a complete breakdown of all aspects of urban activity. On first impression it would appear that the area attacks which laid waste these cities must have substantially eliminated the industrial capacity of Germany. Yet this was not the case. The attacks did not so reduce German war production as to have a decisive effect on the outcome of the war."[1] But at Hiroshima and Nagasaki, cities were leveled and people were annihilated instantly. Whatever had been there was gone. This is simply the nature of nuclear explosives. Their primary coinage is radiation.

At the sun-like temperatures that are characteristic of nuclear explosions, most of the energy produced at detonation goes into radiation in the form of thermal X-rays. This is what is lethal to humans. About a minute after the explosion, half of the energy is released in a giant blast wave and almost all the rest in the form of thermal radiation.[2] After a one-megaton explosion at ground level, an area of some *50,000* square miles around the target area would be uninhabitable because of the radiation; after 6 months, the forbidden area would still be nearly *8,000* square miles.

Discussions of radiation usually involve a number of internationally accepted standards, of which the most important include:

Curie: the rate of disintegration of one gram of radium.

Half-life: time required for a radioactive substance to lose 50 percent of its radioactivity.

Rad: "radiation absorbed dose." One rad is the amount of ionizing radiation that deposits 100 ergs of energy in each gram of biological tissue. This is the measure of how much radiation an individual can absorb.[3]

Rem: A Rad adjusted empirically for "relative biological effectiveness."

The maximum permissible dose per person per year is 500 millirem; the average annual background radiation (medical diagnosis, weapons testing, etc.) is 90-100 millirem. One chest examination produces about 10 millirem.

Rapid kill assessment Part of the jargon that emanates from the *Star Wars* program, this measures the efficiency of a system in terms of how quickly a shot has eliminated its target. The communications system must also be able to discriminate between an actual missile and a dummy and to report its findings instantaneously. All this comes under the heading of what the Pentagon likes to call "birth-to-death" tracking.

Reach Who's in charge? The ability of a president, premier, or prime minister to control battlefield events; *i.e.,* to "reach" from his office to the scene of hostilities. In both World Wars, it became virtually impossible for anyone above the battalion level to exert control. The search-and-destroy tactics employed by U.S. forces in Vietnam were used because the Army had trained itself to use them. They were never chosen by Washington, nor did Washington eliminate them, although those tactics were highly unsuccessful. Despite excellent communications in Vietnam, there was very little reach; decisions were made on the spot.

The absence of reach could have catastrophic consequences for the use of *tactical* battlefield *nuclear weapons.* (See *escalation.*)

Real time What the TV producers call "live": getting information from one command to another without a time lag. But just as labor contract negotiations go through the charade of "setting back the clock" as a deadline approaches, various sections of the armed forces have their own definitions of "real time," allowing for variations of as much as an hour. Consequently, battlefield coordination among ground troops and between ground troops and the air force becomes extremely difficult as high-tech communications reduce real time.

Redundancy A duplication of *nuclear weapons,* or of equipment such as communications and control systems. Some redundancy is necessary; some creates more problems than it solves.

Redundancy in nuclear weapons is not an excuse for the *arms race,* even though some armaments are unnecessary. Every Soviet and American leader has understood that there must be a way of striking back in the event of nuclear *attack.* For example, the U.S. has its submarine fleet; the USSR has its *tactical* missiles aimed at Europe. These are alternative weapons, not redundancies. If all these weapons are added up, each superpower has more than enough *warheads* to wipe out the other's cities. These are redundancies. But the objectives of a nuclear arsenal are not to kill people, but to ensure *deterrence.* Some analysts, however, attest that the size of the superpowers' arsenals are well beyond anything that is required for this purpose.

Redundant C^3I (Command, communication, control and intelligence) systems may create control problems of their own. Duplicate communications networks must be managed so as to coordinate information flows. Otherwise, the results can be chaos or disaster. The Liberty and *Pueblo* debacles of the 1960s were undoubtedly abetted by information mix-ups. In 1985 near disaster and certainly chaos ensued in the U.S. seizure of the *Achille Lauro* highjackers. (See C^3I)

Risk reduction center See *Crisis Center*

Reykjavik The capital of Iceland, where the superpowers met in November 1986 in history's first mini-summit, parleyed, and nearly trashed the future. Both Mikhail Gorbachev and Ronald Reagan, past masters of the art of public relations, were unable for weeks afterward to say precisely what had occurred. Nonetheless, as spokemen for both sides interpreted failure as success and black as white, one outcome was certain—SDI *(Star Wars),* Reagan's *Strategic Defense Initiative,* had worked as a *bargaining chip.* For without restraints on SDI, said Gorbachev, no deal. So, too, said Reagan and went home.

For the Russians, Reykjavik represented the next step in a series of meetings that had begun in Geneva, where the outcome was deadlocked over SDI. During the subsequent brouhaha over the arrest of reporter Nicholas Daniloff, Gorbachev invited Reagan to the meeting in Reykjavik. The Americans assumed that the Soviets were ready to deal on intermediate-range missiles in Europe, which U.S. negotiators had dissociated from SDI in Geneva. And so they rushed to Reykjavik, where the superpowers dangled Utopia before each other and the world and then reversed themselves, thereby substantiating Henry Kissinger's belief that affairs of state are much too serious to be left to chiefs of state at summit meetings.[4]

The ultimate promise was to be a total ban on *ballistic missiles* within ten years. The Reagan administration grabbed at that suggestion as a PR coup, which, unfortunately, would have meant the destruction of a policy that had kept the peace for 40 years—the use of nuclear arms as a *deterrent* against an assumed Soviet conventional attack in Europe. It has been said that while the United States has a *military-industrial complex,* the Soviet Union *is* a military-industrial complex. This is why an effective nuclear deterrent will be needed as long as Russian ambitions remain the same, or the West is not ready to spend the amount required to undo the neglect of conventional forces since World War II.[5]

There is still another argument against the elimination of ballistic missiles: it would destroy two legs of the American *triad,* especially where the U.S. has unmatched *superiority*—in undetectable submarines. However, to separate delusion from possibility, Reykjavik did leave three indications of what might be in reach in future negotiations: the elimination of intermediate-range missiles in Europe which was accomplished in December 1987, some kind of reduction in strategic offensive weapons, and an agreement to limit testing.

Rorsat (Radar ocean reconnaissance satellite) A Soviet "spy" *satellite* that the U.S. does not have. Rorsat is equipped with a radar that scans the oceans and keeps track of all U.S. naval vessels, then transmits its information to Soviet forces. Used in conjunction with Eorsat (Electronic ocean reconnaissance satellite), another exclusively Russian device that monitors radio and radar transmissions from U.S. ships, Rorsat allegedly provides the Soviets with a lock on U.S. naval operations.[6]

Rules of the road A suggested procedure for keeping the peace in space by controlling the uses to which *Satellites* can be put, rather than legislating against the use of *ASATs* (anti-satellite weapons). Both superpowers deployed ground-based ASAT systems in the 1960s and kept them in use for a decade before they were decommissioned, primarily because they were not very effective. Neither superpower has space-based ASATs, but renewed interest in ASATs during the Carter administration led to negotiations with the USSR toward prohibiting such weapons in the late 1970s. It was the Soviets who plumped for "rules-of-the-road" control of satellite use to prevent their employment as launching platforms, rather than ruling them out entirely. It should be noted that there have been successful rules of the road at sea for centuries.

However, developmental work on ASATs continues in both the USSR and the U.S., despite the fact that every administration since Eisenhower, except for the Reagan administration, has favored the prohibition of weapons in space.[7]

RPV (Remotely piloted vehicle) The latest in the Pentagon's bag of high-tech toys, vehicles that go by themselves, and walking robots currently under development. Actually, airborne RPVs have been in use since the 1960s. The versions being developed now, however, carry electrooptical systems that permit them to take pictures of battlefield events while they are occurring and transmit them to command centers.

For example, during the Lebanon War, the Israelis used RPVs in the vicinity of Syrian *missile launchers* to detect missile radar frequencies and transmit the information back to the Israelis, who then programmed their missiles to destroy Syrian defense systems.[8]

Safeguard One in the long line of expensive, flawed anti-missile weapons *(ABM)* that began with Nike and Sentinel. Safeguard was President Nixon's contribution. It cost *$5.7 billion* before it was finally dismantled on its North Dakota site.

When Nixon finally gave the OK to proceed with construction, over the adamant objections of most of the scientific community, the Pentagon was thoroughly familiar with *EMF* (Electromagnetic force), yet it insisted on going ahead. The high-altitude fireballs that Safeguard would have created to knock out Soviet missiles, attacking the continental U.S. would also have knocked out Safeguard's radars, and probably the communications between the president and field installations, while putting *computers* out of commission nationwide. Safeguard was abandoned a year after it was switched on; its deficiencies are a harbinger of some of the problems *Star Wars* would face if undertaken.[1]

Salami tactics A thin slice at a time, applied primarily to possible Soviet tactics in Western Europe in face of the reality that each superpower is now able to blow the other to smithereens. The notion underlying salami tactics is that because *NATO* supposedly has only a nuclear response with which to protect itself, the Soviets might make limited forays that would not elicit such a response. Hence their objectives would be achieved in small increments.

SALT (Strategic arms limitation talks) A series of *arms-control* negotiations between the superpowers aimed at the limitation and reduction of *nuclear weapons.* In May 1972, President Nixon and Leonid I. Brezhnev signed the SALT I Treaty, which restricted *ABM* (anti-ballistic missile) systems. It would haunt the Reagan administration's attempt to launch *Star Wars*, specifically with its ban on the "development, testing or deployment of ABM components which are ... space-based."

Before SALT I, a number of agreements had been signed, prohibiting nuclear arms in Antarctica, in space, and on the sea floors.

A test-ban treaty outlawed atmospheric tests of nuclear *warheads* and a Non-proliferation Treaty tried to set limits on the spread of nuclear weapons. (See *Arms control.*) But is was the burgeoning technology of *verification* that stimulated the SALT agreements. A spy *satellite* can count missiles, ascertain their size, and pinpoint locations. However, it cannot tell how many warheads a single missile carries. To assess comparative strength, the superpowers agreed to count warheads by assuming that a missile carried the maximum possible number of warheads. Some did not carry the maximum, but at least limits were set.

The same year (1972), an Interim Agreement on Offensive Forces was signed; although it has since expired, both parties continue to abide by its provisions. In 1979 President Carter and Brezhnev signed the SALT II treaty, which was never ratified. However, both parties observed its limitations until 1986. In the interim between the two SALT treaties, a number of other agreements were worked out.

The Threshold Test-ban Treaty limited underground testing and the Peaceful Nuclear Test-ban Treaty outlawed such explosions. But the most successful act of cooperation to date is the Standing Consultative Commission set up by SALT I.[2] It examines technical SALT-related matters and is considered an unqualified success. Unfortunately, toward the end of President Reagan's first term, the administration began to break with the treaty. On November 15, 1986, White House spokesman, Larry Speakes, intoned, "SALT II is no longer operational."[3] The final break came with deployment of a *cruise missile* on a B-52 bomber on November 28, 1986, taking the U.S. beyond the weapons limits set by the treaty.[4]

Even so, SALT III negotiations (renamed *START* by the Reagan administration) continued through 1986 and '87, primarily because, like it or not, "Both sides in the arms race are confronted by the dilemma of steadily increased military power and steadily decreased national security," according to Jerome Wiesner, M.I.T. scientist and scientific advisor to several presidents.[5] And then came *Reykjavik.* Billed as a quickie summit meeting to set the agenda for a full summit meeting between Reagan and Soviet leader Mikhail Gorbachev, the mini-meeting ended up in a brouhaha (Wreckjavik) that would confuse the issue of arms control for some time.

The conference produced no spectacular proposals, *e.g.,* no more missiles within ten years, or mutual acceptance of 50 percent cuts in *ICBMs* within five years. Instead, there seemed to be the promise of substantial gains on subjects that had divided the Soviets and the West for years: limitations on ICBMs, a Russian give-back of counting the British and French missiles among medium-range missiles, limitations on *tactical* missiles, possible acceptance of the American position not to limit underground testing, and a real gain in *verification*. All this could happen, it seemed, if the U.S. were willing to be sensible about President Reagan's seemingly impossible dream.

As negotiations continued apace in Geneva, questions were being asked about the worth of arms control negotiations. If they were terminated, would superpower relations suffer? Had the SALT and interim agreements been worth it? The answers comprised a mildly qualified "yes," according to a special Harvard study prepared for the U.S. Arms Control and Disarmament Agency, which set forth a number of postulates about negotiating arms control:

—Arms control agreements were concluded when neither side had a clear advantage. This was especially true of the ABM Treaty of 1972.

—Agreements don't occur when either side wants freedom of action about a weapon because it has tested that weapon, or has invested in it heavily, or both. It was impossible to get an agreement limiting *MIRVs* simply because the U.S. already had deployed them and the USSR was trying to close "the MIRV gap."

—There is very little historical proof that "arms control by denial" has any effect on the behavior of either superpower.

—Over the years, the U.S. has had very little success in trying to use "linkage" (behavior in other policy areas to influence the arms control process). Nor does success in arms control necessarily improve superpower relations.

—None of the agreements that put limits on ICBMs had a "lulling" effect on U.S. behavior.

—The principal dividend from arms control may very well be reduced uncertainty and improved predictability. As the study concluded, "A world without negotiations, agreements, and rules to promote verification would be one of far greater uncertainty" and one more likely to see an unrestrained *arms race*.[6]

Satellite A rocket-launched object shot into orbit around the earth. The Soviet Union began the space age with the launching of *Sput-*

nik on October 4, 1957. The U.S. followed with *Explorer* on January 31, 1958. Since then, some 3,000 satellites have been orbited by various countries, 75 percent are for military use. Between 1959 and 1984, the latter cost about $70 billion, with the 1984 outlay alone standing at some $10.5 billion.[7]

Until the *Challenger* spacecraft disaster, about 100 military satellites were launched each year: 85 by the USSR, 15 by the U.S. The Soviet launchings are more numerous because, on average, U.S. satellites last five to six times longer than their Russian counterparts and are also multipurpose. A U.S. Big Bird satellite stays in space for about 200 days; a comparable Soviet Cosmos satellite lasts about 30 days.[8]

Currently, satellites fly in four different kinds of orbits:

Low orbit: Orbiting below 5,000 kilometers (3,000 miles), these satellites are susceptible to destruction by current *ASAT* weapons. Both superpowers use these orbits for picture-taking, electronic intelligence, meteorology, and geodesy. The Soviets also use the low orbits for communications satellites and their radar ocean scanning.

Highly elliptical or Molniya orbits: Used extensively by the Soviets for early warning and for military and civilian communications. Because they approach the earth closely in part of the orbit, they are especially vulnerable to ASATs.

Semi-synchronous orbits: At 20,000 kilometers (12,000 miles), satellites in these orbits will continue to be invulnerable for at least another decade. Both superpowers use them for their military navigation and targeting systems.

Geosynchronous orbits: At an altitude of 36,000 kilometers (21,600 miles), satellites in these orbits follow the earth and remain at a fixed point on the equator. The U.S. uses these orbits for early warning, intelligence, and military communication. The USSR has only communication satellites in these orbits.

Increasingly, however, as more sophisticated ASAT weapons are developed, U.S. satellite communications systems are becoming so vulnerable that a former secretary of defense for research and engineering has said, "I do not envision that our fixed ground-based systems or our satellite systems would survive an attack."[9] (See *ASAT, Verification.*)

Scenario The script for nuclear war. A tale of developing confrontation that strategists use to forecast the sequence of events leading to the use of *nuclear weapons*. Scenarios are "educated guesses," "guesstimates," or "speculative exercises." They are, in short, what-if approaches to a subject no ones knows very much about—nuclear war.

Scenarios usually don't include public, political, or bureaucratic reactions. And those who create these scenarios have a habit, via probability analysis, of quantifying what cannot be quantified. Scenarios favored among strategists include *bolt from the blue,* a limited *ICBM* attack, a *preemptive* attack, a war in the Middle East, specifically in the Persian Gulf, accidental wars, and the all-time favorite, the chain of events following a conventional Eastern bloc attack on *NATO* forces.

One outstanding scenario illustrates clearly the drawbacks in all the rest. It is the work of Paul Nitze, a prominent strategist and *arms control* expert who has served every administration since Truman's and is now Secretary of State George Shultz's undersecretary for arms control. Nitze's idea is that *"throw weight"* (the weight of the *warheads* and *decoys* that a missile carries) is the measure of *superiority* in a nuclear exchange. His scenario goes like this:

The Soviets *attack* U.S. military targets, destroying enough U.S. missiles to put themselves ahead in throw weight. U.S. authorities immediately know not only how many missiles have been hit, but which ones as well. Soviet forces also have this information.

Next, U.S. forces order a retaliatory strike against the Russians to even up the throw-weight balance. The attack is launched and monitored by a system that has already been subject to thousands of nuclear explosions. Yet all necessary information gets through to the president or his successor. Soviet leaders go through the same exercise, using their communications system, which has also been under nuclear attack. Adding up the throw weights tells them that they have won (Nitze's conclusion).

Nitze's basic idea is that repeated attacks would continue to shift the throw-weight balance, and that these changes could be observed dispassionately by both sets of political leaders. It is not necessary to quarrel with Nitze's assessment of a nuclear exchange as a precise chess game between two unemotional and superbly rational players, each of whom is interested only in evening the score. The blunt fact is that neither superpower has the information system required to implement the scenario. After a nuclear attack, the resulting *EMF* (electromagnetic force), plus destruction, would make communications impossible. Nitze himself would say in 1985, "I do not believe it is possible to have equal forces on both sides."[10]

Scowcroft Commission. President Reagan appointed a bipartisan President's Commission on Strategic Forces in January 1983 "to review the strategic modernization programs of the United States. In particular . . . to examine the future of our ICBM forces and to recommend basing alternatives."[11] To head the commission, he named General Brent Scowcroft, who had worked for Henry Kissinger, served as President Ford's National Security Advisor, and been a member of President Carter's General Advisory Committee on Arms Control.

When the Commission issued its report, it disposed, first, of the question uppermost in the minds of the defense community, the so-called *window of vulnerability,* which it slammed shut. This was the notion that U.S. silo-based missiles were sitting ducks to a Soviet *attack.* Not so, said the report. The USSR would never attack, primarily because the U.S. bomber fleet and submarine-launched missiles could mount a devastating *second strike.*

However, the report continued, better basing was in order, more accuracy for missiles was needed and these dual objectives could not be accomplished with a single missile. Consequently, to solve both problems; the Commission recommended the deployment of a single-warhead, smaller missile that could be kept on mobile *launchers:* the *Midgetman.* For greater power, the report supported the *MX missile* which could be put into Minuteman silos because, after all, the "window" had been shut. Indeed, the Commission did not think that *ABM* defense of the silos was warranted.[12]

Other recommendations were lost in the attention that was paid to the MX and Midgetman missiles; *i.e.,* that the highest priority should be given to updating the nation's Command, Control, Communications, and Intelligence system (C^3I); that development and deployment of the *Trident* II (D-5) submarine-based missile should be continued; that implementation of the *cruise* missile and bomber programs should also be continued. And in a special letter to President Reagan the following April (1984), the commission emphasized the need for arms control so that the superpowers could achieve stability at lower force levels.[13] It should be noted that the administration's arms control policies have disregarded this advice.

In an expanded version of a BBC Radio 3 broadcast in 1985, General Scowcroft reinterpreted a number of the Commission's recommendations and added others. Most importantly, he said: "The expectations for arms control have been too high . . . there are things about strategic defense that can be destabilizing. And so one ought to look very carefully at the whole issue before one launches off in a particular direction . . . I don't think we know nearly enough [to deploy a strategic defense against ballistic missiles]."[14] What the General seemed to recognize was that special interests had kidnapped parts of the report and engraved them to be reprinted for their benefit whenever the occasion arose.

Second strike   The essence of *deterrence:* the capability of absorbing a *first strike* and returning a devastating nuclear *attack.* In short, it is assumed that the existence of the ability to mount a second strike, together with the belief that it will be used, are the factors that deter an adversary from attacking in the first place.

Even if an attack aimed at U.S. missile silos were successful, it would be answered by a devastating response from American bomber- and submarine-based missiles, carrying almost 70 percent of U.S. *warheads.* It is assumed, therefore, that the U.S. has such a second-strike capability. Indeed, its existence prompted the *Scowcroft Commission* to denigrate the concept of a *window of vulnerability.*

There is some thought, however, that a Soviet first strike would be made, not against Minuteman silos, but against the U.S. command and control systems (C^3I). These, it is said, are extremely vulnerable.[15]

Self-deterrence   Another in the long line of concepts grouped around the premise of take-this-take-that nuclear retaliation. A nation that has endured a nuclear *first strike* might be deterred from launching a *second strike* because it fears that the enemy will mount a third.

Before the advent of nuclear arms, it was possible that defeat in war would not annihilate a country. But with the ability to use nuclear arms, the attacker must decide that (1) damage from an opponent's retaliation can be kept within "acceptable" levels, or (2) the enemy will be "self-deterred" from mounting a second strike.[16]

But what are "acceptable" levels of fatalities? It is assumed that because the Soviets suffered 20 million casualties in World War II at least that level of fatalities would be acceptable to them. Armchair estimates of acceptable levels for the U.S. have run as high as the meaningless figures of 50 million and 100 million *prompt* fatalities. Theoretically, it would then require only 50 years for the country to return to "normal."[17]

Simulation   One of the many attempts to know the unknowable; the examination of a situation that can't be examined directly by using some device (e.g. *computer* program, *scenario*) that mirrors the situation.

During the late 1950s, the Rand Corporation (a problem-solving *think tank* funded by the Air Force) was simulating to the nth degree. One group of social scientists divided into Red and Blue teams and role-played the likely outcomes of superpower confrontations. Across the hall, the economists, mathematicians, and scientists calculated their simulations of *kill probabilities,* weapons reliability and so forth.[18] What neither side acknowledged was that one of the dictionary definitions of simulation is "counterfeit."

The nuclear future is indeed unknowable, and rational decision-making cannot be based on simulations that are free of psychological interactions, assume that the enemy thinks as we do, and calculate the consequences of a nuclear exchange to the last fatality.

Single warhead missile   A relatively small, light *ICBM* with only one warhead, as opposed to a *MIRV*ed missile, which carries ten warheads that can all be aimed separately. Such a missile *(Midgetman)* was proposed by the *Scowcroft Commission* in 1984 and has, in fact, been suggested in *arms control* discussions since *SALT* I.

At one point during the SALT I talks, Paul Nitze (later President Reagan's arms control advisor) suggested to his counterpart that the superpowers agree to scrap all their existing missiles and substitute a larger number, say 5,000, of single warhead missiles. They would be too small to MIRV. Neither side gains an advantage, because it would probably lose more missiles than it knocked out. Said Nitze: "This would really work. And my opposite number said, 'I couldn't agree with you more. It would, in fact, do exactly what you said it would do. But we're not going to do it. We like our big weapons. We've put a lot of effort into those big weapons and we're just not going to give them up.' "[19]

SIOP (Single Integrated Operational Plan)   As the number of *warheads* grows, so do the targets increase. This was happening even in the early years of the nuclear age. In 1960 Secretary of Defense Thomas Gates, troubled by the incredible examples of over-kill—several U.S. armed services were targeting one Soviet instal-lation—consolidated the war plans of all the services into one integratid plan, the SIOP (pronounced Sy-Op). Every administra-tion since has altered the plan to fit its own policies.

Gates admitted at the end of his term as secretary that he had not been able to bring the overkill problem within bounds. And Eisen-hower noted that in the interval between his tenure as Army chief of staff and the end of his presidency, the number of bombs targeted on Russia had increased 300 times.[20] Little has changed since then; 30,000 warheads simply mean that many more targeting opportunities.

In the last days of the Carter administration, the president sup-plemented the latest SIOP with PD-59 (Presidential Directive), expressing a whole new strategic approach, which the Reagan ad-ministration adopted, adding its own interpretation via National Security Decision Directive-13.

None of this has ever been released, but enough has leaked to keep the strategic analysis industry going at full tilt. For what the latest (Reagan) version seems to say is that in the event of war, the U.S. objective is to wipe out the adversary's political and military control systems *(Decapitation)*.[21] So far, no one has suggested how the war is going to be ended without decisionmakers. Nor has any-one ever protested the Strangelove-like assumptions on which the SIOP is based:

The "probability of arrival" at targets for weapons carried on bombers is about 77 percent for air-launched cruise missiles, 72 percent for short-range attack missiles, and 60 percent for bombs.

The first warhead allocated to each "aimpoint" will be detonated reliably at an optimum height of burst, destroying surface struc-tures and *killing all the people at the target.* (Italics added.)[22]

SLBM (Submarine-launched ballistic missile) See *ICBM.*

Smart weapons Weapons that do their own "thinking" and get to their targets through incredible flights of technological wizardry. These are the "precision-guided" munitions that are designed to hit and destroy targets at least 50 percent of the time. The 1973 Arab-Israeli War, and clashes between Syrian, and Israeli forces in Lebanon, have proved the worth of these weapons. Their increased use may point the way toward balancing the alleged Soviet conventional superiority in Western Europe, thereby postponing the time when *NATO* would have to resort to *nuclear weapons* to counter a a Soviet attack.[23]

Smart weapons being developed now will ultimately carry multiple-target-seeking *warheads* that could eliminate tanks, artillery pieces, and other vehicles simultaneously. *Cruise missiles* are being equipped with the same kind of capability.[24]

Soft Soft is (1) unprotected and (2) not quite dead. Cities, refineries, factories, and airfields are soft targets. *Warheads* aimed at soft targets don't have to be totally accurate; they could miss New York by 1,000 meters (almost two-thirds of a mile) and still obliterate every living thing and every structure. Missile silos are "hard" targets, built of steel and concrete to withstand explosion-induced pressures of 2,000 pounds per square inch (144 tons per square foot).

The second perversion of soft is used to describe those people who have survived a nuclear attack but have been so burned and irradiated that they will eventually die. They are "soft" fatalities, and of them it is said, "they will envy the dead." Those whom they envy are *"prompt"* fatalities.

Software See *Computer*.

Space mine An armed "space sleuth" would be a better description, for a space mine is a hypothetical small *satellite* carrying an explosive charge.[25] It would be placed in the same orbit as the satellite it is stalking. On command, the mine would move up on its prey and destroy it. Some scientists have argued that unless restrictions on *ASAT* weapons are negotiated between the superpowers, space mines would become a critical threat to satellite systems at the outset of either conventional or nuclear war.[26]

Spasm war Apocalypse: the nuclear war in which the superpowers throw everything they have at each other. As early as the 1960s, it was estimated that if such an all-out *attack* were mounted without restraint and without holding back reserves, the U.S. would have been able to obliterate 360-450 million people throughout the Sino-Soviet world within hours.[27]

Spoofing Feints made as defensive measures to trick the opposition into revealing the location of missile installations.

Stability In nuclear terms, a state in which neither side has the capacity or the incentive to launch a *first strike* against the other and get away with it. As President Reagan suggested midway through his first term in discussing the U.S. *arms control* position, "There will have to be tradeoffs, and the United States is prepared to make them, so long as they result in a more stable balance of forces."[28]

All concepts of stability share several ingredients: a secure *second strike* capability, a reduced reliance on *nuclear weapons* in the overall arms mix, the avoidance of weapons and policies that would upset the balance and threaten the Soviet *deterrent,* and a continuing quest for arms control agreements. According to the Scowcroft Commission report, "stability should be the primary objective both of the modernization of our strategic forces and of our arms control proposals."[29]

No one has been able to improve on an illustration that was first offered in the late 1950s: "Two tribes live in close proximity and [are] armed with poisoned darts. They could not disarm each other, there was no defense and the poison was fatal. However, it took time to be effective, so there was a probability of retaliation. The only rational outcome was for neither tribe to start shooting."[30]

In more familiar terms, it is hoped that stability is not the penultimate scene in an unwritten Western movie wherein the gunslingers face each other with six-shooters strapped to their hips, each waiting for the other to "draw," but rather the ultimate scene where, still armed, they ride off together into the sunset. To reach that scene, both must realize that it is a "far, far better thing" not to shoot. Such is stability.

Standing consultative commission An example of what cooperation between the superpowers could be; a committee established by *SALT* I to examine technical questions related to the control of strategic arms. It has worked quietly, without publicity, ever since and has been judged an unqualified success. It has often been suggested that the SCC's jurisdiction should be extended to SALT II to make a *builddown* workable.

Star Wars See *Strategic Defense Initiative.*

START (Strategic Arms Reduction Talks) The Reagan administration's follow-up to *SALT* II, which it accused of "simply legitimizing the arms race." START would limit each superpower to 5,000 nuclear *warheads* on strategic missiles (half could be on *ICBMs*) and 850 *launchers* for strategic missiles. Under the proposal, however, the numbers would eventually work out to increased *MIRV*ing by allowing more than 10 warheads per ICBM, thereby doing precisely what SALT II had been accused of doing.[31]

Stealth (ATB - Advanced Technology Bomber) The bomber that radar—and curious investigators—can't see. Originally conceived as a bomber with a reduced "radar cross section" (what a radar can see), the "stealthy" design is allegedly being applied to fighter aircraft and *cruise missiles* as well. Not since the Manhattan Project of World War II has a Pentagon project proceeded so successfully in almost total secrecy. Its cost is estimated to be about $5 billion annually. Only a few chosen people, including Senator Barry Goldwater, claim to have seen the Stealth bomber.

Even so, in July 1986 a plastic model of an Air Force stealth fighter appeared in the hobby shops. No one at the Testor Corporation, the model maker, had seen the actual aircraft, but designers had put the model together from bits and pieces that have appeared in the public domain. Knowledgeable observers say that the model resembles the actual plane to a remarkable degree.[32] According to the *Washington Post* of August 22, 1986, there are now about 50 Stealth fighters built and ready for combat. The Pentagon has gone so far as to admit that the program exists.[33]

The Stealth project began during the Carter administration, which revealed the program's existence during the election campaign of 1980. Success of the program will depend ultimately on the technical capability of reducing an object's "radar cross section" (RCS), the development of electronic countermeasures, and the reduction of infrared emissions. The B-52 bomber had a radar cross section of 100 square meters, the B-1B bomber shaved that to one meter, and it is said that the Stealth bomber is down to one tenth of a square meter.

Still, the plane will face other problems if it is to complement the *ICBM* force and create an attack problem for the Soviets. Requirements will include the ability to get off the ground promptly, exemplary speed and acceleration, and sufficent "hardness" to withstand nuclear effects. Allegedly, these requirements are being met. The Stealth process will make *verification* of *arms control* agreements infinitely more difficult.[34] Some observers, however, see the

Stealth bomber less as a way to enhance America's strategic *triad,* and more as an economic weapon that would make obsolete the Soviets' multi-hundred-billion-ruble air-defense system and force them to increase an already swollen defense budget.[35]

Strategic analysis What "nuclear strategists" do; the analysis of how to use what nuclear weapons, when, where, and under what circumstances.

Strategic Defense Initiative (SDI) President Ronald Reagan's vision of a plan to make *nuclear weapons* "impotent and obsolete." Popularly called *Star Wars,* it all began with a speech.

On the evening of March 23, 1983, the president spoke to the American people. He warmed up by talking about the defense budget that had just been unveiled, and warned that anyone who wanted to cut the budget would have to be "candid enough to acknowledge that his cuts mean cutting our commitments to allies, or inviting greater risks, or both." Pointing out that "the United States does not start wars," he explained what *deterrence* meant and the need for it since the dawn of the atomic age.

It works, he said of deterrence, but, with the Soviets' increased capabilities, the requirements for effective deterrence have changed. He was not saying, he underlined, that "the Soviet Union is planning to make war on us"; rather, that "our security is based on being prepared to meet all threats." (See *worst-case assumption.*) Then he proceeded to catalog the Soviet arsenal and how it had expanded over the years. He showed intelligence pictures of Soviet reconnaissance and weapons installations and urged all Americans "to tell your Senators and Congressman that you know we must continue to restore our military strength." Then came SDI.

Because we would have to rely on "mutual threat," even after successful arms reduction agreements, Reagan thought there were other ways to achieve a "truly lasting stability." He had consulted his advisors, he said, including the joint chiefs, and believed "there was a way. Let me share with you a vision of the future which offers hope." "What if . . . we could intercept and destroy strategic ballistic missiles before they reached our own soil or that of our allies?" It would take decades to achieve that goal, he acknowledged, and because of that, we would have to "preserve the nuclear deterrent."

Then he called "upon the scientific community who gave us nuclear weapons to turn their great talents to the cause of mankind and world peace; to give us the means of rendering these nuclear weapons impotent and obsolete." And so, he announced, he was "directing a comprehensive and intensive effort to define a long-term research and development program to begin to achieve our ultimate goal of eliminating the threat posed by strategic nuclear missiles."

More than 25 years earlier, Paul Newman, in an Alfred Hitchcock film, had played the role of an American physicist who pretends to defect to the Soviet bloc so that he can get a special formula known only to an East German scientist. In a press conference scene, Newman says, "We will produce a defensive weapon that will make all offensive nuclear weapons obsolete, and thereby abolish the terror of nuclear war,"[36] Reagan's vision was no more specific than Newman's script and thereby caused infinite confusion.

On March 17, no one knew what was going to be included in the address: not the joint chiefs, not the National Security Council, not the secretary of defense. But six days after the speech, Reagan told a group of six reporters convened in the Oval Office that someday a future president could give the Star Wars weapon to the Soviets.

We do know that Edward Teller, originator of the hydrogen bomb, had four meetings with the president prior to the speech to explore new ways to destroy enemy missiles during an *attack.*[37] Many others contributed bits and pieces, which came from research programs already underway. Reagan obviously had the findings of the President's Commission on Strategic Forces (The *Scowcroft Commission*) available to him. It was made public only days after the speech, and said:

"Applications of current technology offer no real promise of being able to defend the United States against massive nuclear attack in this century . . . the Commission believes that no ABM technologies appear to combine practicality, survivability, low cost and technical effectiveness to justify proceeding beyond the stage of technology development."[38]

In search of a positive vote for the Star Wars concept, President Reagan appointed Dr. James C. Fletcher, former head of NASA, to direct a Future Technologies Study; the Pentagon's Fred Hoffman headed a Future Security Strategy Study. The Fletcher conclusion was easily summed up: "A robust multi-tiered ballistic missile defense system can eventually be made to work." "Eventually" was the key word.[39] The report added that the possibility even of "eventually" depended upon an agreement among the superpowers to reduce offensive arsenals. The Hoffman report went off in another direction, emphasizing the short-term goal of supporting and improving deterrence.[40]

Still, confusion reigned. Three years after the speech, *Time* talked about "a protective shroud of ambiguity."[41] What was Star Wars, and where was it going? Taking a leaf from the Fletcher report, the Pentagon put out the news that "The goal of the SDI is to conduct a program of vigorous research focused on advance defensive technologies that may lead to strategic defense options that could:

- support a better basis for deterring aggression
- strengthen strategic stability
- increase the security of the U.S. and its allies, and
- eliminate the threat posed by ballistic missiles."

The Pentagon concluded that "The SDI seeks, therefore, to exploit emerging technologies that may provide options for a broader based deterrence by turning to a greater reliance on defensive systems."[42]

A number of Star Wars conceptions emerged from the smoke of the battles that raged between the Pentagon and the "arms controllers," who were trying to avoid another surge in the *arms race* by preventing a *breakout* from the restrictions on anti-ballistic missiles set by the 1972 ABM treaty. These conceptual approaches to Star Wars (in no official order or designation), are:

SDI I—Protect everyone and everything with a space-based program; the "leak proof" defense.

SDI II—Protect missile installations with the deployment of anti-ballistic missiles on the ground with, perhaps, some protection of human life, and maintain present deterrent systems.

SDI III—A minimal protective screen after ballistic missiles have been banned by agreement between the superpowers. (This is the "belt-and-suspenders" version.)

SDI IV—A program that turns ABMs into super-high-tech offense weapons, according to some scientists and former Pentagon policy analysts.[43] This is the nightmare, as the Soviets see it.

SDI V—A prompt, phase-one deployment of an anti-missile defense; former Secretary of Defense Caspar Weinberger backed this one.[44]

Apparently, the development of such exotica like *lasers* and rail guns (see *Ballistic missile defense*), which gave SDI its nickname, is gradually slowing down. In place of weapons, SDI V (rapid deployment of anti-ballistic missiles is being pushed under the name of "partial deployment." At a cost of some $100 billion, this limited shield could be in place by 1994, according to Weinberger.[45] In that event, the mistake of accelerating the arms race that was made in developing *MIRV*ed missiles would be duplicated.

Meanwhile, opposition to the management of the SDI program, and its shifting and divergent priorities, was growing. According to Dr. William A. Barletta, a beam-weapon official at the Livermore Laboratory, where much of the exotic-weapons development is going on, the overall program "has the flavor of having a new twist in priorities every few years."[46]

The White House says one thing: In a [January 1985] pamphlet aimed at dispelling some of the confusion about SDI, the White House said: "The combined effectiveness of the defense provided by the multiple layers need not provide 100 percent protection in order to enhance deterrence significantly."

The Defense Department says another thing: "The goal is clear and unchangeable. It is to secure a thoroughly reliable defense against all incoming Soviet missiles, either intermediate or long-range, and to destroy by non-nuclear means, those missiles before they get near any target."[47]

A presidential adviser says still another thing: President Reagan's chief arms control adviser, Paul Nitze, has said: "[we] accept the continuing need for reliance on offensive weapons and the ultimate threat of devastating retaliation as the basis for deterrence."[48]

No wonder the public is confused.

Slightly less than half the people queried had never heard of SDI, according to a *Los Angeles Times* poll conducted in 1985; 56 percent thought that SDI threatened the Soviet Union, and 55 percent opposed appropriations for research on strategic defense.

The New York Times found in the same year that 62 percent thought that the proposed system [!] would work; 48 percent thought that developing SDI would make negotiations between the superpowers easier. Another poll taken in late 1985 found that 48 percent favored the plan while 37 percent had never heard of it.

A *Los Angeles Times* poll in mid-1985 found that 59 percent thought development of SDI would cost too much, even though 58 thought it should be developed.[49] Yet another poll (*Washington*

Post-ABC, July 1985) disapproved of developing space-based weapons. The year before, an ABT poll had indicated that almost half the respondents opposed any system that would let 10 percent of attacking missiles get through.[50]

In early 1987, public opinion analysts were beginning to wonder about the value of opinion surveys on SDI. A big majority claims to know about the SDI program, but only about a fifth know a "great deal." And most people do not understand its purpose, which is understandable, since the experts are not agreed as to what its goal really is. In November 1985, a CBS News/*New York Times* poll indicated that 30 percent thought SDI was supposed to protect the entire population, 28 percent thought it would protect half, 15 percent said less than 10 percent, and 27 percent didn't know.[51]

Finally, the question was asked more precisely. "Supporters say such weapons could guarantee protection of the United States from nuclear attack and are worth whatever they cost. Opponents say such weapons will not work, will increase the arms race, and that the research will cost many billions of dollars. How about you? Would you say you approve or disapprove of plans to develop such space-based weapons? Here, 41 percent of respondents said they approved, and a majority—53 percent—said they disapproved."[52]

Simultaneously, a battle has been going on over SDI's feasibility and whether it should even be attempted in view of the estimated cost of $1 trillion and the foreign policy and defense issues involved. Overall, the pros and cons are as follows:

Supporters of SDI tend to argue from these perspectives:

• The USSR is determined, from all indications, to achieve *superiority* over the U.S. It now has a *first-strike* capability against U.S. *ICBMs.* In the future it is likely to find an answer to submarine invulnerability, thereby undermining America's *triad.*

• Past arms control agreements haven't successfully limited the Soviet arms buildup. The Soviets have deployed far more arms than they need for deterrence.

• SDI has already forced the Soviets to return to the arms control negotiations that they had walked out of in Geneva in 1985. The best prospect for future agreements is to persuade the USSR that its first-strike ICBMs will become obsolete in the face of SDI. The best policy for the future is for both sides to emphasize defense while they negotiate the reduction of offensive weapons.

• Given the asymmetries between the two societies, and the strategic objectives of the superpowers, the arms control process may never benefit the U.S. On the other hand, SDI may permit pursuit of a common interest in the "assured survival" of each society.

The critics of SDI have another view:

• Given all the means to destroy each other, (triad plus *cruise missiles*) that the superpowers possess, the Soviets can't hope to gain a nuclear advantage in the arms race, nor can we.

• By and large, arms control agreements have kept Soviet capabilities below achievable levels. Abandonment of the ABM Treaty, which SDI presupposes, would lead to a more costly and dangerous arms race.

• SDI didn't drive the Soviets back to the negotiating table; instead, it gave them a chance to save face and to stay out of the talks, which were resumed. (See *Summitry, Arms control.*) Moreover, there is no reason to disbelieve the Soviets when they say that SDI has forced them to seek and deploy more offensive weapons. The best way to solve the impasse is to extend the ABM treaty in return for a Soviet agreement to curtail its offensive arsenal.

• Over the long run, the best hope for avoiding nuclear war is not in strategy or new nuclear technologies, but in maintaining a stable deterrence until the political relationship between the two powers can be eased.[53]

Beyond the technical issues, and the very real question of whether the more exotic weapons can be produced in this century, lies a host of domestic and foreign policy questions stemming from a decided lack of policy. In a nation facing financial insolvency, the Reagan administration wants to lock its successors into eventually spending $1 trillion on a set of systems that may never be deployed. Indeed, in early December 1987, defense department insiders were saying that when he retired Secretary Caspar Weinberger had left behind some $300 billion in unfunded defense contracts, a guaranteed way to lock in spending for some time to come.[54]

The search for technological fixes is being used as a substitute for diplomatic negotiations, despite the fact that this quest has fueled the arms race in the past. Ultimately, it will be the political decision, abetted by scientific decisions, that will decide the fate of SDI, as it has decided the fate of other strategic systems over the past 40 years. (See *Ballistic Missile Defense.*)

Strategic reserve What's saved to bomb another day; the nuclear arms the Pentagon holds back from the *SIOP* (war and materiel plans updated by each administration) for "protection and coercion [in the] post-attack environment," according to Admiral Frank B. Kelso, the man who directs the nuclear-loaded submarines. In Congressional testimony, the admiral went on to say, "We plan to deploy a small number of nuclear-armed cruise missiles" [that won't be included in the SIOP]. They're being held for retargeting, if necessary, in the post-SIOP period." These weapons, said Kelso, would help the U.S. "retain a measure of coercive power in the post-exchange environment."[55]

Strategic warning The "pros" separate strategic warning from *tactical* warning of a nuclear *attack*. Strategic warning alerts commanders to an impending attack before it actually happens. Tactical warning advises that the attack is already underway.[56] (See *Early warning.*)

Strategy How we will use, or threaten to use, our weaponry; the use of "all possible means to arrive at ends determined by policy - each means (economic, psychological, weaponry, etc.) being tactical," according to Raymond Aron.[57] This classical definition, which originated far back in military history, was being twisted, almost before the smoke had cleared at Hiroshima, from a word that meant policy to a word that described weapons and their use. Now "strategy," the noun, describes an approach to the use of weapons; and "strategic," the adjective, describes a type of weapon.

In the mid-1950s, according to usage, strategic weapons carried very large *warheads* and *tactical* weapons carried small ones. Today, strategic missiles are those that can span continents *(ICBM)*. Among the tactical weapons are those with shorter ranges, such as battlefield weapons (with ranges as short as 100 miles) and IRBMs (intermediate-range ballistic missiles) that can reach as far as 4,000 miles. Bluntly, a strategic weapon is one that is based in the United States or the Soviet Union, or in nuclear submarines, and can be fired directly into the other country. Tactical weapons are all the rest.

However, strategy as a guide to the nation's military posture, is constantly in flux. There is a world within the CIA, the military, the universities, and the *think tanks* where "strategists" think the unthinkable. They tell how it is *likely* to be, or could be, or should be in the wonderful world of instant nuclear destruction, as each administration shapes strategy to suit its own ideology. The Reagan administration's principal spokesman on strategy was former Defense Secretary Caspar W. Weinberger, who said, "America's basic defense strategy . . . is to deter aggression."[58]

But *deterrence,* according to Weinberger, must also prevent coercion of the U.S. and its allies through threats of aggression: "This we will do by confronting an aggressor with three types of possible responses: Effective defense (defeating a conventional attack with conventional forces); the threat of escalation (countering a conventional attack on NATO with the threat of a nuclear response); and the threat of retaliation (letting the U.S.S.R. have all we've got in response to a Soviet attack).[59] And so the meanings of strategy weave in and out of the worlds of *escalation,* the *nuclear umbrella* and measured responses. Says Yale University's Paul Bracken: "What passes for strategic debate is little more than the construction of a facade of nuclear logic to permit getting on with the day-to-day job of deterrence."[60]

Sufficiency As President Eisenhower, the doctrine's author, first described it in March 1955 at a press conference, once you "get enough of a particular type of weapon, [it may not be important] to have a lot more of it." By the following spring, the doctrine was the official position of the Eisenhower Administration. This time, in response to a reporter who asked whether it wasn't important to have *superiority,* the president replied, "No! I say it is vital to get what we believe we need. That does not mean more than anybody else does."[61]

Henry Kissinger, President Nixon's national security advisor, played with the idea of sufficiency as a substitute for the emphasis on superiority. He defined sufficiency as the forces necessary "to ensure that the United States would emerge from a nuclear war in discernibly better shape than the Soviet Union."[62]

But when David Packard, deputy secretary of defense in the Nixon administration, was asked for a definition of sufficiency, he replied: "It means that it's a good word to use in a speech. Beyond that, it doesn't mean a God-damned thing."[63] Nixon wasn't so sure; he gave it two meanings. One was that sufficiency was enough to deter actual attack; the second was that U.S. forces would be large enough to prevent coercion by the threat of military action.

James Schlesinger, former *think-tank* analyst and defense secretary to President Ford, toyed with the notion, then let it go, just as he abandoned the mouthful "strategic asymmetries" (one of the superpowers is ahead).[64] Sufficiency resurfaced among strategists in the 1980s as "limited *deterrence*," but it is having little vogue among Star Warriors.

Finally, 31 years after President Eisenhower first talked about sufficiency, Mikhail S. Gorbachev promulgated a "doctrine of sufficiency" grounded in the belief that the USSR does not have to match the U.S. weapon for weapon.[65]

Summitry The practice by which heads of state attempt to negotiate the state of the world in public, the principal players being the superpowers. The first such meeting of the Atomic Age was between President Eisenhower and Nikolai A. Bulganin; there have been 13 in all:

July 1955—Eisenhower-Bulganin meeting in Geneva; "the Spirit of Geneva" began to thaw the Cold War.

September 1959—Eisenhower-Khrushchev meeting at Camp David; produced what was called "the Spirit of Camp David."

May 1960—Eisenhower-Khrushchev meeting scheduled for Paris, but scuttled due to Soviet shooting down of U.S. U-2 spy plane, which increased tensions.

June 1961—Kennedy-Khrushchev meeting in Geneva; heated exchanges.

June 1967—Johnson-Kosygin meeting at Glassboro, New Jersey; no progress.

May 1972—Nixon-Brezhnev meeting in Moscow; signed the ABM Treaty limiting the deployment of anti-ballistic missiles.

June 1973—Nixon-Brezhnev meeting in Washington; agreement to complete a new treaty by the following year.

June, July 1974—Nixon-Brezhnev meeting in Moscow and Yalta; signed treaty banning underground testing with yields over 150 kilotons.

November 1974—Ford-Brezhnev meeting in Vladivostok; laid groundwork for *Salt II* treaty, but it was not completed before Carter took over.

June 1979—Carter-Brezhnev meeting in Vienna; signed the second SALT treaty which the U.S. Senate failed to ratify. Nevertheless, the U.S. adhered to its terms until the Reagan administration.

September 1985—Reagan-Gorbachev meeting in Geneva; agreed to meet again.

October 1986—Reagan-Gorbachev meeting in Reykjavik, Iceland; called impulsively, ends in a public relations brouhaha.

December 1987—Reagan-Gorbachev meeting in Washington, D.C.; sign treaty eliminating all INF missiles.

Sunshine unit Where the weird nomenclature of nuclear arms and strategy got one of its initial starts. In the early Fifties, the Atomic Energy Commission (AEC) established "Project Sunshine" to monitor the worldwide dispersion of Strontium 90 from radioactive fallout. A specified amount of Strontium 90 became known as a "sunshine unit." Simultaneously, the AEC began a number of projects in which military personnel were used as guinea pigs and would continue them until the Test-Ban Treaty with the Soviet Union was signed in 1963. According to the Defense Department, between 250,000 and 500,000 military and civilian personnel were involved and exposed to nuclear radiation.

Superiority Who's ahead? The blunt answer is "no one." According to Senator Sam Nunn, chairman of the Senate Armed Forces Committee, there is a "U.S. advantage in submarines, in aircraft carriers, in tactical aircraft, in rapid deployment capabilities, in sea-launched ballistic missiles, in cruise missiles and in bombers."[66] The Soviets are ahead in other parts of the nuclear forest.

But each superpower has enough nuclear forces to blow the other off the face of the earth. Indeed, according to a survey conducted by the Congressional Research Service, "The U.S./Soviet military balance has been relatively stable for more than twenty years, and likely will remain so for some lengthy period. Many of the most impressive Soviet capabilities do not seem to constitute imminent threats, even taken in context with U.S. limitations."[67] In short, the reports of overall Soviet superiority or leading technological achievements that have been used to gain approval for bigger military budgets, upon examination, do not look very credible.

This has been true since Henry Kissinger first asked about superiority, "What do you do with it?" And Admiral E. J. Carrol, now retired, who served on Alexander Haig's *NATO* staff from 1972 to 1979, asserted that "the issue of nuclear superiority is irrelevant in the security equation. In the final analysis, war will come, or will be averted, entirely without respect to any consideration of nuclear superiority."[68] In short, superiority, like similar notions such as *bean count, parity, balance,* and *equivalent megatonnage,* is subject to what one observer called "that curious flexibility about Soviet expertise."[69]

"They're" ahead when the Pentagon needs another infusion of funds. For example, Max Kampelman, U.S. arms control negotiator, and Zbigniew Brzezinski, former National Security Advisor, say that "many Soviet missile silos are reloadable [and] and are set up for launching three salvos to our one."

"We're" ahead when the Pentagon, or its cohorts in the country's research labs and deep-think tanks, want to boast about the might of American technology. To the Kampleman-Brzezinski claim, the Pentagon says that even if it were true, "U.S. retaliatory capabilities could destroy any ICBM reload facilities long before a second Soviet salvo could be fired."[70]

More importantly, who gets there first? Whose *arms race* is it, anyway? The answer is clear and unequivocal. In a list of 40 initiatives in the strategic arms race, ranging from the first atomic bomb tests and the deployment of intercontinental bombers to the deployment of *MIRV*ed missiles and long-range *cruise missiles,* the U.S. leads in every instance. The Soviet Union trailed for periods ranging from 1 to 17 years (the latter case being that of an anti-*satellite* weapon) and still has not caught up in 8 areas.[71] This is what President Johnson was talking about when he said of the space program: "If nothing else had come out of it except the knowledge we've gained from space photography, it would be worth ten times what the space program has cost. Because tonight we know how many missiles the enemy has, and it turned out our guesses were way off. We were doing things we didn't need to do. We were building things we didn't need to build. We were harboring fears we didn't need to harbor."[72] That was in March 1967!

Surgical strike The term was coined during the Kennedy administration to describe a sudden, swift attack on a particular target. Indeed, the historian Arthur Schlesinger, Jr., who allegedly coined the phrase, said that the use of the word "surgical" to describe a military operation was "spurious." "War, as the late W. T. Sherman pointed out, is not surgical."[73]

This term was used most recently to describe the Reagan administration's 1986 attack on Libya, in which almost one-third of the planes didn't reach their destination and 5 out of 18 planes didn't release their bombs due to malfunction of the release mechanisms.[74] In short, the label didn't fit the package.

Surprise One of the niceties of the current stage of nuclear preparedness is the fact that surprise is not possible. It should not to be confused with a *first strike* or *preemptive strike,* say the professionals, who claim a surprise attack is the least *likely* way for a nuclear war to start.

If a country has had some warning of a nuclear attack and its forces are alerted, what follows is not a surprise attack. But if its forces have not been alerted, what ensues is a surprise attack. Thus a nuclear surprise attack "(1) would be launched before the outbreak of conventional war; (2) would catch the enemy's forces unalerted; (3) would catch the country's leaders in Moscow or Washington before they could be evacuated,"[75] and (4) will never be launched simply because the element of surprise has been eliminated entirely by spy *satellites.* (See *Verification.*)

Survival Who's left after a nuclear attack; estimates range from hardly anyone to almost everyone. For some time, Pentagon planners have been nourishing the notion that it is possible to survive and fight again another day—in short, to win a nuclear war. According to former Defense Secretary Robert McNamara, "The Pentagon is full of papers talking about the preservation of a 'viable society' after nuclear conflict. That 'viable society' phrase drives me wild. I keep trying to comb it out, but it keeps coming back."[76]

After the "winners" come the "rebuilders." They point to Hiroshima as an example of how civilization can bootstrap itself into the future, coming back from total devastation to normalcy in, say, 20 or 30 years. What's omited is that there was a nation and a whole world left to help the city back onto its feet. In a contemporary nuclear exchange, there would be no one left to help, especially if the effects of *nuclear winter* are considered.

All kinds of estimates have been made of the actual casualties to be expected in a nuclear *attack* on the U.S. One such projection assumes that in an all-out confrontation the Soviets would use about half of their *warhead* arsenal and the attack would be over in a matter of hours. The results in terms of human life would be staggering. Counting both those who would be killed outright and those who would linger for some weeks after the attack, over 100,000,000 people would die. That's more than half the population.

Doctors would not survive in sufficient numbers to help very much. Medical supplies and hospitals would have disappeared. Food would be in extremely short supply, and many of the deaths would result from starvation. *EMP* would have destroyed all the country's electronic and electrical equipment. Machinery needed to clear rubble and start some kind of reconstruction would be useless because of the unavailability of gasoline and oil. Ultimately, if reconstruction were possible, it would probably require some 50 years, and it is likely that ensuing social, economic, physical, and political structure would bear little relation to what we know today.[77] It is quite possible that the living would indeed envy the dead. This, perhaps, is why *NASA* as seriously considered putting large quantities of bone marrow into orbit, so that a supply would be available after a nuclear exchange for the treatment of radiation victims![78]

Sympathetic detonation Missile suicide, the offense's defense against the defense's offense. It would supposedly occur within 5/8 of a mile of a target that is being attacked by *ICBMs* and is envisioned as the final layer of a *ballistic missile defense.* The defensive technique, also known as swarm-jet, is to fire a large number of small rockets at the incoming *RV* (reentry vehicle, *warhead*). But if the attacker fused his RVs so that they would detonate on being attacked, the defense would be foiled. (See *SDI.*)

Systems analysis A system of what-if analysis (see *Scenario*) that grew out of World War II's operations research, which asked "what is the best that can be done?" given the existing equipment and its characteristics. Systems analysis asks instead, "what kind of equipment with what characteristics" will do the job. But operations research knew what it was dealing with—the known quantity of fighting wars at that time.

Systems analysis, however, is trying to plan equipment to confront the environment of nuclear war, about which it knows exactly nothing. It stands or falls on its assumptions, many of which make little sense, because there is no way to measure them. Like wargaming on *computers,* scenario-building, and the other what-if analytical devices, systems analysis is a remarkable tool for examining the elements of a situation. Nevertheless, it cannot penetrate the imponderables of reactions and consequences in hostile situations where nuclear explosives are used.[79]

T, U, V

Tactical The kind of nuclear weapon that *NATO* expects to use to turn back a Soviet conventional attack across the European East-West boundary line. All the other nuclear weapons are strategic weapons. (See *Strategy*.) They are the *ICBMs* that can be fired between superpower homelands or from submarines. But the difference between tactical and strategic weapons is not as clear as this sounds, because it has created one of the major battles about nomenclature.

Tactical weapons are not necessarily something soldiers can carry in knapsacks. They can be bigger than the Hiroshima bomb. They are not destined exclusively for anti-tank use; they can be targeted at cities. And they are not always called tactical weapons. They may be called theater or battlefield weapons. But whatever they are called, one observer said, "a tactical nuclear weapon is one that explodes in Germany." And that is why they are the ultimate military stupidity.

For the fact is, "Tactical nuclear weapons cannot defend Europe; they can only destroy it . . . nobody knows how to fight a tactical nuclear war. Twenty years of effort by many military experts have failed to produce a believable doctrine for tactical nuclear warfare," according to Alain Enthoven, one of America's leading military analysts.[1]

Finally, the obtuse reasoning that surrounds the supposed use of "tactical" nuclear weapons overlooks what the Russians say about it. According to General Mikhail Milshstein, a military spokesman who has represented the USSR in SALT negotiations, "Our doctrine regards nuclear weapons as something that must never be used. They are not an instrument for waging war in any rational sense. They are not weapons with which one can achieve foreign policy goals. But if we are forced to use them, in reply to their first use by an aggressor, we shall use them with all their consequences for the punishment of the aggressor."[2] And the ultimate, telling argument was offered by Dr. Georgy Arbatov, a full member of the

154

Soviet Central Committee and director of the main Russian think-tank on U.S.-Soviet relations: "All sane leaders now say that we cannot hope to fight, nor hope to win, a nuclear war. We are now also saying that Europe is too fragile, not just for a limited nuclear war, but even for a modern conventional war—not with 150 nuclear reactors and countless chemical plants on our continent."[3]

Tactical warning A warning that hostile missiles are on their way. A *strategic warning,* however, indicates that an attack is being readied. In both instances, *satellites* would provide the warning information.

Technology What the U.S. is presently ahead in: the application of scientific principles to the achievement of a practical goal. Originating in what Jacques Ellul, the French sociologist, called "a civilization that is committed to the quest for continually improved means to carelessly examined ends,"[4] the U.S. has set the tone and the pace of the *arms race,* sometimes to the advantage of its national security, sometimes not.

Currently, the box score looks something like this. Of 20 outstanding technologies used in the design of weapons, the U.S. is ahead in 14 and shares first place in 3 with the Soviets, who are moving ahead in 3 (conventional *warheads,* nuclear, and optics), according to former Defense Secretary Caspar Weinberger in his annual report to Congress for Fiscal Year 1988.[5]

Some developments are truly awesome—and frightening. For example, in a speech on October 14, 1969, General William C. Westmoreland said, "I see battlefields that are under 24-hour real or near-real time surveillance of all types [I see what's happening as it happens]." This is partially in effect now. He also spoke of weapons with "first-round kill probabilities approaching zero." What he meant was weapons that virtually never miss. And they have been available for some time. Over 800 sorties were flown and 2,000 tons of conventional bombs dropped on the famous Thanh Hoa Bridge in North Vietnam, and it still stood. Then *laser*-guided bombs were introduced, and 8 sorties dropped the bridge on the first mission.[6]

Some technologies help other technologies. For example, *computers* have taken over the peacetime world; they also direct wartime weapons. The Soviet computer ES 1060 was first produced in 1978 and is roughly equivalent to the IBM 360, which was introduced in the U.S. in the mid-1960s.[7]

With these advantages, however, the U.S. is continually searching out the technological "fix" as a substitute for political bargaining. In the process, says Dr. Henry Kendall, an M.I.T. physicist and 11-year consultant to the Pentagon, "stunning technical successes have translated into unbearable national security headaches and have raised the risk of nuclear war."[8] One of these was the development of *MIRV*ing, which put 10 warheads instead of 1 on the end of a missile. The reason for this development was to counter the Soviets' achievement of an *ABM* system. Now, all Soviet *ICBMs* are MIRVed. We had blindly followed what Nobel physicist Hans A. Bethe called "the technological imperative" without regard for the consequences.[9]

Think tank Where most of all the *scenarios* and *strategic analyses* come from; an organization staffed with specialists in the physical and social sciencies devoted to the analysis of national issues and problems. The first so-called think tank was probably the Rand Corporation, a non-profit organization formed in cooperation with the U.S. Air Force to undertake contract research. The Army has a similar arrangement with the Operations Research Office at Johns Hopkins University, and the Navy has an Operations Evaluation Group at M.I.T. The Institute of Defense Analysis works for the joint chiefs of staff and the secretary of defense.

The original concept has broadened to include a number of universities. Moreover, the study of Soviet policy and behavior is being carried on at universities like Harvard and Columbia. And organizations like the Brookings Institution, which was originally founded to produce economic studies, have broadened their activities to include strategic analysis as well as Russian studies.

With the advent of the Reagan administration, a number of think tanks with a conservative cast have become more prominent. Foremost among them are the Hoover Institution, Georgetown University's Group for Strategic Studies, and the Heritage Foundation.

Throw weight The business end of a nuclear missile: the combined weight of guidance equipment, *decoys* and *warheads* that a missile can lift. Throw weight is a concept that grew out of the negotiations that followed the first *SALT* treaty, which Nixon and Brezhnev signed in 1972. SALT I instituted numerical limitations on the arsenals of the superpowers; what was needed was a way to measure missile potentials in order to strive for *parity* rather than *superiority* between the superpowers.

The Carter administration, however, came to believe that missile performance rather than throw weight, or even *MIRV*ing, is the important variable in developing a capability to overwhelm silo-based missiles.[10] Now, again, the pendulum is swinging back toward superiority. Paul Nitze, who originally pushed the idea of throw weight after the SALT I treaty, and is at this writing a consultant to the Reagan *START* negotiating team in Geneva, said on a BBC Radio broadcast in 1985, "I do believe that it is possible to deny the Soviet Union a usable superiority . . . I think the world would be better off, you know, if the West had superiority . . . I do not believe it is possible to have equal forces on both sides."[11]

Time-urgent hard targets Close to deserving the nuclear obfuscation award from the U. S. standpoint is this euphemism for Soviet missile silos. Sometimes the words are pushed around to come out as "hard-target kill capability." One can hear this in the lecture halls of leading universities, [12] or on television programs [13] in which the speaker will add the aside "we all know what that is." In this instance, "capability" is the clue. What he means is the ability of a nuclear weapon to knock out a reinforced enemy missile silo.

Transitional deployment options (TDOs) Weinbergerese for "How to get *Star Wars* going without anybody really noticing." This notion was projected by a defense undersecretary in 1985 testimony before the Senate Armed Services Committee:

TDOs "may be relatively near term technological opportunities, perhaps based in single layers of defense, or on relatively early versions of technologies that can be the early basis for later growth in system capability. Or if they are effective and cheap enough, they might serve for a limited lifetime against early versions of the Soviet threat, while the SDI technology program continues to work on staying abreast of qualitative changes in the threat. Such an approach would incorporate a process for evaluating the transitional deployment options in terms of their 'robustness' against realistic countermeasures, their ability to survive direct attack on themselves, their cost and their compatability with our long-range strategic goals."[14]

Translation: "Transitional deployment options" can be several things. They may be technologies that we can develop relatively quickly. They may have to do with only one layer of defense (Star Wars is supposed to have three), or they may be the beginning of something that will be pretty big later on. If they work and they're cheap enough, we can use them for a while against early versions of the "Soviet threat" (to build their own Star Wars) if, in fact, there is a threat. (See *Superiority*.) Meanwhile, the Star Wars technology program can work on keeping up with the alleged threat. We would also get time to decide whether the TDOs were effective, whether they were able to see through any *decoys* that were put up to fool them, whether they could stand a direct *attack* themselves, and whether they were cheap enough and fit into the country's long-range strategic goals.

Triad   The three major components of *nuclear weapons* and forces of both superpowers: land-based *ICBMs*, bombers, and nuclear-armed submarines that make up each country's strategic nuclear forces.

The American triad, which forms an effective *deterrent* against *attack* (see *Scowcroft Commission*), grew like Topsy, as each of the armed services grabbed for a place at "the nuclear trough" in the postwar era. The Army was already in the act when, in the early 1950s, the Navy conducted two nuclear explosions on the Bikini atoll in the Pacific. One was underwater, one was atmospheric, and neither had any scientific justification whatever.

The battle among the forces continued well into the Eisenhower administration. Herbert York, Eisenhower's director of defense research, would say later that of six missile-development programs conducted in those years, three had no justification at all.[15] With the arrival of the Kennedy administration, the concept of a "triad" was enshrined as Holy Grail in the Pentagon. "Synergism" was discovered, and it became irrefutable doctrine that the deterrent effects of the triad were greater than the sum of the three legs. Each superpower puts its bet on a different component of the triad. The Soviets emphasize the missile leg of their triad; the U.S. is relying on the undetectability of its submarines (a single Poseidon missile, for example, could destroy Leningrad). Countering a Soviet *first strike*, a dozen Poseidon subs, each with 16 missiles aboard, could eliminate the 200 largest cities in the Soviet Union. In so doing, we would destroy a third of the Soviet population and 75 percent of its industry. Raise the ante to 20 Poseidons and all industry would disappear, along with every military installation in the USSR. that could be a threat to the U.S. The U.S. keeps that number of subs, with 4,000 nuclear weapons, at sea at all times. Sixteen subs, with another 3,000 missiles, are ready to go to sea on command. But the Soviets have only 10 subs with 850 weapons at sea.[16] (See *Trident*.)

Trident A program that includes the Trident *ballistic missile* submarine (SSBN), the Trident I (C-4) missile, and the Trident II (D-5) missile, which looks like it might be the most deadly weapon in either superpower arsenal. The whole program is thought to cost around $70 billion, much of which ($26 billion) is allocated for the D-5 missile.[17]

Replacing the older Poseidon submarine, the Trident is going into service at the rate of 1 per year. Initial equipment consists of 24 Trident I missiles, which will be replaced with D-5s. In addition, 12 Poseidon boats are being converted to carry 16 Trident Is. Altogether, the U.S. ballistic missile submarine fleet will consist of 36 vessels carrying 648 missiles with 5,760 *warheads*. Current plans call for a final deployment of 20 Trident submarines carrying 480 D-5 missiles.

The D-5 is being touted as the most accurate missile around and the one to beat. Weighing in at 475 *kilotons,* it has an 82 percent single-shot *kill probability* (the chances are it can wipe out its target 82 out of 100 times) against a silo *hardened* to withstand overpressures of 6,000 pounds per square inch; this is five times the accuracy of Trident I. Accuracy, more than power, is what makes for a lethal weapon. Under consideration is the possibility of equipping the D-5 with *NAVSTAR* recievers, which would enable it to receive navigational corrections in flight. Thus the D-5's *MIRVs* will become *MARVs*.

Apparently, what's going on is an attempt to make the D-5 as responsive, accurate and destructive as any *ICBM* around, thereby making two legs of the *triad* interchangeable and forcing the question of whether or not the D-5 is, in effect, a *first-strike* weapon and is not being built simply for *second strike capabilities*. Surely, the Soviets are asking precisely that question.[18]

Tripwire Included in a larger force, this is a smaller force whose presence calls bigger reserves into action—the original rationalization for the presence of American troops among *NATO* forces in

Europe. NATO forces including U.S. troops would resist the advance of Soviet forces while, it was originally thought, *SAC* (Strategic Air Command) forces armed with *nuclear weapons,* would do their work. At that time, Europeans reasoned that the presence of American troops guaranteed the use of SAC.

Today, NATO conventional forces (including U.S. troops) would resist a Soviet attack with conventional forces until they were beginning to lose, when *tactical* nuclear weapons would be brought to bear, theoretically keeping hostilities limited (see *Limited war*). In both instances, ground troops provide the nuclear "tripwire."

Usability paradox A rationalization of how reasonable men might act in a nuclear confrontation. In the early days of the nuclear age, the paradox was described this way by Bernard Brodie, one of the first nuclear analysts:

"It is a curious paradox of our time that one of the foremost factors making deterrence really work and work well is the lurking fear that in some massive confrontation crisis, it [deterrence] might fail. Under these circumstances, one does not tempt fate."[19] In short, if one superpower contemplates the use of nuclear forces but fears the other might really use them, he shouldn't even think about it.

Today the paradox has been broadened. Now it includes the necessity to prevent the easy triggering of nuclear weapons by forestalling accidental use and inhibiting the decentralization of political authority to fire. The paradox may then be rephrased: if one superpower knows the other won't use his nuclear weapons except to retaliate, conventional war becomes more likely.

User friendly A term that originated in the wonderful world of *computers,* meaning that the computer has been designed to ease the pain of operation and is now being applied to the litany of weapons envisioned for *Star Wars.* What could be more user-friendly than weapons that one superpower uses to shoot down the other's nuclear weapons while the attacker uses up his arsenal, is forced to replace it, and thereby bankrupts himself. This gobbledygook is essentially what former Secretary of Defense Caspar W. Weinberger calls "competitive strategies."[20] Indeed, the notion that the *arms race* can be pursued so far as to induce the USSR to spend itself into bankruptcy is being incorporated into the Defense Department's planning and budgeting process.[21]

Verification Who's *cheating*? "Verification" is a judgemental process that uses the results of "monitoring" (the collection of pertinent data) to decide whether the terms of a treaty are being met. According to the President's Commission on Strategic Forces, "The essential test of an effective verification system is that it will detect with a high degree of confidence any set of violations which would have a significant impact on the strategic balance. The Commission believes that goal is within our reach."[22] It is already here. Advances in both seismology and "national technical means" (*satellite* reconnaissance and other systems), once the stuff of science fiction, are available, and they work.

On-site inspection to detect nuclear explosions seems to be unnecessary. And, statements to the contrary notwithstanding, no one wants it. The Soviets have always resisted any kind of inspection as an intrusion on their secrecy and an invitation to spying. The U.S. has been similarly uncooperative, most recently during the Carter administration. But it is said that the Soviets could change their minds, because now they have nothing to fear from inspection. According to the leading seismologist with the U.S. Geological Survey at Menlo Park, California which keeps a weather eye on the Andreas Fault, "There are many tens of papers in the seismological literature which, taken together ... prove without a doubt that available seismological evidence does not support the case for Soviet cheating."[23]

Just in case the evidence didn't hold up, a private American organization made arrangements with the Soviet Academy of Sciences to monitor Soviet underground nuclear tests—the only ones allowed under the 1963 Test Ban Treaty. (It prohibited tests in the atmosphere, in space, and underwater.)[24] But within weeks of this arrangement, the Kremlin announced that it had put together *seismic means and satellite intelligence* to detect three unannounced American underground tests, and the administration admitted that it was so. The Soviet spokesman added that "These tests only went to prove that there is no problem of verification."[25] And there isn't, especially for the U.S.

In 1960 America orbited its first "spy" satellite. For 18 years there was no acknowledgment that such devices existed. Then, in 1978, in an attempt to ease the public's mind about the *SALT* II treaty then being negotiated, President Carter revealed that such satellites existed. We "would not have to rely on trust," he said, because we had "photographic satellites" that would catch the Russians every time.[26] How good are these satellites and what do they actually do?

According to William E. Burrows, director of the Science Reporting Program at New York University, *it is by and large agreed that "no major weapon has been developed by the USSR that has gone unnoticed, unanalyzed and uncataloged by the United States, and that no nuclear explosion has gone unrecorded and unmeasured"*[27] (emphasis added). Nevertheless, the question is raised continually, about how authorities can be certain that instances of cheating have not occurred.

Surveillance work is being done by satellites that can listen, satellites that can take pictures of a license plate from hundreds of miles above the earth, satellites that can produce pictures almost in *real time* (at the same time an event is occurring). There are also surveillance systems on ships at sea and at land-based locations around the world. In short, "virtually no significant event can take place on the earth's surface undetected," according to a former deputy director of the CIA.[28] The Union of Concerned Scientists even grades this performance. It points out that if the development of a new Soviet weapons system needs three phases, each of which has an 80 percent chance of being spotted, there is less than a 1 percent chance that the U.S. would fail to spot any of the phases.[29]

Indeed, so much is being found that the Pentagon sees fit to publish *Soviet Military Power,* a 143-page manual, every year. It includes locations of nuclear stockpiles, ammunition depots, and concentrations of petroleum products. It lists type and performance for every fighter, bomber, and missile. It shows *ABM* and radar locations around Moscow, even *cruise missiles,* with comparisons between U.S. and USSR performance. Moscow has pooh-poohed *Soviet Military Power;* it has never quarreled with the numbers.[30]

With verification of such a high order, the faltering of *arms-control* negotiations on this issue obviously says a good deal about the sincerity of the negotiators.

Vertical proliferation The growth in the number of nuclear weapons in one country, as opposed to *horizontal proliferation,* the growth in the number of countries with nuclear weapons. It is thought that the increasing numbers of nuclear weapons among the "have" nations influences *proliferation* among the "have not" nations, if only for the sake of prestige.

W, X, Z

Walk-in-the-woods A dramatic attempt to break a deadlock in the *INF* (intermediate-range nuclear forces) negotiations in Geneva in 1982. The attempt failed for reasons that are still unclear, but its daring and its "what if" possibilities have intrigued commentators ever since. In the spring of 1987, the "walk" would become the subject of a hit Broadway play. On February 28, 1987, Mikhail Gorbachev offered to sign an agreement "without delay" to eliminate all intermediate-range nuclear missiles within five years.[1] That's what "the walk" had been all about.

If the walk was an act of desperation, it was also the act of experienced *arms-control* negotiators who believed that they alone could achieve what had escaped the crowd of negotiators at Geneva. The Soviet involved was Yuli Kvitsinsky, his nation's chief negotiator at the Geneva meetings. His U.S. counterpart was Paul Nitze, who had served every administration since Truman's. The walks took place in July 1982, in the Jura Mountains, outside Geneva. What brought the two there was a complicated set of factors—superpower jockeying and an obdurate Reagan administration attitude toward arms control. As the "walkers" viewed the situation, it involved infighting among the *NATO* allies, as well as attempts by both superpowers designed more to gain public opinion advantages than to set arms limits.

The basic U.S. problem was how to get five recalcitrant NATO nations to accept new weapons on their territories, while talking the USSR into cutting its force of SS-20 mobile, *MIRV*ed missiles that threatened Western Europe. Furthermore, the weapons that America made the subject of bargaining were still being developed; the Russian missiles were in place. The proposed American missiles, the Pershing II, and the Tomahawk *cruise missile,* were suggested as bargaining tools. And, if they were eventually deployed, they could not do any more than other weapons already in place.

European nations weren't buying the symbolism. To them it looked as if the weapons were intended to enable Americans to fight

163

a *limited* nuclear war—limited to Europe. As the deadline for deployment of the Pershings and Tomahawks approached (December 1983), the pressure which the deadline was supposed to put on the Russians shifted to the Americans, and the whole situation invited the Russians to make propaganda hay.

Meanwhile, the Reagan administration, in an attempt to put something on the table before the deadline, proposed the so-called *"zero option."* In exchange for canceling the Pershing and cruise missile deployments, the Soviets would have to dismantle all their SS-20s throughout the USSR, including those aimed at Asian targets. As expected, the Russians said *"nyet"* quickly and angrily. And by mid-1982, it began to look as if they were going to take a walk. Hence the quieter walk in the woods.

Nitze based his approach on the idea that the Soviets didn't need more than 100 SS-20 missiles to cover every conceivable target in Europe. Anything beyond that was a waste of money. Therefore, the U.S. would trade a reduction in its Pershings and cruise missiles for the SS-20 surplus. Ultimately, what the walkers worked out as a proposal was that the Soviets would have a monopoly in the IRBMs (intermediate-range missiles) and the U.S. would have a monopoly in cruise missiles. In short, if the deal was accepted, each superpower could claim that it had not sacrificed its principles and simultaneously achieve its notion of equality. Finally, Nitze and Kvitsinsky agreed that their written memorandum would be known as "a joint exploratory package for the consideration of both governments."[2]

Both men went home. The Russian turndown did not come through for some time; neither did the American. An initially favorable U.S. reaction was quickly turned around, and Nitze was chewed up, not only by Pentagon forces, but by President Reagan's love for what he called "fast fliers" (nuclear missiles) as against "slow fliers" (cruise missiles). He wanted to keep the Pershing IIs because they were fast fliers. Obviously, he had not read the comments of a Soviet specialist on nuclear weapons:

"So what if the [cruise missile] takes hours to reach its targets. If we are the target and we don't know it's coming until it explodes, which is the whole point of its deceptive means of approach after all, then we have zero warning. In our judgment about what constitutes a first-strike threat, we care about warning time, not flight time."[3]

War fighting An aberration of *deterrence;* the unbelievable concept that a nuclear war can be fought and won, and that, therefore, a "war-fighting" capacity must be maintained as part of the nation's deterrent capability. That, at least, is the word according to Defense Secretary Caspar W. Weinberger. Like most Pentagonians, however, he put it in reverse. "The United States cannot prepare only for a 'short war'."[4] All this, despite the awful toll of 155-165,000,000 deaths in the United States alone that would follow from an all-out nuclear exchange between the superpowers.[5] This estimate does not include the devastating effects of nuclear winter that would follow.

The impossibility of war-fighting was recognized nearly 30 years ago, when the only *nuclear "weapon"* available was an intercontinental bomber. The logic was incontestable Bernard Brodie observed in the 1950s: "Too much depends on what the other fellow does—how accessible or inaccessible he makes his own retaliatory force and how he makes his attack if he decides to launch one. However much we dislike the thought, a win-the-war strategy may be impossible because of the circumstances outside of our control."[6]

Today's Navy doesn't agree. In an article approved beforehand by Defense Secretary Weinberger and published by the United States Naval Institute, Admiral James D. Watkins, Chief of Naval Operations, says that if a major conventional conflict broke out between the superpowers, the U.S. Navy has plans to attack Soviet nuclear weapon submarines. The Admiral wants the Soviet Union to know that it will face the prospect of prolonged global conflict if it so much as reaches for a gun, however conventional.[7]

Warhead See *nuclear weapons.*

Window of vulnerability The concept that America's nuclear arsenal of *Minuteman* missiles deployed in concrete silos are sitting ducks for a Soviet *first strike.* Since the Soviets would not need to use all of their missiles to knock out most of America's forces, the theory went, the USSR could blackmail the U.S. into doing whatever it demanded. This vulnerability threat was used to secure funds for the *MX missile.* It would replace the old Minuteman missiles, and the MX would be placed in their silos. But according to Admiral Eugene Carroll, now retired, "the window of vulnerability is the son of the missile gap."[8]

President John Kennedy rode to an election victory and justified a larger defense budget with the notion that there was a dangerous "missile gap." This meant that the USSR had considerably more missiles than the U.S. and was therefore in a position to attack at will—and win. Soon after the election (some say before the election), it became known that the Russians had 4 missiles to America's 50.

Similarly, President Reagan's *Scowcroft Commission* (President's Commission on Strategic Forces), which was formed in 1983 to study the state of the nation's nuclear arsenal, admitted that there was no such thing as the window of vulnerability, although two years later, on a BBC Radio program, Scowcroft would fudge:

"People say the Scowcroft Commission did away with the window of vulnerability. We didn't. What we said was, you have to look at this with a certain amount of perspective; and one perspective is the ability to do, in fact, what technically the weapons can do, in other words your operational confidence in being able to do it. And the second part, as we addressed this question of vulnerability, was this: that for now and for some time into the future, the missile forces and the bomber forces lend survivability to each other. The Soviets cannot attack both of them simultaneously."[9]

The notion of such a window was voiced in the 1970s as an attack on the *SALT* II negotiations, and as an argument in behalf of the MX missile. It was almost as walleyed then as it is now, for the Soviets' "window" is wider—almost 3-1/2 times wider than the U.S. window.

Two-thirds of the 7,500 Soviet strategic *warheads* are concentrated on 668 missiles, while only one quarter of America's warheads are in 1,054 silos.[10] This is undoubtedly what Henry Kissinger was getting at when he confessed that "My own view was that the Soviets were more vulnerable to a first strike than we; most of their strategic force was land-based and fixed."[11] And, it should be pointed out, the window of vulnerability has never taken into account the large number of invulnerable *Trident* II missiles on nuclear submarines. (See *Strategic Defense Initiative*.)

Worst-case assumption "The Russians are coming, the Russians are coming!" What started as the necessity faced by military planners to prepare for the worst outcome of an engagement has infected superpower relations since the beginning of the *Cold War*. The military planner played his wargames to test "capabilities" against an enemy whom he assumed was the epitome of aggressiveness and who was winning the game. Once he had done that, worst-case attitudes were bound to infect political and international relations, as indeed they did, when *deterrence,* a military strategy, was elevated into a maxim of superpower relations. Both the Soviets and the U.S. use worst-case analysis, and the latter case is especially instructive, simply because the U.S. is a relatively open society.[12] Several distortions arise from its use.

The enemy's capability is elevated to the status of a "threat" that is used to persuade the public, Congress, and the White House (if it didn't start there) that certain military expenditures are required to counter the threat. Indeed, the threat becomes part of the strategic litany, as it is in Defense Secretary Weinberger's annual reports to the Congress. Finally, the repeated political use of the "threat" turns it into an axiom that is used to justify a foreboding picture of the adversary's intentions. Why did the Soviets deploy the SS-20 missile in Europe? Why does the U.S. want Pershing missiles there? Obviously, their intentions are evil; ours are only protective and benign. Similarly, *detente* is a delusion and a trap; *arms control* initiatives are intended to have a narcotic effect.

Perhaps the most damaging use of worst-case analysis is in current projections of the intentions of Soviet and Warsaw Pact forces in Europe. We think those forces are more than the Russians need for defense and, therefore, their intentions must be imperialistic. All *NATO* and U.S. political and force planning is based on that assumption. But the fact is that neither NATO nor the Pentagon has ever estimated Soviet defense requirements. Taking the Soviet point of view, Western analysts would have to assume a NATO *first strike.* Any Soviet planner who failed to make that assumption would be awarded a one-way ticket to the Gulags. But once the Soviets' worst-case assumption is made, it is not a long step to the conjecture that current Soviet forces, rather than a "threat," are merely adequate for their nation's defense and deterrence.[13]

X-ray laser See *laser.*

Zero option The arms-control proposal that the Reagan Administration offered to the Soviets in 1981-82 because it assumed the Soviets wouldn't say, "yes." The option grew out of a proposal made by European protest movements to prohibit the Soviet intermediate range SS-20 missiles already in place and the U.S. Pershing and cruise missiles that were about to deployed. The Reagan Administration grabbed at the suggestion as a way of undercutting the Soviet image among NATO political groups simply because the Soviets would have to turn down any such idea.

That is precisely what they did, according to the British military analyst, Lawrence Freedman. "All this was politically very clever, though the influence either on the course of the domestic political debate in Europe or on the arms control negotiations was less than had been expected."[14]

And this is precisely the kind of approach that Gorbachev took in the Spring of 1987 when he offered to scrap his SS-20's for the removal of all Pershing and cruise missiles from Europe. NATO countries withdrew objection to "denuclearizing" Europe, and an agreement was signed in December 1987. (See *Arms control, Summitry.*)

ACRONYMS

The alphabet soup of Armageddon: words, pronounceable or otherwise, that are formed from the first initials of descriptive phrases. The following list is based on the Department of Defense list of acronyms contained in annual reports to Congress by the secretary of defense for the fiscal years 1987 and 1988.

AAW Anti-air warfare

ABM Anti-ballistic missile

ACM Advanced cruise missile

ACS Artillery computer system

ADCAP Advanced capability (torpedo)

ADP Automated data processing

AFAP Artillery-fired atomic projectile

AFATDS Advanced field artillery data system

AFSATCOM Air force satellite communications

AID Agency for international development

AIM Air-intercept missile

ALCM Air-launched cruise missile

ALMV Air launched miniature vehicle

AMRAAM Advanced medium-range air-to-air missile

APOMS Automated propeller optical measurement system

ASAT Anti-satellite

ASPJ Airborne self-protection jammer

ASROC Anti-submarine rocket

ASW Anti-submarine warfare

ATA Advanced tactical aircraft

ATACMS Army tactical missile system

ATB Advanced technology bomber

ATF Advanced technology fighter

ATM Anti-tactical missile

AUTOVON Automatic voice network

AWACS Airborne warning and control system.

BCS Battery computer system

BFV Bradley fighting vehicle

BICES Battlefield information collection and exploitation system

BMD Ballistic missile defense

BMEWS Ballistic missile early-warning system

C-4 Trident I missile

C³ Command, control, and communications

C³CM Command, control, and communications countermeasures

C³I Command, control, communications, and intelligence

CELV Complementary expendable launch vehicle

CEM Combined effects munitions

CINC Commander in chief

CIWS Close-in weapons system

COMSEC Communications security

CONUS Continental U.S.

D-4 Trident II missile

DCA Dual-capable aircraft

DCS Defense communications system

DDG Guided missile destroyer

DDN Defense data network

DEW Directed-energy weapons/Distant early warning

DIA Defense intelligence agency

DoD Department of Defense

DSCS Defense satellite communication system

EC Electronic combat

ECM Electronic counter-measures

ELF Extremely low frequency

EMP Electromagnetic pulse

EW Electronic warfare

FAASV Field artillery ammunition support vehicle

FFG Guided missile frigate

FLIR Forward-looking infrared radar

FMC Fully mission capable

FSS Fast sea-lift ships

FTS Full-time support

FY Fiscal year

GLCM Ground-launched cruise missile

GPS Global positioning system

GWEN Ground wave emergency network

HARM High-speed anti-radiation missile

HEMTT Heavy expand-ed mobility tactical truck

HF High frequency

HMMWV High-mobility multipurpose wheeled vehicle

IAMP Imagery acquisition and management system

IAP Improved accuracy program

ICBM Intercontinental ballistic missile

IFF Identification, friend or foe

IIR Imaging infrared

IMA Individual mobilization augmentees

IONDS Intergrated operational nuclear detonation system

IUS Inertial upper stage

INCA Intelligence communications architecture

INEWS Integrated electronic warfare system

INF Intermediate range nuclear forces

IR Infrared

JCS Joint Chiefs of Staff

JSTARS Joint surveillance, target attack radar system

JTDE Joint technology demonstrator engine

JTFP Joint tactical fusion program

KEW Kinetic energy weapons

LAMPS Light airborne multipurpose system

LANTIRN Low-altitude navigation/targeting infrared system/night

LAV Light amored vehicle

LAV-AF Light armored vehicle, air force

LF Low frequency

LRINF Longer range intermediate-range nuclear forces

LRTNF Long-range theater nuclear forces

LVT Assault amphibian vehicle

MAF Marine amphibious force

MAW Marine aircraft wing

MBFR Mutual and balanced force reductions

MCE Modular control equipment

MCS Maneuver control system

MiG Mikoyan-Gurevich [aircraft]

MILSTAR Military strategic and tactical relay system

MIRV Multiple independently targetable reentry vehicle.

MLRS Multiple-launch rocket system

MPS Maritime positioning ship

MSE Mobile subscriber equipment

MULE Modular universal laser equipment

MX Missile experimental

NATO North Atlantic Treaty Organization

NAVSTAR Navigation satellite timing and ranging

NCA National command authorities

NCS National communication system

NDS Nuclear detonation detection system

NEACP National Emergency airborne command post

NIS NATO identification system

NMCC National military command center

NORAD North American aerospace defense command

NPG Nuclear planning group

NTPF Near-term prepositioning forces

OSIS Oceb surveillance information system

OTH Over the horizon

OTH-B Over-the-horizon backscatter (radar)

PARC Perimeter acquisition radar attack characterization system

PAVE PAWS Phased array radars

PGM Precision guided munitions

PLRS Position, location, and reporting system

PLSS Position location strike system

R&D Research and development

ROK Republic of Korea

RO/RO Roll on/roll off

RPV Remotely piloted vehicle

RRF Ready Reserve Force

RV Reentry vehicle

SA/BM Systems analysis-/battle management

SAC Strategic Air Command

SALT Strategic arms limitation talks/treaty

SAM Surface-to-air missile

SATKA Surveillance, acquisition, tracking and kill assessment

SDI Strategic Defense Initiative

SDIO Strategic Defense Initiative Organization

SHORAD-C^2 Short-range air defense command and control

SINCGARS-V Single-channel ground and airborne system, VHF

SLBM Submarine-launched ballistic missile

SLC Submarine laser communications

SLCM Submarine-launched cruise missile

SLKT Survivability, lethality, and key technologies

SM Standard missile

SNF Short-range nuclear forces

SOSUS Sound surveillance system

SRAM Short-range attack missile

SSATS Surface ship advance sonar

SSBN Ballistic missile submarine, nuclear powered

SSGN Cruise missile attack submarine, nuclear powered

SSKP Single-shot kill probability

SSN Attack submarine, nuclear powered

START Strategic arms reduction talks

SU Sukhoy (aircraft)

SUBROC Submarine rocket

SURTASS Surveillance towed-array sonar system

TACAMO Airborne strategic communications system

TACTAS Tactical towed-array sonar

TAOC Tactical air operations center

TFW Tactical fighter wing

TGSM Terminally guided submunitions

TOW Tube launched, optically tracked, wire guided anti-tank missile

UHF Ultra high frequency

VHF Very high frequency

VHSIC Very high speed integrated circuit

VLA Vertical launch ASROC

VLS Vertical launch system

VLSI Very large-scale integration

V/STOL Vertical/short take-off and landing

WIS WWMCCS Information systems

WWMCCS Worldwide military command and control system

SOURCE NOTES

PREFACE

1. Paul Bracken, *The Command and Control of Nuclear Forces* (Yale University Press, New Haven, 1983), p. 239.
2. Morton H. Halperin, *Nuclear Fallacy* (Ballinger Publishing Co., Cambridge, Mass., 1987), p. 25.
3. Richard Reeves, *The Reagan Detour* (Simon & Schuster, New York, 1985), p. 12.
4. Harold Brown, U.S. Department of Defense *Annual Report to the Congress,* FY 1979, p. 106.
5. *Ibid.*
6. Caspar W. Weinberger, U.S. Department of Defense *Annual Report to the Congress,* FY 1987, pp. 291, 313.
7. Quoted in Gerard H. Clarfield and William W. Wiecek, *Nuclear America* (Harper & Row, New York, 1984), p. 307.
8. Lawrence Freedman, *The Price of Peace* (Henry Holt & Co., New York, 1986), p. 43ff.

INTRODUCTION

1. Quoted in Gregg Herken, *The Winning Weapon* (Vintage Books, New York, 1982), p. 3.
2. Joshua M. Epstein, *Strategy* and *Force Planning: The Case of the Persian Gulf* (Brookings Institution, Washington, D.C. 1987), pp. 99, 104.
3. Morris Schwartz, "The Social-Psychological Dimensions of the Arms Race," in Paul Joseph, ed., *Search for Sanity* (South End Press, Boston, 1984), p. 278.
4. Jon Connell, *The New Maginot Line* (Arbor House, New York, 1986), p. 277.
5. *Ibid.* p. 583.
6. Thomas C. Schelling, "Abolition of Ballistic Missiles," *International Security*, Summer 1987, p. 179.
7. William J. Broad, *Star Warriors* (Simon & Schuster, New York, 1986), p. 137.

8. Fred Kaplan, *The Wizards of Armageddon* (Simon & Schuster, New York, 1983), p. 375.

9. Walter Pincus, "A Successful Soviet First Strike is Nearly Impossible," *Washington Post,* March 2, 1986.

10. Richard L. Berke, "Unarmed Soviet Test Missile is Reported to Land in China," *New York Times,* September 17, 1986.

11. Matthew L. Wald, "Troubles Infest System for Making Plutonium," *New York Times,* December 12, 1986, p. 1.

12. Michael R. Gordon, "U.S. Reports Failure in Recent Soviet Test of Big New Missile," *New York Times,* April 15, 1986; "Second Soviet Missile Mishap is Reported by U.S. Officials," August 18, 1986.

13. Craig Covault, "Soviet Military Space Flight Fails," *Aviation Week and Space Technology,* October 27, 1986, p. 24.

14. Covault, "Soviet Proton Booster Fails; Reconnaissance Satellite Fails," *Aviation Week and Space Technology,* February 9, 1987, p. 26.

15. John H. Cushman, Jr., "Pentagon Study Faults Planning on Grenada," *New York Times,* July 12, 1986, p. 1.

16. Bill Keller, "U.S. Plans Were Made on Open Line," *New York Times,* October 15, 1985.

17. Bruce G. Blair, *Strategic Command and Control* (Brookings Institution, Washington, D.C., 1985), p. 262.

18. Ibid, p. 266.

19. William G. Hyland, *Mortal Rivals* (Random House, New York, 1987), p. 209.

20. Andrew Cockburn, "The Stinger is No Stinger," *New York Times,* July 22, 1986.

21. Arthur T. Hadley, *The Straw Giant* (Random House, New York, 1986), p. 162.

22. Connell, *The New Maginot Line,* p. 38.

23. Editorial, "The Death of a Gun," *New York Times,* August 28, 1986, p. A22.

24. John L. Gaddis, *Strategies Of Containment* (Oxford University Press, New York, 1982), p. ix.

25. Michael Charlton, *The Star Wars History* (BBC Publications, London, 1986), p. 35.

26. *Ibid*, p. 36.

27. Peter T. Kilborn, "Submarine Case to Lift U.S. Costs," *New York Times,* July 28, 1987, p. D1.

28. Quoted in Lawrence Freedman, *The Price of Peace* (Henry Holt, New York, 1986), p. 200.

29. "The Long Nuclear Peace," *The Economist,* February 22, 1986, p. 16.

30. Freedman, p. 203.

31. Michael Mandelbaum and Strobe Talbott, *Reagan* and *Gorbachev* (Vintage Books, New York, 1987), p. 43.

32. Seweryn Bialer, *The Soviet Paradox* (Knopf, New York, 1986), p. 19.

33. Mandelbaum, p. 47.

34. Bialer, pp. 329ff. (What follows here relies heavily on the analysis in *The Soviet Paradox).*

35. Leonard Silk, "Soviet Arms v. Growth," *New York Times,* October 15, 1986, p. 8.

36. John K. Fairbank, *The Great Chinese Revolution* (Harper & Row, New York, 1986), p. 8.

37. Richard J. Barnet, "Reflections: The Four Pillars," *The New Yorker,* March 9, 1987, pp. 76ff.

A

1. Quoted in Paul Joseph, ed., *Search For Sanity* (South End Press, Boston, 1984), p. 116.

2. Graham T. Allison, Albert Carnesale, Joseph S. Nye, Jr., *Hawks, Doves and Owls* (W.W. Norton, New York, 1985), p. 142.

3. Lord Zuckerman, "The Prospects of Nuclear War," *New York Review,* August 15, 1985.

4. Kosta Tsipis, *Arsenal: Understanding Weapons in the Nuclear Age* (Simon & Schuster, New York, 1983), p. 167ff.

5. Bernard Brodie, *Strategy in the Nuclear Age* (Princeton University Press, N.J., Princeton, 1959), p. ix.

6.Gerald H. Clarfield and William M. Wiecek, *Nuclear America* (Harper & Row, New York, 1984), p. 292.

7. Solly Zuckerman, *Nuclear Illusion and Reality* (Random House, New York, 1983), p. 51.

8. John Tirman, ed., *The Fallacy of Star Wars* (Vintage Books, New York, 1984), p. 18.

9. Lawrence Freedman, *The Price of Peace* (Henry Holt, New York, 1986), p. 219.

10. John D. Morrocco, "Pentagon Will Develop Defense Against Soviet Tactical Missiles," *Aviation Week & Space Technology,* January 19, 1987.

11. Michael R. Gordon, "Arms and the Man's Language," *New York Times,* February 6, 1987.

12. Lawrence Freedman, *The Price of Peace* (Henry Holt, New York, 1986), p. 217.

13. Paul Boyer, *By the Bomb's Early Light* (Pantheon Books, New York, 1985), p. 102.

14. Gregg Herken, *Counsels of War* (Knopf, New York, 1985), p. 49.

15. Bernard Gwertzman, "U.S. and Soviet 'Out of Sync', *"New York Times*, June 1, 1986.

16. *The World Almanac and Book of Facts 1987* (Pharos Books, New York, 1986), p. 338.

17. Anthony Lewis, "Who are the Realists?," *New York Times,* August 8, 1985.

18. Richard E. Nuestadt and Ernest R. May, *Thinking in Time* (The Free Press, New York, 1986), p. 123ff.

19. William W. Kaufman, *A Reasonable Defense* (Brookings Institution, Washington, D.C., 1986), p. 40ff.

20. Tom Gervasi, *The Myth of Soviet Missile Supremacy* (Harper & Row, New York, 1986), p. 201.

21. John Polanyi, in *The Nuclear Crisis Reader,* ed. Gwyn Prins (Vintage Books, New York, 1984), p. 57.

22. Wayne Biddle, "Drawing a Bead on a Target in Space," *New York Times,* The Week in Review, p. 2.

23. "A Code for Satellite Bashers," *The Economist,* Sept. 14, 1985, p. 19.

24. *Strategic Defenses,* Office of Technology Assessment, Congres-

sional Board of the 99th Congress, (Princeton University Press, Princeton, N.J., 1985, p. 3ff.

25. *The Economist,* Jan. 11, 1986; *Manchester Guardian,* Jan. 5, 1986.

26. Kosta Tsipis, *Arsenal* (Simon & Schuster, New York, 1983), p. 79ff.

27. *Daedalus,* "Weapons in Space", Spring 1985, pp. 65, 121ff.

B

1. Editorial, "The Strategic Bomber Mess," *New York Times,* February 23, 1987.

2. Albert Carnesale, *et al. Living With Nuclear Weapons* (Harvard University Press, Cambridge, Mass., 1983), pp. 122, 126.

3. Gwyn Prins, ed., *The Nuclear Crisis Reader* (Random House, New York, 1984), p. 25ff.

4. Lord Gladwyn, "Writing out Fate in the Stars," *Manchester Guardian Weekly,* October 26, 1986.

5. David Fairhall, "Superpower Arms in Balance," *Manchester Guardian Weekly,* November 16, 1986, p. 8.

6. Richard A. Stubbing *The Defense Game* (Harper & Row, New York, 1986), p. 19.

7. The Harvard Nuclear Study Group, *Living with Nuclear Weapons* (Harvard University Press, Cambridge, Mass., 1983), p. 24.

8. Thomas Schelling, *The Strategy of Conflict* (Oxford University Press, New York, 1960), p. 194.

9. Alun Chalfont, *Star Wars,* (Weidenfeld and Nicholson, London, 1985), p. 60.

10. Lawrence Freedman, *The Evolution of Nuclear Strategy* (St. Martin's Press, New York, 1983), p. 360.

11. William L. Shirer, *The Rise and Fall of the Third Reich* (Simon & Schuster, New York, 1960), p. 1009.

12. William J. Broad, "Star Wars Traced to Eisenhower Era," *New York Times,* October 28, 1986, p. C1.

13. Hans A. Bethe, *et al.,* "BMD Technologies and Concepts in the 1980's," *Daedalus,* Spring 1985, p. 53.

14. Leslie H. Gelb, "Star Wars Advances: The Plan vs. the Reality," *New York Times,* December 15, 1985, p. 1.

15. "Ballistic Missile Defense Technologies," Congressional Office of Technology Assessment, September 1985, p. 32.

16. Broad, "Star Wars Traced to Eisenhower Era," *New York Times*, October 28, 1986, p. C1.

17. Thomas C. Schelling, "What Went Wrong with Arms Control?," *Foreign Affairs,* vol. 64, No. 2, p. 231.

18. Gerald H. Clarfield and William Wiecek, *Nuclear America,* (Harper & Row, New York, 1984), p. 324.

19. Michael Mandelbaum, *The Nuclear Question* (Cambridge University Press, Cambridge, 1979), p. 24.

20. Lord Zuckerman, *Star Wars in a Nuclear World* (William Kimber, London, 1986) p. 56.

21. William W. Kaufman *A Reasonable Defense* (Brookings Institution, Washington, D.C., 1986), p. 53.

22. *The Command and Control of Nuclear Forces* (Yale University Press, New Haven, 1983), p. 73.

23. Bernard Brodie, *Strategy in the Missile Age* (Princeton University Press, Princeton, 1959), p. 289.

24. Michael Mandelbaum and Strobe Talbott, *Reagan and Gorbachev* (Vintage Books, New York, 1987) p. 134.

25. William J. Broad, *Star Warriors* (Simon & Schuster, New York, 1985), p. 138.

26. "Weapons in Space," *Daedalus,* Summer 1985, p. 240.

27. Paul Joseph, *Search for Sanity* (South End Press, Boston, 1984), p. 141.

28. Paul Feldman, "Cancer Strikes Where Nuclear Bomber Crashed," *Manchester Guardian Weekly,* December 21, 1986.

29. Brodie, *Strategy in the Missile Age,* pp. 160-165, 403.

30. Robert Jastrow, *How to Make Nuclear Weapons Obsolete* (Little Brown, Boston, 1985), p. 106.

31. William P. Bundy, *The Nuclear Controversy* (New American Library, New York, 1985), p. xvi, 156.

32. Nigel Calder, *Nuclear Nightmares* (Viking Press, New York, 1979), pp. 5, 30, 49.

33. Carl Sagan, "Nuclear War and Climatic Catastrophe," in William P. Bundy, ed., *The Nuclear Controversy,* p. 139.

34. Hans A. Bethe, *et al.,* "Space Based Ballistic Missile Defense," *Scientific American,* October 1984.

C

1. Will Brownell, "GWEN System Part of Flawed Scenario for Fighting Nuclear War," *Castine Patriot,* Castine, Me., July 11, 1985.

2. President Kennedy's remark when he was given the news at the height of the Cuban Missile crisis that a U-2 plane had gone off course and was over Russian territory. Quoted in Arthur M. Schlesinger, Jr., *A Thousand Days* (Houghton Mifflin Co., Boston, 1965), p. 828.

3. Bruce G. Blair, *Strategic Command and Control* (Brookings Institution, Washington, D.C., 1985), p. 73.

4. Bill Keller, "U.S. Plans Were Made on Open Line," *New York Times, Oct. 15, 1985.*

5. *Arthur T. Hadley, The Straw Giant* (Random House, New York, 1986), p. 27.

6. *Ibid.,* p. 247.

7. Editor's Note, *Science Digest,* September 1985, p. 4.

8. Lord Zuckerman, "The Prospects of Nuclear War," *New York Review,* Aug. 15, 1985, p.

9. Kosta Tsipis, "It's Not Just the President Who Can Release Armageddon," *Manchester Guardian Weekly,* June 23, 1985.

10. Graham T. Allison, *et al, Hawks, Doves and Owls* (W. W. Norton, New York, 1985), p. 150.

11. Richard Halloran, "How Leaders Think the Unthinkable," *New York Times,* Sept. 2, 1986.

12. Richard Norton-Taylor, "Minister Quizzed on Banning of Star Wars Book," *Manchester Guardian Weekly,* Sept. 21, 1986.

13. Tom Gervasi, *The Myth of Soviet Military Supremacy* (Harper & Row, New York, 1986), p. 129.

14. Gervasi, *Myth of Soviet Military Supremacy,* p. 243.

15. Memorandum to the president on "Responding to Soviet Viola-

tions (RSVP) Policy Study," the Secretary of Defense, November 15, 1985.

16. Lord Zuckerman, *Star Wars in a Nuclear World* (William Kimber, London, 1986), p. 85.

17. Raymond J. Garthoff, "U.S.-Soviet Radar Dispute Tests Treaty Good Faith," Letters, *New York Times,* February 14, 1987.

18. Charles Mohr, "Soviet Arms Pact Breaches: Charges Questioned," *New York Times,* June 6, 1986.

19. Michael R. Gordon, "Joint Chiefs Find No Cheating," *New York Times,* February 8, 1986.

20. Michael R. Gordon, "U.S. Aide Says Soviet Has Kept Most Pacts," *New York Times,* Jan. 10, 1986.

21. Michael Charlton, *The Star Wars History* (BBC Publications, London, 1985), p. 72.

22. Daniel Ellsberg, "Nuclear Weapons and Global Intervention," in Paul Joseph, ed., *Search for Sanity* (South End Press, Boston, 1984), p. 43.

23. Thomas A. Schelling, *Arms and Influence* (Yale University Press, New Haven, 1966), p. 93.

24. William J. Broad, "Economic Collapse Tied to Atom War," *New York Times,* June 21, 1987, p. 24.

25. William M. Arkin and Richard W. Fieldhouse, *Nuclear Battlefields* (Ballinger Publishing, Cambridge, Mass., 1985), p. 82.

26. William P. Bundy, ed., *The Nuclear Controversy* (New American Library, New York, 1985), p. 18.

27. Robert Jastrow, *How to Make Nuclear Weapons Obsolete* (Little Brown, Boston, 1985), pp. 18, 34.

28. Seweryn Bialer, *The Soviet Paradox* (Knopf, New York, 1986), p. 119.

29. Gregg Herken, *Counsels of War* (Knopf, New York, 1985), p. 262.

30. William H. Kincade, *"Arms Control or Arms Coercion?,"* Foreign Policy, Spring, 1986, p. 25.

31. Raymond Aron, *Clausewitz,* (Prentice Hall, Englewood Cliffs, N.J., 1985), p. 326.

32. William J. Broad, *Star Warriors* (Simon & Schuster, New York, 1985), p. 65.

33. Charles Mohr, "Scientist Quits Anti-missile Panel, Saying Task Is Impossible," *New York Times,* July 12, 1985.

34. Lord Zuckerman, *Star Wars in a Nuclear World,* p. 82.

35. Kosta Tsipis, *Arsenal* (Simon & Schuster, New York, 1983), p. 172.

36. David E. Sanger, "Software Fears on Star Wars," *New York Times,* July 4, 1985, p. D2.

37. Jon Connell, *The New Maginot Line* (Arbor House, New York, 1986), p. 226.

38. *Ibid.*

39. X [George F. Kennan], "The Sources of Soviet Conduct," *Foreign Affairs,* July 1947.

40. Kennan, *Memoirs, 1925-1950* (Little Brown, Boston, 1967), p. 362ff.

41. *Ibid.,* p. 367.

42. Herman Kahn, *Thinking About the Unthinkable* (Horizon Press, New York, 1962), p. 64.

43. Albert Carnesale, *et al. Living with Nuclear Weapons* (Harvard University Press, Cambridge, Mass., 1983), p. 147.

44. Charlton, *The Star Wars History,* p. 56.

45. Michael Mandelbaum and Strobe Talbott, *Reagan and Gorbachev* (Vintage Books, New York, 1987), p. 81.

46. Bernard Brodie, *Strategy in the Missile Age* (Princeton University Press, Princeton, N.J., 1959), p. 156.

47. Bruce G. Blair, *Strategic Command and Control* (Brookings Institution, Washington, D.C., 1985), p. 26.

48. Allan Krass and Dan Smith, "Fallacies in Deterrence and Warfighting Strategies," in Paul Joseph, ed., *Search for Sanity* (South End Press, Boston, 1984), p. 31.

49. Herken, *Counsels of War,* p. 301.

50. Quoted by Robert W. Tucker, "The Nuclear Debate," in *The Nuclear Controversy,* p. 254.

51. Christopher Paine, "Reagatomics, or How to Prevail," *The Nation,* April 9, 1983.

52. Carnesale, *Living with Nuclear Weapons,* p. 34.

53. *Congressional Record:* 98th Congress, 2nd Session, vol. 130, No.8, Feb. 1, 1984.

54. Hillard Roderick, ed., *Avoiding Inadvertent War: Crisis Management* (University of Texas at Austin, 1983), pp. 4, 135.

55. Quoted in G. H. Clarfied & W. M. Wiecek, *Nuclear America* (Harper & Row, New York, 1984), p.

56. Michael Gordon, "Issue of Sea-Launched Cruise Missiles Is Revived," *New York Times,* June 18, 1986.

57. Tsipis, *Arsenal,* p. 161.

58. Peter Clausen, *et al. In Search of Stability* (Union of Concerned Scientists, Washington, D.C., 1986), p. 7.

D

1. L. R. Beres, "Nuclear Errors and Accidents," in Paul Joseph, ed., *Search for Sanity* (South End Press, Boston, 1984), p. 147.

2. Lord Zuckerman, *Nuclear Illusion and Reality* (Random House, New York, 1983), p. 19.

3. Leon Wieseltier, *Nuclear War, Nuclear Peace* (Holt, Rinehart & Winston, New York, 1983), p. 40.

4. Helen Caldicott, *Missile Envy* (Bantam Books, New York, 1984), p. 200.

5. Gregg Herken, *Counsels of War* (Knopf, New York, 1986), p. 300.

6. John Steinbrunner, "Nuclear Decapitation," in Paul Joseph, ed., *Search For Sanity,* p. 181.

7. Nigel Calder, *Nuclear Nightmares* (Penguin Books, New York, 1981), p. 42.

8. *Ibid.,* p. 43.

9. Carl Sagan, "Nuclear War and Climatic Catastrophe," in W. P. Bundy, ed., *The Nuclear Controversy* (New American Library, New York, 1985), p. 150.

10. Lawrence Freedman, *The Evolution of Nuclear Strategy* (St. Martins Press, New York, 1983), p.250.

11. William W. Kaufman, *A Reasonable Defense* (Brookings Institution, Washington, D.C., 1986), p.1.

12. Quoted in Freedman, *Evolution of Nuclear Strategy*, p. 164.

13. Seweryn Bialer, *The Soviet Parodox* (Knopf, New York, 1986), p. 308.

14. President and Fellows of Harvard College, "Learning from Experience with Arms Control," for U.S. Arms Control and Disarmament Agency, September 1986, p. 10-18.

15. Quoted in Albert Carnesale *el al, Living with Nuclear Weapons* (Harvard University Press, Cambridge, Mass., 1983), p. 32.

16. Lord Zuckerman, *Star Wars in a Nuclear World* (William Kimber, London, 1986), p. 35.

17. Bernard Brodie, *War and Politics* (Macmillan, New York, 1973) p. 430.

18. Joseph, ed. *Search for Sanity,* p. 22.

19. E. J. Carroll, "Nuclear Weapons and Deterrence," in G. Prins, ed., *Nuclear Crisis Reader* (Random House, New York, 1984), p. 8.

20. Herken, *Counsels of War,* p. 133.

21. Alun Chalfont, *Star Wars* (Weidenfeld & Nicholson, London, 1985), pp. 81, 83.

22. "Iraq Ascribes a Key Defeat in '86 to Misinformation from the U.S.," *New York Times,* January 19, 1987.

23. Ann E. Weiss, *The Nuclear Question* (Harcourt Brace Jovanovich, New York, 1981), p. 123.

24. G. H. Clarfield & W. M. Wiecek, *Nuclear America* (Harper & Row, New York, 1984), p. 201.

25. Freedman, *Evolution of Nuclear Strategy,* p. 434, n.3.

26. John D. Morrocco, "Defense Official Challenges Continuing SICBM Development," *Aviation Week & Space Technology,* March 16, 1987, p. 16.

27. Elizabeth Drew. "Letter from Washington," October 27, 1986, *New Yorker,* p. 129.

28. Leon Wieseltier, *Nuclear War, Nuclear Peace* (Holt Reinhart & Winston, New York, 1983), p. 43.

29. Herman Kahn, *On Thermonuclear War* (Princeton University Press, Princeton, N.J., (1960), p. 24, n.10.

30. Prins, ed., *Nuclear Crisis Reader,* p. 122.

31. "U.S. Sues over Device on MX," *New York Times,* August 27, 1987.

32. William J. Broad, *Star Warriors,* p. 165.

33. Solly Zuckerman, "Reagan's Highest Folly," *New York Review,* April 9, 1987, p. 37.

34. Carl Sagan, "Nuclear War and Climatic Catastrophe," in *The Nuclear Controversy,* p. 145.

E

1. Bruce G. Blair, *Strategic Command and Control* (Brookings Institution, Washington, D.C., 1985), p. 125.

2. Helen Caldicott, *Missile Envy* (Bantam Books, New York, 1985), p. 32.

3. W. M. Arkin and R. W. Fieldhouse, *Nuclear Battlefields* (Harper & Row, New York, 1985), p. 31.

4. *Castine Patriot,* Castine, Me., July 11, 1985.

5. Carnesale, *Living with Nuclear Weapons,* p. 119.

6. Blair, *Strategic Command and Control,* p. 29.

7. Richard Halloran, *To Arm a Nation* (Macmillan, New York, 1986), p. 326.

8. Zbigniew Brzezinski, *Game Plan* (Atlantic Monthly Press, boston, 1986), p.

9. Tom Gervasi, *The Myth of Soviet Military Supremacy* (Harper & Row, New York, 1986), p. 152.

10. Lawrence Freedman, "The First Two Generations of Nuclear Strategists," in Peter Paret, ed., *Makers of Modern Strategy* (Princeton University Press, Princeton, N.J., 1986), p. 764.

F

1. Gregg Herken, *Counsels of War,* (Knopf, New York, 1985), p. 93.

2. William J. Broad, *Star Warriors* (Simon & Schuster, New York, 1986), p. 194.

John Tirman, ed., *The Fallacy of Star Wars* (Random House, New York, 1984), p. 115.

3. Lawrence Freedman, *The Evolution of Nuclear Startegy* (St. Martin's Press, New York, 1983), p. 367.

4. McGeorge Bundy, "The Unimpressive Record of Atomic Diplomacy," in G. Prins, ed., *The Nuclear Crisis Reader* (Vintage, New York, 1984), p. 49.

5. Herken, *Counsels of War,* p. 269.

6. Graham T. Allison, *et al., Hawks, Doves and Owls* (Norton, Boston, 1985), p. 56.

7. Daniel Ellsberg, "Nuclear Weapons and Global Intervention," in P. Joseph, ed., *Search For Sanity* (South End Press, Boston, 1984), p. 50.

8. McGeorge Bundy, *et al.,* "Back from the Brink," *The Atlantic Monthly,* August 1986.

9. Lord Zuckerman, *Star Wars in a Nuclear World* (William Kimber, London, 1986), p. 32.

10. Leon Wieseltier, *Nuclear War, Nuclear Peace* (Holt, Rinehart & Winston, New York, 1983) p. 65.

11. Caspar W. Weinberger, U.S. Dept. of Defense Annual Report to the Congress, 1987, p. 30.

12. Freedman, *Evolution of Nuclear Strategy,* p. 109.

13. Paul Bracken, *The Command and Control of Nuclear Forces* (Yale University Press, New Haven, 1983), p. 226.

14. Kosta Tsipis, *Arsenal* (Simon & Schuster, New York, 1983), p. 122.

15. William M. Arkin and Richard M. Fieldhouse, *Nuclear Battlefields* (Ballinger, Cambridge, Mass., 1985), p. 82.

16. Helen Caldicott, *Missile Envy* (Bantam Books, New York, 1985), p. 187.

G

1. Lawrence Freedman, *The Evolution of Nuclear Strategy* (St. Martin's Press, New York, 1983).

2. The Importance of Being Nice, Retaliatory, Forgiving and Clear," *The Economist,* November 9, 1985, p. 99.

3. Lord Zuckerman, "Strategy or Romance," *New York Review,* July 18, 1985, p. 12.

4. "SDIO [Strategic Defense Initiative Organization] on Verge of Producing Kinetic Kill Vehicle," *Aviation Week and Space Technology,* February 9, 1987, p. 24.

5. *Ibid.*

6. David E. Sanger, "Many Experts Doubt Star Wars Could Be Effective by the Mid-90's," *New York Times,* February 11, 1987, p. B 13.

7. Office of Technology Assessment, *Strategic Defenses* (U.S. Government Printing Office, Washington, D.C., 1985).

8. Hans A. Bethe, *et al.,* "Space-based Ballistic-missile Defense," in *Arms Control and the Arms Race* (Scientific American, New York, 1985), p. 134.

9. Serge Schmemann, "Great Glasnost Turns Some Soviet Heads" *New York Times,* Nov. 9, 1986.

10. Alun Chalfont, *Star Wars* (Weidenfeld & Nicholson, London, 1985) p. 42.

11. Solly Zuckerman, *Nuclear Illusion and Reality* (Vintage Books, New York, 1983), p. 78.

12. John H. Cushman, Jr., "Applying Military Brain to Military Brawn Again," *New York Times,* December 17, 1986.

H

1. Office of Technology Assessment, *Strategic Defenses* (U.S. Government Printing Office, Washington, D.C., 1985), p. vi.

2. John C. Toomay, "The Case for Ballistic Missile Defense," in "Weapons in Space," *Daedalus,* Summer 1985, p. 219.

3. Robert J. Lifton, letter published by Physicians for Social Responsiblity, Washington, D.C., 1985.

4. William R. Van Cleave, Earl C. Ravenal, *U.S. Defense Strategy: A Debate,* in George Hudson, Joseph Kruzel, eds., *American Defense Annual: 1985-1986* (D.C. Heath & Co., Lexington, Mass., 1985), p. 33, 34.

5. Joshua M. Epstein, *Strategy and Force Planning* (Brookings Institution, Washington, D.C., 1987), p. 99.

6. Paul Joseph, ed., *Search for Sanity* (South End Press, Boston, 1984), p. 4.

7. Lawrence Freedman, *The Evolution of Nuclear Strategy* (St. Martin's, Press, New York, 1983), p. 111.

I

1. Stephen E. Ambrose, *Eisenhower the President* (Simon & Schuster, New York, 1984), p. 247.

2. Raymond Aron, *Clausewitz* (Prentice Hall, Englewood Cliffs, N.J., 1985), p. 328.

K

1. Fred Kapan, *The Wizards of Armageddon* (Simon & Schuster, New York, 1983), p. 380.

2. Caspar W. Weinberger, U.S. Dept. of Defense Annual Report to the Congress, FY 1987, p. 290.

3. *Aviation Week and Space Technology,* September 15, 1986, p. 18.

4. Paul Bracken, *The Command and Control of Nuclear Forces* (Yale University Press, New Haven, 1983), p. 203.

5. Bruce G. Blair, *Strategic Command and Control* (Brookings Institution, Washington, D.C., 1985), p. 147.

L

1. Office of Technology Assessment, "Ballistic Missile Defense Technologies," (U.S. Government Printing Office, Washington, D.C., 1985, p. 323.

2. *Ibid.*

3. Reported by Hans Bethe, Yale University, April 6, 1987.

4. William J. Broad, *"Who's Ahead Now in Nuclear Arms?",* *New York Times,* March 1, 1987.

5. Charles Mohr, "Some Light on Weapon Terminology," *New York Times,* June 17, 1986.

6. *Aviation Week and Space Technology,* Dec. 8, 1986, p. 22.

7. Helen Caldicott, *Missile Envy* (Bantam Books, New York, 1985), p. 14.

8. Nigel Calder, *Nuclear Nightmares* (Penguin Books, New York, 1980), p. 104.

9. Bruce G. Blair, *Strategic Command and Control* (Brookings Institution, Washington, D.C., 1985), p. 236.

10. Bruce Russet and Fred Chernoff, "Arms Control and the Arms Race," *Scientific American,* 1985, p. 127.

11. W. M. Arkin, R. W. Fieldhouse, *Nuclear Battlefields* (Ballinger Publishing Co., Cambridge, Mass., 1985), p. 31.

12. Peter D. Zimmerman, "Pork Bellies and SDI," *Foreign Policy,* No. 63, p. 77.

13. McGeorge Bundy, "To Cap the Volcano," *Foreign Affairs,* Oct. 1969, p. 10; quoted in *Daedalus,* Summer 1985, p. 244.

14. Leon Wieseltier, *Nuclear War, Nuclear Peace* (Holt, Rinehart & Winston, New York, 1983), p. 50.

15. Peter Clausen, Allan Krass, Robert Zirkle, *In Search of Stability* (Union of Concerned Scientists, Cambridge, Mass., 1986), p. 60.

16. Richard Neustadt and Ernest May, *Thinking in Time* (The Free Press, New York, 1986), p. 142.

17. "Review and Outlook," *Wall Street Journal,* July 24, 1985, p. 20.

18. Bernard Brodie, *Strategy in the Missile Age* (Princeton University Press, Princeton, N.J., 1959), p. 305.

19. Lawrence Freedman, *The Evolution of Nuclear Strategy* (St. Martin's Press, New York, 1983), p. 101.

20. McGeorge Bundy, George F. Kennan, Robert S. McNamara, Gerard Smith, "Nuclear Weapons and the Atlantic Alliance," in William P. Bundy, ed., *The Nuclear Controversy* (New American Library, New York, 1985), p. 27.

21. Martin Walker, "Gorbachev Speech a Major Change in Soviet Ideology," *Manchester Guardian Weekly,* March 1, 1987, p. 8.

22. S. M. Keeny, Jr. and W. K. H. Panofsky "Mad Versus Nuts," in *Nuclear Controversy,* p. 15.

23. "Soviets Display MiG-29 During Exchange Visit with Finland," *Aviation Week and Space Technology,* July 7, 1986, p. 28.

M

1. "Weapons in Space" *Daedalus,* Spring 1985, p. 33.

2. Robert S. McNamara, *The Essence of Security;* cited in Peter Paret, ed., *Makers of Modern Strategy* (Princeton University Press, Princeton, N.J., 1986), p. 758.

3. Alun Chalfont, *Star Wars* (Weidenfeld & Nicholson, London, 1986, p. 61.

4. William L. Shirer, "Perilous Pipe Dream," letter to the *New York Times,* October 10, 1986.

5. Helen Caldicott, *Missile Envy* (Bantam Books, New York, 1985), p. 186.

6. Stephen E. Ambrose, *Eisenhower the President* (Simon & Schuster, New York, 1984), p. 172.

7. G. H. Clarfield & W. M. Wiecek, *Nuclear America* (Harper & Row, New York, 1984), p. 429.

8. *Anti-satellite Weapons, Countermeasures and Arms Control*, U.S. Office of Technology Assessment (Princeton University Press ed., Princeton, N.J., 1986, p. 58.

9. Michael R. Gordon, "Air Force to Test a Weapon in Space," *New York Times,* Feb. 20th, 1986.

10. According to a Pentagon official: "I know of no one in this building who wants that thing"; cited in Richard Halloran, "Old Disputes on the MX Erupt Anew," *New York Times,* News of the Week, December 21, 1986.

11. A mobile Midgetman force "needs an arms control component. You have to get reductions in Soviet warheads and throw weights or you're in trouble." Congressman Les Aspen, Chairman of the House Armed Services committee. "The Midgetman Missile," briefing paper published by the Union of Concerned Scientists, August 1985.

12. Paul Walker and John Wentworth, "Midgetman: missile in search of a mission." *Bulletin of the Atomic Scientists,* November 1986, p. 19.

13. Stephen E. Ambrose, *Eisenhower the President,* p. 612.

14. G. H. Clarfield and W. M. Wiecek, *Nuclear America* (Harper & Row, New York, 1984), p. 245.

15. Paul B. Stares, *The Militarization of Space* (Cornell University Press, Ithaca, N.Y., 1985), p. 51.

16. Arthur T. Hadley, *The Straw Giant* (Random House, New York, 1986), p. 201.

17. Robert S. McNamara, *Blundering into Disaster* (Pantheon Books, New York, 1986), p. 66

18. Clarfield and Wiecek, *Nuclear America,* p. 318.

19. Bernard Brodie, *Strategy in the Missile Age* (Princeton University Press, Princeton, N.J., 1971), p. 164.

20. Desmond Ball, "Can Nuclear War Be Controlled?" in Paul Joseph, ed., *Search For Sanity* (South End Press, Boston, 1984), p. 169.

21. Annual Report to the Congress, Fiscal Year 1987, p. 39.

22. "Weapons in Space," *Daedalus,* Spring 1985. p. 56.

23. "First 10 MX Missiles Placed on Alert" (AP), *New York Times,* Dec. 24, 1986, p. D16.

24. Richard Halloran, "Old Dispute on the MX Erupts Anew," *New York Times,* Dec. 21, 1986.

N

1. Dean Acheson, *Present at the Creation,* p. 495.

2. Richard A. Stubbing, *The Defense Game,* p. 349.

3. S. M. Keeny, Jr., and W. K. H. Panofsky, "Mad Versus Nuts" in William P. Bundy, ed., *The Nuclear Controversy* (New American Library, New York, 1985), p. 13.

4. William M. Arkin, "No Use for No First Use," *Bulletin of the Atomic Scientists,* November 1986, p. 4.

5. James Meacham, "The Sentry at the Gate," *The Economist,* August 30, 1986, pp. 1-22.

6. McGeorge Bundy, "Back From the Brink," *The Atlantic Monthly,* August 1986, p. 35.

7. Kurt Gottfried *et al.,* "No-first-use of Nuclear Weapons," *Scientific American,* March 1984.

8. Leon Wieseltier, *Nuclear War, Nuclear Peace* (Holt, Rinehart & Winston, New York, 1983), p. 68.

9. *Ibid.,* p. 46.

10. Alun Chalfont, *Star Wars* (Weidenfeld & Nicholson, London, 1985), p. 34.

11. George Weigel, "A Long March," *Wilson Quarterly,* vol. II, No. 1, p. 122.

12. Carnesale, *Living with Nuclear Weapons.*

13. "Weapons in Space," *Daedalus,* Summer 1985, p. 279.

14. William J. Broad *Star Warriors* (Simon & Schuster, New York, 1986), p. 15.

15. James Gleick, "Less Drastic Theory Emerges on Freezing after a Nuclear War," *New York Times,* June 22, 1986.

16. *Ibid.*

17. Carl Sagan, "Nuclear War and Climatic Catastrophe," *Foreign Affairs,* Winter 1983/1984.

18. W. M. Arkin, R. W. Fieldhouse, *Nuclear Battlefields* (Ballinger Publishing Co., Cambridge, Mass., 1985).

19. "Fires in West Aiding Study of Nuclear War," *New York Times,* October 20, 1987.

20. Michael D. Lemonick, "A Third Generation of Nukes," *Time,* May 25, 1987, p. 36.

21. Keeny and Panofsky, "Mad Versus Nuts," p. 4.

22. Paul Joseph, ed., *Search For Sanity* (South End Press, Boston, 1985, p. 588.

P

1. Jon Connell, *The New Maginot Line* Arbor House, New York, 1986), p. 155.

2. Kosta Tsipis, *Arsenal* (Simon & Schuster, New York, 1983), p. 187.

3. Albert Carnesale, *et al., Living with Nuclear Weapons* (Harvard University Press, Cambridge, Mass., 1983), p. 119.

4. Steven Kull, "Nuclear Nonsense," *Foreign Policy,* Summer 1985. p. 28.

5. Quoted in Lawrence Freedman, *The Evolution of Nuclear Strategy* (St. Martin' Press, New York, 1983), p. 369.

6. Kull, p. 41.

7. *Ibid.,* p. 27.

8. Quoted in William J. Broad, *Star Warriors* (Simon & Schuster, New York, 1985), p. 73.

9. Hans A. Bethe, *et al.,* "Space-based Ballistic-missile Defense," *Scientific American,* October 1984.

10. Graham T. Allison, *et al.*, *Hawks, Doves and Owls* (Harvard University Press, Cambridge, Mass., 1985), p. 189.

11. Paul Joseph, ed., *Search For Sanity* (South End Press, Boston, 1983), p. 159.

12. Matthew Bunn and Kosta Tsipis, "The Uncertainties of a Preemptive Nuclear Attack," *Scientific American*, November 1983.

13. Bernard Brodie, *Strategy in the Missile Age* (Princeton University Press, Princeton, 1965), p. 234.

14. Leon Wieseltier, *Nuclear War, Nuclear Peace* (Holt, Rinehart & Winston, New York, 1983), p. 42.

15. Richard Halloran, "Use of Small Reactors for Power in Wide Nuclear War is Explored," *New York Times*, March 27, 1987.

16. Herman Kahn, *Thinking about the Unthinkable in the 1980s* (Simon & Schuster, New York, 1984).

17. Joseph Nye, *Nuclear Ethics.* The Free Press, New York, 1986), p. 76.

18. Paul Joseph, ed., *Search for Sanity* (South End Press, Boston, 1984), p. 131.

19. John Maynard Keynes, *A Treatise on Probability* (Harper & Row, New York, 1921), pp. 285, 322.

20. G. H. Clarfield and W. M. Wiecek, *Nuclear America* (Harper & Row, New York, 1984), p. 124.

21. Carnesale, *Living with Nuclear Weapons,* p. 215; Daniel Yergin, "The Terrifying Prospect," in *"Search for Sanity,"* p. 193.

22. Nigel Calder, *Nuclear Nightmares* (Penguin Books, Ltd., Middlesex, England, 1981), p. 150.

23. Congressional Budget Office, background paper, "Counterforce Issues for the U.S. Strategic Nuclear Forces," January 1978, p. 50.

R

1. Quoted in Bernard Brodie, *Strategy in the Missile Age* (Princeton University Press, Princeton, N.J., 1959), p. 121.

2. Kosta Tsipis, *Arsenal* (Simon & Schuster, New York, 1983), p. 44.

3. Glossary of Radiation Terms, *Bulletin of the Atomic Scientists,* August-September 1986, p. 12.

4. Stanley Hoffman, "An Icelandic Saga," *New York Review of Books,* November 20, 1986, p. 15.

5. Brent Scowcroft, *et al.,* "A Way Out of Reykjavik," *New York Times Magazine,* p. 76.

6. Robert Jastrow, *How To Make Nuclear Weapons Obsolete* (Little Brown, Boston, 1985), p. 59.

7. Office of Technology Assessment, *Strategic Defense* (Princeton University Press ed., Princeton, N.J., 1986), p. 26.

8. Frank Barnaby, The Automated Battlefield (The Free Press, New York, 1986) p. 89ff.

S

1. William J. Broad, *Star Warriors* (Simon & Schuster, New York, 1985), p. 55.

2. Albert Carnesale, *et al., Living with Nuclear Weapons* (Harvard University Press, Cambridge, Mass., 1983), p. 93.

3. Michael R. Gordon, "Going Beyond the Limit with Strategic Arms," *New York Times,* Nov. 16, 1986.

4. John D. Morrocco, "Deployment of Cruise Missiles on B-52 Exceeds SALT II Limits," *Aviation Week and Space Technology,* Dec. 8, 1986, p. 22.

5. Bruce Russet, ed., *Arms Control and the Arms Race* (W.H. Freeman, New York, 1985).

6. Albert Carnesale and Richard Haas, "Learning from Experience with Arms Control," Harvard Office of Sponsored Research, Cambridge, Mass., Sept. 1986, p. 10.

7. Paul B. Stares, *The Militarization of Space* (Cornell University Press, Ithaca, N.Y., 1985), p. 14.

8. Frank Barnaby, *The Automated Battlefield* (The Free Press, New York, 1986), p. 112.

9. Bruce G. Blair, *Strategic Command and Control* (Brookings Institution, Washington, D.C., 1985), p. 201.

10. Michael Charlton, *The Star Wars History* (BBC Publications, London, 1985), p. 59. *See also* Paul Bracken, *The Command and Control of Nuclear Forces* (Yale University Press, New Haven,

1983), p. 120; Paul Nitze, "Assuring Strategic Stability in an Era of Detente," *Foreign Affairs,* Jan. 1986, p. 207; Gary D. Brewer and Bruce G. Blair, "War Games and National Security with a Grain of SALT," *Bulletin of the Atomic Scientists,* June, 1979, p. 18.

11. Brent Scowcroft, letter to the president, 6 April 1983.

12. Report of the President's Commission on Strategic Forces, April 1984, p. 17.

13. Scowcroft letter to the president, March 21, 1984.

14. Charlton, *Star Wars History,* p. 103.

15. Bruce G. Blair, *Strategic Command and Control* (Brookings Institution, Washington, D.C., 1985), p. 208.

16. Graham T. Allison, *et al., Hawks, Doves and Owls* (Norton & Co., New York, 1985), p. 61.

17. Herman Kahn, *Thinking About The Unthinkable in the 1980's* (Simon & Schuster, New York, 1984), p.

18. Fred Kaplan, *The Wizards of Armageddon* (Simon & Schuster, New York, 1983), pp. 201, 202.

19. Transcript of a BBC Radio broadcast (Radio 3, 1985) in Charlton, *Star Wars History,* p. 67.

20. Gregg Herken, *Counsels of War* (Knopf, New York, 1985), p. 126.

21. Bracken, *Command and Control,* p. 75.

22. William M. Arkin and Richard W. Fieldhouse, *Nuclear Battlefields* (Ballinger Publishing Co., Cambridge, Mass., 1985), p. 91.

23. Arthur T. Hadley, *The Straw Giant* (Random House, New York, 1987), p. 197.

24. Kurt Gottfried *et al.,* "No First Use of Nuclear Weapons," *Scientific American,* March, 1984.

25. Office of Technology Assessment, *New Ballistic Missile Defense Technology* (Princeton University Press, Princeton, N.J., 1986), p. 321.

26. John Tirman, ed., *The Fallacy of Star Wars* (Vintage Books, New York, 1984), p. 228.

27. Lawrence Freedman, *The Evolution of Nuclear Strategy* (St. Martin's Press, New York, 1983), p. 235.

28. Quoted in William P. Bundy, ed., *The Nuclear Controversy* (New American Library, New York, 1985), p. 157.

29. Brent Scowcroft, "Report of the President's Commission on Strategic Forces," Washington, D.C., April 1983.

30. Freedman, *Evolution of Nuclear Strategy,* p. 192.

31. Paul Joseph, ed., *Search For Sanity* (South End Press, Boston, 1984), p. 429.

32. T. A. Heppenheimer, "Stealth," *Popular Science,* September 1986, p. 74.

33. "Stealth Fighter," *The Economist,* August 30, 1986.

34. Peter Clausen, *In Search of Stability* (Union of Concerned Scientists, Cambridge, Mass., 1986), p. 39.

35. Zbigniew Brzezinski, *Game Plan* (Atlantic Monthly Press, Boston, 1986), p. 185.

36. Michael Mandelbaum and Strobe Talbot, *Reagan and Gorbachev* (Vintage Books, New York, 1987), p. 125.

37. William J. Broad, "Reagan's Star Wars Bid," *New York Times,* March 4, 1985, p. 1.

38. Report of the President's Commission on Strategic Forces, pp. 9, 12.

39. Freedman, *The Price of Peace,* p. 242.

40. Jon Connell, *The New Maginot Line* (Arbor House, New York, 1986), p. 257.

41. "Star Wars at the Crossroads," *Time,* June 23, 1986, p. 16.

42. U.S. Department of Defense, "Report to the Congress on the Strategic Defense Initiative," 1985.

43. Broad, "Antimissile Weapon Spurs Debate on Potential for Offensive Strikes," *New York Times,* February 2, 1987.

44. Paul Mann, "Arms Control Protests Force Delay in Next Stage of SDL Research," *Aviation Week and Space Technology,* February 16, 1987, p. 16.

45. John H. Cushman, Jr., "Star Wars Setup Likely by '94, Weinberger Says," *New York Times,* February 25, 1987, p. A-11.

46. Broad, "Star Wars Push Dimming Prospect for Exotic Arms," *New York Times,* March 9, 1987, p. 1.

47. Richard Halloran, *To Arm a Nation* (Macmillan, New York, 1987), p. 307.

48. Robert S. McNamara, *Blundering into Diaster* (Pantheon Books, New York, 1986), p. 97.

49. Halloran, p. 318.

50. Keith B. Payne, *Strategic Defense* (Hamilton Press, Lanham, Md., 1986), p. 233.

51. Michael Bard, "Strategic Thoughts about SDI," *Public Opinion,* March/April 1987, p. 19.

52. Connell, *New Maginot Line,* p. 245.

53. "Ballistic Missile Defense Technologies," Congressional Office of Technology Assessment, 1985, p. 6-7.

54. Flora Lewis, "A Lethal Defense Legacy," *New York Times,* December 1, 1987, p. 27.

55. Quoted in *Search for Sanity,* p. 14.

56. Bracken, *Command and Control of Nuclear Forces,* p. 5.

57. Raymond Aron, *Clausewitz,* (Prentice-Hall, Englewood Cliffs, N.J. 1985), p. 396.

58. Caspar W. Weinberger, U.S. Dept. of Defense Annual Report to the Congress, RY 1988, p. 42.

59. *Ibid.,* p. 44.

60. Bracken, *Command and Control of Nuclear Forces,* p. 239.

61. Quoted by Clarfield and Wiecek, *Nuclear America,* p. 159.

62. Herken, *Counsels of War,* p. 266.

63. Freedman, *Evolution of Nuclear Strategy,* p. 341.

64. Herken, p. 268.

65. Philip Taubman, "A Sense of Strategy," *New York Times,* July 24, 1987.

66. McNamara, *Blundering into Disaster,* p. 41.

67. John M. Collins, "US-Soviet Military Balance 1980-1985," Congressional Research Service, Spring 1985, p. 283. The investigation actually started by comparing the period from 1960 to 1980, and noting:"Comprehensive, unbiased views of the U.S./Soviet military balance are scarce. Many (perhaps most) studies of that subject manipulate information and substitute assumptions for missing facts to create preferred impressions."

68. E. J. Carroll, "Nuclear Weapons and Deterrence," in G. Prins, ed., *The Nuclear Crisis Reader* (Vintage Books, New York, 1984), p. 13.

69. Broad, *Star Warriors,* p. 172.

70. Tom Gervasi, *Myth of Soviet Military Supremacy,* p. 13.

71. *Ibid.,* p. 400.

72. Quoted in William E. Burrows, *Deep Black* (Random House, New York, 1987), p. vii.

73. William Safire, "Different Strikes," *New York Times Magazine,* June, 1986.

74. Charles Mohr, "Some Planes Didn't Drop Their Bombs," *New York Times,* April 17, 1986.

75. Allison, *Hawks, Doves and Owls,* p. 54.

76. Clarfield and Wiecek, *Nuclear America,* p. 258.

77. Tsipis, *Arsenal,* p. 75.

78. "Shuttle May Take Bone Marrow into Space in Radiation Study," New York Times, February 11, 1985, p. 11.

79. Kaplan, *The Wizards of Armageddon,* pp. 86ff.

T, U, V

1. A.C. Enthoven, "U.S. Forces in Europe," *Foreign Affairs,* vol. 53(3), pp. 513ff.

2. Interview, *New York Times,* August 28, 1980.

3. Martin Walker, "Kremlin Sees Opportunities for Deal—If US Really Wants One," *Manchester Guardian Weekly,* March 29, 1987.

4. Jacques Ellul, *The Technological Society* (Knopf, New York, 1964), p. vi.

5. Annual Report to the Congress, FY '88, pp. 43-44.

6. Frank Barnaby, *The Automated Battlefield* (The Free Press, New York, 1986), p. 14.

7. "Science and the Citizen," *Scientific American,* March 1986, p. 58.

8. Union of Concerned Scientists, *Nucleus,* vol. 7 no. 4, p. 3.

9. L. Ackland and S. McGuire, eds. *Assessing the Nuclear Age* (Educational Foundation for Nuclear Science, Chicago, 1986).

10. Bruce Russet and Fred Chernoff, eds., *Arms Control and the Arms Race* (Scientific American, New York, 1985), p. 15.

11. Michael Charlton, *The Star Wars History* (BBC Publications, London, 1986), p. 59.

12. Yale University Medical School, New Haven. February 14, 1986.

13. "Firing Line," Public Broadcasting System, October 20, 1985.

14. Fred S. Hoffman, testimony before the U.S. Senate Armed Services Comm., March, 1985.

15. G. H. Clarfield & W. M. Wiecek, *Nuclear America* (Harper & Row, New York, 1984), pp. 123, 237.

16. Tom Gervasi, *The Myth of Soviet Nuclear Supremacy* (Harper & Row, New York, 1986), p. 10.

17. *Trident II Missiles,* Congressional Budget Office, July 1986, p. 32.

18. Peter Clausen *et al., In Search of Stability* (Union of Concerned Scientists, Washington, D.C., 1986), p. 27ff.

19. Bernard Brodie, *War and Politics* (Macmillan & Co., New York, 1973), p. 430.

20. Caspar W. Weinberger, U.S. Dept. of Defense Annual Report to the Congress, FY 1988.

21. Paul Mann, "U.S. Formulates Strategic Doctrine for High Technology," *Aviation Week and Space Technology,* June 15, 1987, p. 110.

22. Brent Scowcroft, Chairman, President's Commission on Strategic Forces, to the president, March 21, 1984, p. 7.

23. William E. Burrows, *Deep Black* (Random House, New York, 1986), p. 345.

24. Michael R. Gordon, "Two Powers Agree to Discuss Ways to Verify A-tests," *New York Times,* July 10, 1986, p. 1.

25. *Ibid.,* "Kremlin Reports U.S. A-tests, Citing Ease of Detection," *New York Times,* August 30, 1986, p. 1.

26. Quoted in Tom Gervasi, *The Myth of Soviet Military Supremacy* (Harper & Row, New York, 1986), p. 254.

27. Burrows, p. 336.

28. Gervasi, p. 252.

29. "Arms Control Verification," (Union of Concerned Scientists, Cambridge, Mass., 1985), *briefing paper,* p. 3.

30. Burrows, p. 334ff.

W, Z

1. Bill Keller, "Moscow, In A Reversal, Urges Quick Arms Pact on Missiles in Europe," *New York Times,* March 1, 1987, p. 1.

2. Strobe Talbott, *Deadly Gambits* (Knopf, New York, 1984), pp. 116-151. A shorter version of the incident appears in Talbot, "Buildup and Breakdown," in William P. Bundy, ed., *The Nuclear Controversy* (New American Library, New York, 1985), pp. 181-192.

3. Talbott, p. 132.

4. Caspar W. Weinberger, U.S. Dept. of Defense Annual Report to the Congress, FY 1988, p. 46.

5. Albert Carnesale, *et al., Living with Nuclear Weapons)* Harvard University Press, Cambridge, Mass., 1983), p. 145.

6. Bernard Brodie, *Strategy in the Missile Age* (Princeton University Press, Princeton, N.J., 1959), p. 277.

7. Michael G. Gordon, "Officials Say Navy Might Attack Soviet A-Arms in Nonnuclear War," *New York Times,* January 7th, 1986, p. 1; January 12, 1986, p. 8. Paul Joseph, ed., *Search for Sanity* (South End Press, Boston, 1984), pp. 17.

9. Michael Charlton, *The Star Wars History* (BBC Publications, London, 1986), p. 105.

10. Joseph, p. 299.

11. Tom Gervasi, *The Myth of Soviet Military Supremacy* (Harper & Row, New York, 1986), p. 132.

12. See *Report of the President's Special Review Board (The Tower Commission), special edition* (Bantam Books, New York, 1987).

13. R. L. Garthoff, "Worst-Case Assumptions," in G. Prins, ed., *The Nuclear Crisis Reader* (Vintage Books, New York, 1984), p. 98ff.

14. Lawrence Freedman, *The Price of Peace* (Henry Holt, New York, 1986), p. 86.

BIBLIOGRAPHY

Ackland, Len and McGuire, Steven, eds. *Assessing the Nuclear Age.* Chicago: Educational Foundation for Nuclear Science, 1986.

Allison, Graham T., Carnesale, Albert; Nye, Joseph S., Jr. *Hawks, Doves and Owls.* New York: W.W.Norton, 1985.

Ambrose, Stephen E. *Eisenhower the President.* New York: Simon & Schuster, 1984).

Arkin, William M. and Fieldhouse, Richard W. *Nuclear Battlefields.* Cambridge, Mass.: Ballinger Publishing Co., 1985.

Aron, Raymond. *Clausewitz.* Englewood Cliffs: Prentice-Hall, 1985.

Barnaby, Frank. *The Automated Battlefield.* New York: The Free Press, 1986.

Betts, Richard K. *Nuclear Blackmail and Nuclear Balance.* Washington, D.C.: Brookings Institution, 1987.

Bialer, Seweryn. *The Soviet Paradox.* New York: Knopf, 1986.

Binkin, Martin. *Military Technology and Defense Manpower.* Washington, D.C.: Brookings Institution, 1986.

Blair, Bruce G. *Strategic Command and Control.* Washington, D.C.: Brookings Institution, 1985.

Boyer, Paul. *By the Bomb's Early Light.* New York: Pantheon Books, 1985.

Bracken, Paul. *The Command and Control of Nuclear Forces.* New Haven: Yale University Press, 1983.

Broad, William J. *Star Warriors.* New York: Simon & Schuster, 1985.

Brodie, Bernard. *Strategy for the Missile Age.* Princeton, N. J.: Princeton University Press, 1959, 1965.

Brzezinski, Zbigniew. *Game Plan.* New York: Atlantic Monthly Press, 1986.

Bundy, William P., ed. *The Nuclear Controversy.* New York: New American Library, 1985.

Burrows, William E. *Deep Black*. New York: Random House, 1986.

Calder, Nigel. *Nuclear Nightmares*. New York: Viking Press, 1979.

Caldicott, Helen. *Missile Envy*. New York: Bantam Books, 1984.

Carnesale, Albert *et al*. The Harvard University Nuclear Study Group. *Living with Nuclear Weapons*. Cambridge, Mass.: Harvard University Press, 1983.

———— Learning from Experience with Arms Control, for the U.S. Arms Control and Disarmament Agency. Cambridge, Mass.: Harvard University Press, 1986.

Chalfont, Alun. *Star Wars*. London: Weidenfeld & Nicholson, 1985.

Charlton, Michael. *The Star Wars History*. London: BBC Publications, 1986.

Clarfield, Gerard H. and Wiecek, William W. *Nuclear America*. New York: Harper & Row, 1984.

Clausen, Peter, *et al. In Search of Stability*. Cambridge, Mass.: Union of Concerned Scientists, 1986.

Connell, Jon. *The New Maginot Line*. New York: Arbor House, 1986.

Dunne, Keith & Straudenmeir, William O. *Alternative Military Strategies for the Future*. Boulder, Colo.: Westview Press, 1985.

Ellul, Jacques. *The Technological Society*. New York: Alfred Knopf, 1964.

Epstein, Joshua M. *Strategy and Force Planning*. Washington, D.C.: Brookings Institution, 1987.

Fairbank, John K. *The Great Chinese Revolution: 1800-1985*. New York: Harper & Row, 1986.

Freedman, Lawrence. *The Evolution of Nuclear Strategy*. New York: St. Martin's Press, 1981.

———— *The Price of Peace*. New York: Henry Holt, 1986.

Gaddis, John L. *Strategies of Containment.* New York: Oxford University Press, 1982.

Garthoff, Raymond L. *Detente and Confrontation.* Washington, D.C.: Brookings Institution, 1985.

Gervasi, Tom *The Myth of Soviet Military Supremacy.* New York: Harper & Row, 1986.

Hadley, Arthur T. *The Straw Giant.* New York: Random House, 1986.

Halloran, Richard. *To Arm a Nation.* New York: Macmillan, 1986.

Halperin, Morton H. *Nuclear Fallacy.* Cambridge, Mass.: Ballinger Publishing Co., 1987.

Herken, Gregg. *The Winning Weapon.* New York: Vintage Books, 1982.

Hudson, George E. and Kruzel, Joseph, eds. *American Defense Annual, 1985-1986.* Lexington, Mass.: D. C. Heath & Co., 1985.

Hyland, William G. *Mortal Rivals.* New York: Random House, 1987.

Jastrow, Robert. *How To Make Nuclear Weapons Obsolete.* Boston: Little Brown & Co., 1983.

Joseph, Paul, & Rosenbloom, Simon, eds. *Search For Sanity.* Boston: South End Press, 1984.

Kahn, Herman. *On Thermonuclear War.* Princeton, N.J.: Princeton University Press, 1960.

―――― *Thinking About the Unthinkable.* New York: Harrison Press, 1962.

―――― *Thinking About the Unthinkable in the 1980's.* New York: Simon & Schuster, 1984.

Kaplan, Fred. *The Wizards of Armageddon.* New York: Simon & Schuster, 1983.

Kaufman, William W. *A Reasonable Defense.* Washington, D.C.: Brookings Institution, 1986.

Kennan, George F. *Russia, the Atom and the West.* New York: Harper & Bros., 1957.

———— *Memoirs, 1925-1950.* Boston: Little Brown, 1967.

———— *The Nuclear Delusion.* New York: Pantheon Books, 1976.

The Cloud of Danger. Boston: Little Brown, 1977.

Keynes, John M. *A Treatise on Probability.* New York: Harper & Row, 1921.

McNamara, Robert. *Blundering into Disaster.* New York: Pantheon Books, 1986.

Mandelbaum, Michael. *The Nuclear Question.* New York: Cambridge University Press, 1979.

Mandelbaum, Michael and Talbott, Strobe. *Reagan and Gorbachev.* New York: Random House, 1987.

Molander, Earl A., ed. *What About the Russians and Nuclear War?* New York: Pocket Books, 1983.

Morison, Samuel Eliot. *The Oxford History of the American People, Vol.3.* New York: New American Library, 1962.

Neustadt, Richard E. and May, Ernest R. *Thinking in Time.* New York: The Free Press, 1986.

Nye, Jr., S. *Nuclear Ethics.* New York: The Free Press, 1986.

Office of Technology Assessment. *Strategic Defenses.* Princeton, N.J.: Princeton University Press, 1986.

Paret, Peter, ed. *Makers of Modern Strategy.* Princeton, N.J.: Princeton University Press, 1986.

Payne, Keith B. *Strategic Defense.* London: Hamilton Press, 1986.

Prins, Gwyn, ed. *The Nuclear Crisis Reader.* New York: Random House, 1984.

Quester, George H. *The Future of Nuclear Deterrence.* Lexington, Mass.: D. C. Heath & Co., 1986.

Reeves, Richard. *The Reagan Detour.* New York: Simon & Schuster, 1985.

Rhodes, Richard. *The Making of the Atomic Bomb.* New York: Simon & Schuster, 1987.

Roderick, Hilliard, ed. *Avoiding Inadvertent War.* Austin: University of Texas, Lyndon B. Johnson School of Public Affairs, 1983.

Russet, Bruce, ed. *Arms Control and The Arms Race*. New York: W.H. Freeman & Co., 1985.

Schelling, Thomas C. *Arms and Influence*. New Haven: Yale University Press, 1966.

Schlesinger, Jr., Arthur M. *A Thousand Days*. Boston: Houghton Mifflin, 1965.

Shirer, William L. *The Rise and Fall of the Third Reich*. New York: Simon & Schuster, 1960.

Spector, Leonard S. *Nuclear Proliferation Today*. New York: Random House, 1984.

Stares, Paul B. *The Militarization of Space*. Ithaca, N.Y.: Cornell University Press, 1985.

———— *Space and National Security*. Washington, D.C.: Brookings Institution, 1987.

Stubbing, Richard A. and Mendel, Richard A. *The Defense Game*. New York: Harper & Row, 1986.

Talbott, Strobe. *Deadly Gambits*. New York: Knopf, 1984.

Teller, Edward. *Better a Shield Than a Sword*. New York: The Free Press, 1987.

Tirman, John, ed. *The Fallacy of Star Wars*. New York: Random House, 1984.

Tsipis, Kosta. *Arsenal: Understanding Weapons in the Nuclear Age*. New York: Simon & Schuster, 1983.

Tucker, Robert W. *The Nuclear Debate*. New York: Holmes & Meier, 1985.

Weinberger, Caspar W. U.S. Department of Defense *Annual Report to the Congress,* FYs 1987 & 1988.

Weiss, Anne E. *The Nuclear Question*. New York: Harcourt Brace, 1981.

Zuckerman, Solly. *Nuclear Illusion & Reality*. New York: Random House, 1983.

Zuckerman, Lord. *Star Wars in a Nuclear World*. London: William Kimber, 1986.

INDEX

206